A Portrait of Fryn

A Portrait of Fryn

A Biography of F. Tennyson Jesse

JOANNA COLENBRANDER

ANDRE DEUTSCH

First published 1984 by
André Deutsch Limited
105 Great Russell Street
London WC1

Copyright © 1984 by Joanna Colenbrander

ISBN 0 233 97572 1

Typeset by Inforum Ltd, Portsmouth
Printed in Great Britain
by St Edmundsbury Press,
Bury St Edmunds, Suffolk

To Sybout

CONTENTS

—••€)(3••—

LIST OF ILLUSTRATIONS

Eustace Tennyson d'Eyncourt Jesse and his daughter Wynifried Margaret, who was to become first Fryniwyd, then Fryn.

Stella (top) and May.

Fryn by Jean de Bosschère. He used her as a model when he was illustrating a children's book written by himself, which she translated.

Tottie – H.M. Harwood – soon after he and Fryn got married.

Fryn at about the time of her marriage.

At Cut Mill (top) and at Sabi Pas.

Three homes. Top, Cut Mill. Bottom, Sabi Pas (left) and Pear Tree Cottage.

Tottie, by the French caricaturist G. Augsbourg.

Author's Note and Acknowledgments

LONG BEFORE there was any question that I might write a life of Fryn – F. Tennyson Jesse – I had been in the habit of inserting a letter, a paragraph or an article into a red box labelled *Autobiography* that stood on a shelf of her workroom at Pear Tree Cottage in St John's Wood. As her secretary, I had been doing the same to several other box files, called *Nare*, *Burma* and *Prison Anthology*; *Women in Crime*, *Sequel to the Alabaster Cup* and *Psychette*: projects ranging from fiction through history and crime, and back to fiction again. Each box contained its notebook also, where any relevant phrase, uttered or heard by or about Fryn on the subject chosen, could be entered by either of us for possible future use.

In a letter to her husband Tottie, the playwright H.M. Harwood, in 1945, Fryn had written: 'And I have six books still in me!' This claim had related to her desire to promote a uniform edition of all her books, published and to come – novels, short stories, crime studies and poetry. She counted on this to bring her name back before the public after the damaging hiatus caused by her war work for the Ministry of Information.

At intervals, one of the boxes would be worked on, or merely glanced through and returned to comparative oblivion, and it was in this way that *The Alabaster Cup*, a semi-autobiographical novel, grew in 1950 from the story of old Nare, Fryn's pet-name for the Nan of her childhood; and that *Sequel to the Alabaster Cup* was abandoned as too sensitive to handle in 1951. It was in this way too that *The Dragon in the Heart* came into being in 1956, from data spanning the two wars and the tragic story of Fryn's Paris heroine, *Psychette*. I was well aware, therefore, which of the projects would be the next to burgeon, even before the writing of the Trials of Evans and Christie for murder was completed in 1956; after which the red box began rapidly to fill up with letters, cuttings and youthful mementoes of Fryn's own life.

Though by that time she was all but blind, I perversely continued to assume that she would somehow succeed in doing the intrepid thing she so dearly wanted to do: complete at least the first of the two volumes of autobiography on which she had set her heart. When in the summer of 1958 Fryn died with the writing scarcely begun, it did not at once occur to me that I must be the one to carry on with it; only that someone must. True, I had pored over her memoirs from age three to eighteen; her diaries from nineteen to twenty-one; her papa's great scrapbooks called the *Annales Tennysoniani*. I had copies of all her books, stories and essays; the files of her letters received for years back, and the carbons of those sent. I had the review cuttings, and her notebooks, and my own. And for ten years I had seen her almost daily, listened to her talking to her family and her staff, to lawyers, policemen, actors, tradesmen, painters, fellow writers and beloved lunch-guests; above all, talking to me by the hour, entrancing me with conversation so richly entertaining that it was an art form. Certainly I knew a great deal about her work and her life, the early part and the end especially.

My first thought was that, if Tottie could be persuaded to bestir himself to write the second face to a joint biography – if he could fill in their middle years, which were indistinct to me – I could then save his time and strength by dovetailing the two together. It would still be Fryn's story that would result, though a different version from the one she herself would have written. At the same time, it might be his best chance of coming back from the shadows. And even when I found he would not, and would rather die and trust it all to me to do, I thought there would surely be experienced writers eager to make use of the mass of material I could feed to them. Perhaps Robert Gore-Browne, Tottie's oldest friend, who had written several biographies and had shared those middle years with them? Perhaps Tiger, Moira Tighe, Fryn's secretary for eighteen years before me? I was widely assured too that some hack would soon come clamouring for the chance! But time passed and nobody did.

It was then, in reply to a bulletin from me on how the bereaved Tottie was coping with his solitude, that I had a letter from Archibald Batty. He had met the Harwoods in Burma in 1921, when he was ADC to the Governor there and Fryn was beginning work on *The Lacquer Lady*, and he had later joined Tottie's team at the Ambassador's Theatre. He wrote: 'Thank you for the most satisfactory postscript I have ever read in my life. I hope you have a future even longer than your name and that you are planning to devote it to biography, for which you obviously have a flair. But if this seems too long and plodding a chore, may I remind you of the Obituary Departments in all the national papers? My only fear is that you would bring such a breath of life to the departed that a number of interments would have to be postponed.'

These astonishing and heartening words worked upon me like a mental laxative. I must confess to having felt not unlike the nun on the Mississippi steamer, as quoted in this book from Fryn's diary, when she said: *'Je suis docile, mais je tiens encore'*; yet even she had relieved herself of her burden at last. I began at once to do the 'long and plodding' chore on my own account that I had expected to do for another. It was only after Tottie's death in 1959, and many months of work, that it became evident to me that there were vital gaps in my knowledge, of which I knew so little that I did not even know where to go to fill them – except to May King, Fryn's housekeeper-companion of over forty years' standing. And from May, as I soon discovered, although she loved nothing better than to talk of those high-flying days with nostalgia, information of value would come only in droplets, for she rejoiced almost equally in her power to withhold, would tell only if I promised her never to write one word for publication in her lifetime.

Conceding temporary defeat, I decided to hoard all the preliminary work in a tropical trunk, to take tea sometimes in May's new flat which I had found for her round the corner from Pear Tree Cottage, and to allow the precious drops to collect in peace when they would, like cupping a gum-tree. In the meantime I could attend to earning my share of a living again, and to enjoying the presence of Martine, a dear daughter my husband had brought with him when we married in 1952. She would shortly be leaving St Paul's School for Girton College, Cambridge, and would be over the hills and far away all too soon.

When I joined the administrative staff of a local school in 1960, I did not yet anticipate that my promise to May could not be ratified until 1978, when she died at the age of ninety-two and I could begin seriously to collate what had been accumulating in the trunk: her droplets alone – some of them like manna – had ultimately over-spilled two fat notebooks such as the one in Fryn's red box. It has since taken me almost as long to diminish as it took to collect, echoing a familiar dictum of Fryn's to would-be writers that the art is not in what you put in but in what you take out.

Far the greatest number of quotations in this book come from the letters, notebooks, diaries and conversations of F. Tennyson Jesse herself. As Fryn's papers, and the newspapers and articles from which cuttings were taken, are seldom dated or otherwise identified, it has sometimes been impossible to be precise as to their origin. Rather than distract the eye with a surfeit of references, I have entered footnotes only for quotations other than these. Naturally, I sought and received help of various kinds from many sources, and all of these – including those no longer living – I want to thank:

Archie: the late Archibald Batty, MVO, OBE. He was aide-de-camp to Sir Harcourt Butler, Governor of Burma, when *The Lacquer Lady* by F. Tennyson Jesse was in infancy; his first stage success was in *The Transit of Venus* by H.M. Harwood; and his was the spur that induced me to start the writing.

Grace Hubble: the late Mrs Edwin Hubble, widow of the Mount Wilson astronomer. She wrote that nothing had brought her such satisfaction since he died as working on Edwin's papers; could I not set to work at once on Fryn's, for she too should not be forgotten.

Tiger: the late Miss Moira Tighe, Fryn's secretary for the greater part of eighteen years, who wrote to me from Kenya when Fryn died: 'Have you thought of writing Fryn's biography? Somebody should', and for offering me her own Hollywood and Mississippi diaries of their travels.

May: the late Miss A.M. King. For invaluable information given me over the years, bridging the gaps in my knowledge at Fryn's death in 1958; for memories of Papa and Stella too, and of the four homes she shared with Fryn: Gordon Place, Cut Mill, Sabi Pas and Pear Tree Cottage. Also for leaving me the peacock screen designed by the sculptor Bruce Douglas to commemorate the publication of *The Lacquer Lady*, and the family photograph albums, which provide illustrations for this text.

The late Miss Alethea Garstin, daughter of the painter Norman Garstin and sister of Dennis and Crosbie Garstin – the latter known later as 'Patlander' of the Mudlarks series in Punch – for her letters recalling life at Newlyn and the School of Art.

Damit: the late Mrs Percy Bell, for memorabilia of many kinds, of Fryn and her sister Stella, and of the Newlyn School of Art in Cornwall and Fryn's first home at 46 Gordon Place.

Enid Bagnold: the late Lady Jones, for her recollections of 'the lovely, kind, golden Fryn, and how gay she was'.

Joan O'Connor: Mrs Osiakovski, playwright, for her youthful impressions of Fryn being lionized in the days of her London début.

Dame Rebecca West: the late Mrs Henry Andrews, for memories of her own and Fryn's youthful beginnings in Fleet Street, of the secret marriage to Tottie Harwood and the psychological complications which developed; also for her permission to quote her review of Fryn's first novel *The Milky Way* and her obituary – 'the most graceful thing one woman could say of another', as Grace Hubble commented.

Cathleen Nesbitt: the late Mrs Cecil Ramage, for remembering Fryn as a part of her youth: 'those months at the Ambassador's Theatre, at Sabi Pas in the South of France, and all those happy times at Cut Mill and Pear Tree Cottage!'

Virginia: the late Mme Vernon, for her reminiscences of life at Sabi Pas and later, and for her insight into Fryn's volatile temperament.

Marjorie Greig: now Mrs Cyril Budd, for recalling the flavour of life at Cut Mill, Bosham, in particular. Also for giving me the oil painting of Fryn in Provence, by Elizabeth Stanhope Forbes ARWS, which is reproduced on the jacket of this book.

Joe Jackson: the late Sir Leofric Jackson, Assistant Commissioner Scotland Yard, who came to Pear Tree Cottage to prime me with recollections of Fryn's rare expertise in the realm of crime.

Letty: Mrs Colin Cameron Kirby, for her descriptions of Fryn's puzzling psychological state and attempted suicide at Prestbury in the second world war.

Peter Cotes and his wife Joan Miller, for contributing countless memories of their friendship with Fryn and Tottie, and for allowing me to quote from their files on the production of *A Pin to See the Peepshow* from the novel by F. Tennyson Jesse, dramatized in collaboration with H.M. Harwood.

Fryn's cousin Charles: the late Sir Charles Tennyson, who kindly vetted the first half of the typescript as it went along, and was to have written a foreword had he lived to see it finished. Also for permission to quote passages from *The Tennysons: Background to Genius*, written with Hope Dyson, and from *Life's All a Fragment*.

Joe Gaute: J.H.H. Gaute of Harraps, who generously gave his time and experience to reading the first half of the typescript, and advising me as to the form it should take, which advice I have tried to follow.

Ruth Harris: Mrs Christopher Harris, Tottie's half-sister, for her valuable descriptions of the younger branch of the Harwood family, and her impressions as a child of the courtship of Tottie and Fryn.

La Wareing: Miss Elsie Wareing, Osteopath, for her recollections of untold hours devoted to the household at Pear Tree Cottage, spent relieving pain, and for her valuable advice on the nature of Fryn's migraine and other ills.

Lucy Hair: widow of the late Gilbert Hair, prison governor, for her memories of Fryn, Stella and Tottie.

I also want to thank the following for permission to reprint copyright material:

Macmillan Publishing Company: for permission to quote passages from *Stanhope A. Forbes ARA and Elizabeth Stanhope Forbes ARWS* (Cassell and Company Limited) 1906, by Mrs Lionel Birch, married to the painter at Newlyn 'Lamorna' Birch.

Oppenheim-John Downes Memorial Trust for permission to quote from E. Philips Oppenheim's *The Pool of Memory* (Hodder and Stoughton) 1941 – for him comments on Tottie as playwright.

Weidenfeld and Nicolson for permission to quote from Jocelyn Baines's *Joseph Conrad* 1960 – for his description of migraine sufferers and other mental disorders to which authors are especially prone.

Part One

—⋅⋅❦)(❦⋅⋅—

Spring

ONE

—◆◦)(◦◆—

Annales Tennysoniani

FRYNIWYD TENNYSON JESSE was the second of the three daughters born to the Reverend Eustace Tennyson d'Eyncourt Jesse and his wife Edith Louisa, née James. She was not christened Fryniwyd but Wynifried Margaret; though that is neither here nor there, for one of the first things she did was to simplify her style to Fee. This was to be elaborated upon by a succession of nursemaids into Whiny Fee, Fatty Fee and even Miss Fee, before the happy day when she found that Fryn was all she needed to carry her through life.

Fryn's father, Eustace Jesse, was the second son of Captain Richard Jesse of the Royal Navy. There is a large photograph of Richard in one of Eustace's scrap-books of cuttings and mementoes, the *Annales Tennysoniani*. It shows a handsome, bearded man with light-coloured eyes set wide apart. He wears a frock-coat on which medals are pinned, and Eustace has written: 'The medals were given him for taking out the life-boat at Tenby, South Wales, where he was on the Coastguard, during terrific storms. The small medal, gold, was given him by Napoleon III – "Medaille de Sauvetage".' Richard had accompanied Sir John Ross on his last Arctic Expedition. He was the son of the Reverend William Jesse, Vicar of Margaretting in Essex.

On the opposite page, Eustace's mother appears, on her head a net mantilla worn well back over chastely middle-parted hair. The lobes of her ears are uncommonly long and carry long chain ear-rings, and Eustace has set down: 'Mrs Emily Jesse, daughter of George Clayton Tennyson, Vicar of Somersby in the County of Lincoln. When seventeen she was engaged to Arthur Henry Hallam, the subject of Tennyson's *In Memoriam*. She was born at Somersby in 1811. She was one of the founders of "The Dog's Home". She talked metaphysics, without being aware of it. She had a great knowledge about wild birds. She had very large eyes and a rich deep voice. Like all the Tennysons she could speak French and Italian.' This portrait always reminded Fryn of 'the thin part of Laurel and Hardy,' so she said, and it is true that something plaintive and stoic has crept into the expression of the dark, symmetrical face.

Beside it, a cut-out profile, postage-stamp size, is labelled: 'Eustace Jesse. Queen's College, Oxford, 1875–76'. The young face of Eustace is almost a facsimile of his mother's, but lacks her strength. Where her brow is serene, his is clouded. Long afterwards, Fryn said of him: 'My father was sweet and silly, with a scissors-and-pastepot mind.'

The reverend Dr George Clayton Tennyson, LLD, Fryn's great-grandfather, was the scholarly elder son of George Tennyson, MP, of Bayons Manor near Market Rasen in Lincolnshire, descended from the old Norman d'Eyncourt family who trace back to John of Gaunt – 'But only on the distaff side, my dear,' as Eustace said when he was guiding Fryn through the intricacies of their descent, from Edward I who married a daughter of the King of France.

The elder George was an autocrat, whose drive as a politician and skill as a lawyer had brought him land and influence, but failed to bring him rapport with his first-born son. Manoeuvring him into the Church against his will, he disinherited him in favour of his younger son Charles, the Rt Hon Charles Tennyson d'Eyncourt, JP, DL, PC, MP, MA Cantab, who shared his father's strenuous ambitions and assumed by Royal Licence the additional surname and arms of d'Eyncourt.

The eleven children who grew up in the old Rectory of Somersby were tall, beautiful, imaginative and eccentric. Most of them were 'more or less true poets'; all of them 'enjoyed weak health but strong constitutions',* in that they never ceased either to be ill or to think themselves so, but all lived to be old. They had fine minds, too, but by inherited tendency they were unable to make full use of their strength, mental or physical. Periodically, they had to 'switch off', to lie fallow, and some of them lay fallow all their lives.

George had married Elizabeth Fytche in 1805, and they had produced one of these phenomenal beings every year or so until 1819. Wild though they were, they were of a gentle breed; the unruly strain inherited from their father was tempered by the piety and mysticism

* *The Tennysons: Background to Genius*, Sir Charles Tennyson and Hope Dyson, Macmillan, 1974.

of the beautiful Elizabeth, and her loving indulgence bred in them a great closeness to one another but did nothing to help them to cope with the world outside. Feverish stresses between the penurious household of the 'tribe' at Somersby and the prosperous one up at the Manor rendered most of them unfit for anything but dreams. They faced the world with defiance, dressed outlandishly, and carried their magnificent persons with a flamboyant disregard of criticism. Each of them laboured at times under obsessive religious convictions, and each was subject to moods of morbid despondency. Despite their tender hearts and their delightful sense of fun, they were spoken of as 'the black-blooded Tennysons.'

The learned Rector, rejected and disparaged, at intervals lost his mental balance entirely, but he had encouraged his children's poetic inclinations and educated them himself in the classics. Alfred was the third child, and Fryn's grandmother Emily was two years younger. When Alfred brought home from Cambridge for the long vacation his dearest friend, Arthur Henry Hallam, a fine poet too and son of the distinguished historian Henry Hallam, Arthur 'lay and read the Tuscan poets on the lawn' and exchanged promises with Emily. In 1833, before they could be married, he died of an aneurism in the brain while travelling with his father in the Tyrol, and Emily collapsed with grief and shock.

Alfred expressed his sorrow over the man he 'held as half divine' in the lovely lament, *In Memoriam*, described by Gladstone as 'the richest oblation ever offered by the affection of friendship.' Its eventual publication turned the tide in his affairs, when Queen Victoria appointed him Poet Laureate. Providentially, his Uncle Charles of Bayons Manor, who had squandered his fortune without avail in attempting to recover the ancient d'Eyncourt barony, died in 1861 and was thus spared the chagrin of seeing one of 'that Somersby tribe' receive the friendship of the Queen and, in 1884, a barony all his own. But, for all Alfred's triumphant success and stupendous looks, he had a vulnerable nature, flayed by criticism. Phases of low health and spirits alternated with bursts of great vigour, and he suffered from overwhelming hypochondria. He had a taste for the macabre, and a family legend came down to Fryn that he read the Newgate Calendar as a bed-book.

Apart from his two elder brothers, Frederick and Charles, who continued to write and to earn high praise for their poetry and who had already left home, the family remained with their mother long after their father's death in 1831. By 1841 they had moved to Boxley Hall in Kent, and Emily Tennyson married Richard Jesse there on 24 January 1842, when she was just over thirty and he some years younger. Oddly dressed and with hair in long ringlets, she looked 'singular and elflike' at their wedding. He looked his brave and handsome self, 'talking fast and with a pale good-humoured face.'*

Jesse is an illustrious name; from the first Jesse, father of royal David. Fryn's Jesse ancestors were writers: naturalists, theologians, historians, minor poets. Richard Jesse's father, William, the 'country parson' of the caption to his photograph, was also Domestic Chaplain to the Earl of Glasgow and writer of several theological works. Before him there was grandfather William and great-grandfather William, and so on straight back to the reign of Elizabeth I. Living at Chilmark in Wiltshire, each duly appeared at Trinity College, Oxford, and carried off his prize for learning. Their brides came from Somerset, Dorset or Wiltshire, and one of their daughters was known as the Rose of Somerset. For ten generations, the Jesse pedigree at the College of Arms shows these Williams, the eldest sons, living into their eighties. Many were clergymen, and invariably something else besides. Richard's grandfather had a bird museum and was called the Apostle of the Woods; his brother was a soldier and wrote a life of Beau Brummel; his nephew was Naturalist to the Zoological Society for the Abyssinian Expedition of 1868 and wrote on natural history.

John Heneage Jesse, Fryn's great-uncle, wrote thirty volumes of social and literary history and essayed drama and poetry as well, including a collection of verses called *Tales of the Dead*. His father was the great naturalist, Edward Jesse, private secretary to the Earl of Dartmouth and a gentleman of the Ewry to George IV, who called him 'My Handsome Ewer'. His height was six foot four inches, and there is a bust of him in the Brighton Pavilion. He became Surveyor General of the Royal Parks and Palaces and Eustace noted in the *Annales Tennysoniani*: 'The Duke of Clarence, afterwards that Buffoon William IV, wanted to cut down an avenue of trees in Richmond Park, but Edward Jesse refused him, and the Duke did not like it. Those Hanoverians were a common, boorish lot.'

In addition, there is a photograph of a man with a great bony nose very like Emily's and Eustace's, and eyes and beard very like

* *The Tennysons*, Sir Charles Tennyson and Hope Dyson.

Richard's, labelled: 'George R. Jesse, author of "History of the British Dog".'

Many of these Jesse books were in Fryn's bookcases from her girlhood days in London. She offered them to the London Library in the end, and she left her prized Tennyson collection to members of the Tennyson family or to the Tennyson Research Centre at Lincoln. Among these were 'All my Tennyson books and the *Annales Tennysoniani*; the miniature of Arthur Henry Hallam and the daguerreotype of my grandmother Emily Tennyson with her husband Captain Richard Jesse RN and their elder son Arthur Henry Hallam Jesse; the daguerreotype of my father as a little boy of three, looking like a beautiful little girl in a frock; and the pearl spray brooch given by Arthur Henry Hallam to my grandmother Emily.'

Emily and Richard had two sons. Their first was born at Boxley Hall on 18 January 1843, a year after the wedding and just ten years after the death of Arthur Henry Hallam. Sixty years later he was buried in a common grave in the Old Highgate Cemetery, in August 1903. What happened to him in between appears in a letter Fryn wrote to her cousin, Sir Charles Tennyson:

'Of course I can tell you all about my Uncle Arthur. My grandmother had christened him, their first-born son, Arthur Henry Hallam. How my grandfather liked that I don't know, but he had to put up with it. It looks as though my grandmother had (if I may express myself vulgarly) the bulge on my grandfather. Eventually, Uncle Arthur went into the Army, purchasing a Commission, but he once disgraced himself by abandoning his Regiment in mid-air, so to speak, forming fours – or whatever these people do – while he helped an old woman over a stile. When he left the Army he went to Somerset House, where he sat in a daze of alcohol. He drank himself steadily but very slowly to death . . . When I was a little girl I thought him a great bore, as he would try to be funny and you know how children hate that.'

An earlier description of the young Arthur appears in a letter of July 1856 from Emily's brother-in-law, the scholarly and fastidious Edmund Lushington: '. . . he is the most intolerable 14-year-old . . . in almighty shamelessness in manner and clatter, that ever amazed quiet people – but there may be something better too, with all that.'

It would seem that Arthur Henry Hallam's 'half-divine' quality had failed to perpetuate itself in his namesake, and that Uncle-worship was evidently not Fryn's 'thing'. She did revere her great-

Uncle Alfred, though, and she set some store on having a saint and a poisoner in her line of descent: 'the former was St Louis IX of France, and the latter was the sister of Gian Galiazzo Visconti, the Viper of Milan, who married Thomas Holland Earl of Kent, a forbear of mine.'

Ten years after Arthur's birth, Eustace was born on 19 September 1853. Since he is not registered among the Births in England and Wales, he may have first seen the light in Italy or in France where his father served. In the 1860s his parents were living at Rosemount in Flask Walk, Hampstead. Alfred Tennyson had installed his mother, Elizabeth, next door at Rose Lodge in New End Square. The two houses are linked at an obtuse angle, like Siamese twins sharing one kidney, and a communicating door was broken through the party wall. Both Arthur and Eustace Jesse will have known their grandmother and many of the constantly visiting uncles and aunts, for she remained the adored kernel of the family until she died in 1865.

Writing to Sir Charles, Fryn said: 'My father was educated in France until he was eight or nine and was perfectly bi-lingual. I should imagine he never had any particular brains, but he had beautiful manners and he was very sensitive. He told me that never once as a child does he remember his mother having held him in her arms or caressed him . . .' All the same, he thought her very handsome, for 'he admired a woman with what he called "a fine nose" and was vain of his own which was identical. My little short straight nose was a great blow to him, though not to me.'

That Emily was not wholly an iceberg is indicated by her popularity with her Tennyson nephews and nieces for the amusing way she had with word games and nonsense verses. She was as credulous and soft as her mother, too, in bribing brutal boys to stop beating their beasts, and was as often blackmailed. Still, there is Emily's own word for it, when sympathising with another's bereavement: 'I don't want any new emotion. I know what it is to feel like a stone.'* At all events, when Fryn came to know her father, she found him in great need of demonstrative affection.

From 1873 to 1875 Eustace was at St Mary's Priory, Cogges, Witney, under the care of a private tutor, the Reverend James Payne. He was then entered at Queen's College, Oxford. By his rowing prowess there he assembled a collection of tankards, engraved with the name of R.E.R. Jesse as bow, and showing the three eagles of

* *The Tennysons*, Sir Charles Tennyson and Hope Dyson.

Queen's College and a pair of crossed oars. One has a scrolled shield as well, with three prancing horses, and bears the legend: HAUD DEJECTUS EQUUM DUCI JUBET. Somehow all these tankards found their way to Fryn. Her free rendering of the motto was: NOTHING DAUNTED HE ORDERED ANOTHER HORSE TO BE BROUGHT, but she was to adapt this more freely later on, to NOTHING DAUNTED HE ORDERED ANOTHER HOUSE TO BE BOUGHT, the better to fit her husband.

Despite his increasing tendency to asthma, this was obviously a happy, active time for Eustace, and when he transferred to Durham University in 1877, listed as a 'student of Arts, Richard Eustace Russell Jesse' he was in the second boat for University College Boat Club in the scratch fours. By the end of the year he was President of the Union Society, elected under the name of Eustace Tennyson d'Eyncourt Jesse. He had assumed by Royal Licence the additional surnames of Tennyson and d'Eyncourt, much in the manner of his great-uncle the Rt Hon Charles Tennyson d'Eyncourt and presumably for the same reason: an urge to recognize the royal blood he felt flowing in his veins. As this became diluted, it seems to have given its vessels a disturbing problem of identity, for which a positive solution had to be found. Eustace revelled in the resuscitated name and took to signing it whenever opportunity offered.

The Durham University Calendar shows him in the Pass List. He was given a title for Deacon's Orders in 1878, and a title for Holy Orders the following year, and took up his first curacy at St Paul in South Hampstead.

It must have been in the course of these hopeful years that Eustace, on a visit to Cornwall, met and courted his first love, for he was in his later twenties when he began writing a series of sonnets mourning her death, of which this one was written in 1881:

ON FINDING A DEAD ROSE IN HER BOOK

All faded are thy petals, lowly rose,
Thy beauty vanished and thy fragrance fled!
The vision of thy blossom brings the dead
Once more before my sight, and darkly throws
The veil of sadness o'er my longing eyes
When hours of night and morning-moments meet.
I plucked thee from thy stem, and moved to greet
My treasured love, who smiled in sweet surprise.
Thy burning petals glowed upon her breast,

And fluttered gently as she kissed thy leaf:
Thy lot proved happy though thy life was brief;
So like to hers, the fairest and the best.
Thus dear to me thy bruised fragments seem,
The fond remembrance of a vanished dream.

In the *Annales Tennysoniani*, near to the formidable likeness of Emily, there is a portrait which has a shining beauty. In this lovely picture of a girl in white, the head is held high, pale hair waves loosely at the temples under a mantilla of lace. She could be twenty. A photograph of a gravestone is on the page beside her, with the words in Eustace's hand: 'Fell asleep at Penzance May 1881, "May she rest in peace, and light perpetual shine on her".' Fryn discovered later that her father's fiancée had been one Elizabeth Woodburn, 'a very great beauty, who had died of what was known as galloping consumption and was buried at Penzance.'

Eustace had been enthusiastically taking rubbings of the brasses at Durham and, on going to St Mary Magdalen, Lincoln, after some two years at Hampstead, he became expert, contributing illustrations to *The Builder* and other publications. While at Lincoln he explored the Tennyson country, visiting Somersby and Bayons Manor with his Uncle Horatio, the youngest of the Somersby Tennysons, in 1883 and 1884. On leaving Lincoln in 1885, with an MA from Durham University, he arrived at St Peter's Church, the Parish Church of Kirkley in Suffolk, as Rector-Designate.

After an initial serious bout of asthma, which delayed him into the New Year, he 'read himself in' as Rector and prepared to move into the Pro-Rectory on Richmond Terrace. Then, with a home of his own and a church of his own, he took leave to fetch a wife. He returned with a pale slender girl.

During a visit to his parents the year before, Eustace had met Edith James, second of the five children of Mr and Mrs Henry James, then living at The Elms in Croydon. He had gone to the same church she attended, had caught sight of her slight figure and the delicate neck where tendrils of soft hair stirred at each genuflexion. Later, he told Fryn how they had been instantly and mutually in thrall, he thirty-three, Edith nineteen; uplifted by the High Anglican service and the heart-swelling pulse of the organ.

A photograph in the *Annales* shows a low white house among

lawns, labelled 'where my wife and I first met'. There Eustace, still a curate, was received without enthusiasm as Edith's suitor. Her father was a self-made man who had left Cornwall as a youth to seek his fortune, and had prospered. His eldest son Jack was in the Army. The younger boys, Somers and Squire, were still at school, as was Margaret, the youngest of the family. Apart from Edith, whose pious aspirations rose above anything the others would have found comfortable, they were robust, enterprising people, altogether of this world. Still, Edith was attracted by the ascetic good looks of Eustace, and eventually her father and mother were prevailed upon. *The Times* of 18 February 1886, in a list headed Ecclesiastical Appointments, announced: 'The Rev Eustace Tennyson d'Eyncourt Jesse, MA, Rector of Kirkley, South Lowestoft: Patron, Mr Henry James', and stock to the value of £10,000 was made over to Edith as her marriage settlement. The wedding was at St Saviour's Church, Croydon, and Eustace and Edith spent their honeymoon in London, at the Westminster Palace Hotel. He noted that 'It was little more than a Sunday out, with a few days on either side.'

Back at Kirkley, the new Rector was almost immediately in the thick of a battle. It must have occurred to him that he was entering a stronghold of Nonconformity. Perhaps he deluded himself that it would be a stimulating challenge to become a Daniel in the lion's den? But the attacks upon him came from a source difficult to parry – unsigned letters published in the local papers. One of them declared that 'the Parish of Kirkley is fast becoming notorious. The Rector is astonishing his parishioners by his ignorance and superstition. Because he has not sprinkled a few drops of water upon two or three score children, he insults their parents and shocks common sense by declaring that these tender little babes belong to heathendom.'

Another letter urged a Catholic priest to look to his laurels, 'for the incense burnt at Kirkley Church is as sweet smelling as that which is wafted from the censers at the Church of Our Lady of the Sea.' It ended: 'Here is a riddle for the curious: What is the difference between a Romanist and a Ritualist?'

The victim defended himself adroitly in the pulpit. Often he gave as good as he got. He published reasoned articles in the parish magazine. But everything he said or did was mocked. 'I should like to deal gently with the gentleman, but he should not try to make out that every clergyman of the Church of England who does not wear a black dressing-gown in the streets is breaking the canon.' As well as foes, he gained champions who railed against his persecutors in letters to the editor, accusing them of an intolerant and rancorous spirit. With every year the correspondence proliferated, wounding and exhausting. And the Rector did not have the advantage of his attackers in being nameless and faceless; his vulnerable head was stuck up to be potted at.

Not all his critics were actuated by ill-will; many were genuinely distressed by his innovations and what they considered excesses. And he continued to give them fresh cause. As well as introducing music and flowers, lights and incense, into his unaccustomed edifice, he introduced poetry into his sermons – sometimes his uncle's poetry and sometimes his own – or took his place at the organ. This earned the usual knockabout treatment: 'He did his part admirably, but he must really try and keep cool and remember that stamping and beating time and gesticulating is neither reverent nor edifying.'

In the five years from 1886, moreover, came crucial personal changes: his wife bore him three children and both his parents died. On Twelfth Night, 6 January 1887, Stella was born in Kirkley, and Edith took her baby to Croydon, where she could be taken care of by her own old nursemaid Ethel, while she rested in the easy well-run house of her parents.

Before Edith's planned return to her husband's side, Eustace's mother died on 25 January 1887. A friend, Thomas Purnell, wrote in his obituary on Emily in the *Athenaeum*: 'She was one of those women – and it is hoped that all of us meet with one or two such in life – who excite in us the feelings at once of a brother, a son, a lover. The misery of others was always of deep concern to her and her love for animals was almost a passion.'

Late at night, on 1 March 1888, Fryn was born at Holly Bowers in Chislehurst, to which the James family had moved. Edith had naturally again taken Stella with her, and when the time came to bring their new baby home to Eustace, she left the fourteen-month-old Stella behind. This was to become the pattern for the future; the Pro-Rectory was too small and too full while the extrovert Stella was in it. Alone, Fryn made little disturbance. Her wide-open, wide-apart eyes were everywhere, but her tongue was singularly still. An immense dome of forehead under flaxen down was matched by chubby cheeks, giving her the look of a baby owl.

While the experience of Eustace as a family man was taking on greater complexity, there was no easing off for Eustace the pastor. To pay for the restoration of the church, he arranged a series of organ recitals, in which one programme included Mendelssohn's 'O rest in the Lord', a vocal solo sung by the Rector himself. By fits and starts as his health dictated, numerous ambitious campaigns were tackled. He inaugurated a system of free nursing for the sick poor and, like his mother, he took a very active interest in the work of the Society for the Prevention of Cruelty to Animals, being particularly concerned for beaten donkeys and for horses in tight bearing-reins. And there was humour in him; the kind of humour Emily had had. It took the form of verbal twists or malapropisms such as : 'people in the garbage of monks with tonsils on their heads', which made him fall about with laughter. He collected them in his scrapbooks and used them in his sermons. He had an inquiring mind, set like a terrier on unearthing peculiar titbits of information. But his intelligence was unleavened by common-sense. His turbulent energy lacked stamina; when not in full spate it abruptly dwindled to nothing and left him spent. All too often he had to lie fallow.

On Christmas Day 1889, Captain Richard Jesse died, having long retired. It was perhaps fortunate that he did not have to watch the sands running out for his younger son; the career of the elder must have brought him disillusion enough, and he had never quite succeeded in laying the ghost of Arthur Henry Hallam.

A Musical Service was held in the spring of 1890, to establish a fund for providing a curate, and the church was filled in every part; every available space, sitting and standing, being occupied. 'The performance of the Messiah was one of the richest musical treats ever enjoyed in Kirkley', it was reported. 'The greatest tribute I can pay Mr Jesse is to say that the poor of his flock love him. If he would only pay less heed to rites and ceremonies, his church would become a centre of light and sweetness.' But Eustace had a curiously provocative streak in his nature; he could not resist tilting at windmills. It had caused him to couch his advertisement for the so-greatly-desired curate: 'Brother priest desired . . . must be Catholic; able to cope with much ignorant but honest dissent . . .'! Not surprisingly, this brought a storm of protest. Yet he did at last acquire a curate, and an assistant curate who 'having private means can work for Love'.

At a sale of work, launched by 'the indefatigable Rector' in a marquee on Lowestoft esplanade, for which the programme was printed in Ye Olde English characters, Edith served at Ye Floral Bower, supported by her young sister Margaret, for Edith was expecting her third child. Babs was born at home, and Stella went blithely off again with her Auntie Margaret to Holly Bowers. Fryn, over two years old and not yet walking, stayed quietly where she was. On 26 July 1890 Edith Mary Ermyntrude 'came to gladden her father's heart', as he put it. Until her coming he had felt that children, and girls especially, were 'the affair of the mother', but Babsie was the apple of his eye.

In truth the Rector was by no means indefatigable. In January 1891, faithful members of the congregation offered him an arm-chair in token of their esteem and regard. His dearest hope, the provision of a Rectory house by a grant from the Ecclesiastical Commissioners, was well on its way to becoming real, but already he knew he would never occupy it. His health had collapsed under the various strains and he was voluntarily giving up the living.

After Kirkley, Eustace's high-flying days were over. As to Edith, she lapsed into chronic invalidism; the outrage to her lofty religious stance matched by the outrage to her sexual nature. She wanted no more children and had come to resent Eustace and his unwelcome love-making. Edith was twenty-five then, and the nape of her neck where it met the soft hair was the seat of cruel migraine. The time and the place broke their stand against Nonconformity, but much of the damage done they did to each other, so that quarrels became the order of the day. Eustace never ceased, even in old age, to argue how right his fight against dissent had been. In Fryn's words, in those after years, 'his was the rightness of a stopped clock.'

No name was put to his illness. He gave out that he would spend the approaching winter abroad in the sun. His father-in-law, who had paid for the living, never quite forgave him, and he was never again *persona grata* in his wife's parental home. Shortly before the household packed up and left the Pro-Rectory, Fryn became aware for the first time of herself within her surroundings. It was a purely sensual impression of a shaft of yellow sunshine striking into the room, and of a nursemaid – called in the local dialect Gartie – cutting into a slab of butter and giving some to her and some to her sister Stella. Fryn had shifted herself slightly in her high-chair to ease the familiar weight of the iron supports strapped to her legs, and had watched the yellow of the butter flare as the light rays stabbed it. Stella had protested: 'La, Gartie! If I eat any more I shall b-b-barst!' She was to be whisked off to Chislehurst before the Suffolk dialect vied with the stammer to become part of her. She went alone to the rich relations, while the rest of the family went to the first of many dingy lodgings.

TWO

—••E)(3••—

The Look Backwards

AN 'infinite succession of lodgings', which left an indelible impression of dreariness on Fryn's mind, began at Balham. And a new acquaintance who was to become the chief figure of her childhood was Miss Hannah Mercy Roberts, known to her fondly as Nan. Nan lived in a lovely old house at the top of Church Street, Kensington, where she looked after her uncle, who had retired from a firm of music publishers. She had advertised offering her services free occasionally to a mother with young children and Edith had accepted with alacrity, for at Kirkley both she and Eustace had joined that strange aristocracy in their generation, the aristocracy of illness. 'Even as a small child,' wrote Fryn in her unpublished memoir, *The Look Backwards*, 'I observed it with curiosity. Its people cherished ill-health and saw it as a great spiritual or social attribute.'

Eustace had been urged by a fellow cleric, to whose lodgings in Balham they had come, to go to South Africa; anybody as distinguished as he would certainly be offered a Dean's gaiters there. So to South Africa they were going, leaving Stella behind. Stella came to see them before they went away, and was lifted up to stand on the dining-room table to show off a new dress, while Fryn watched her admiringly as she stood there laughing.

Fryn's legs were in irons because she had rickets, but after Stella left she climbed up on to a three-cornered dustbin painted a dingy flesh-pink, built into the corner of the little back garden. She wanted to practise flying and thought that, if she locked her hands firmly beneath her legs and jumped, she could sit on her hands and remain in the air. She tried it many times perseveringly, and could not in the least see why she always fell to the gravel.

No child can thrive in an emotional vacuum, and Fryn loved her mother slavishly, asking only that she should bear with her, for she knew baby Ermyntrude was her father's favourite. She had few toys, but treasured an engine and tender made of unpainted oak, and was heart-broken that it should be left behind when they sailed for Cape Town in December 1891. They experienced such heavy gales that the pilot could not be landed, but Fryn did not notice this, so she already promised to be a good sailor. On the voyage, a steward called Bobby made friends with her. Bobby was a ventriloquist, and had two people living inside the cupboard in his cabin. Fryn talked to them quite boldly and they would answer from the cupboard, but her courage vanished when Bobby begged her to put her arm in and shake hands with them.

The first night in Cape Town, Eustace had his worst attack of asthma yet, and nobody there ever offered him a Dean's gaiters. So they went on round the Coast to Grahamstown, where Fryn had a Hottentot nurse called Betsy. Betsy slept on the floor, rolled up in a mat, and told Fryn weird stories of her childhood that changed every time. Edith said she was a terrible liar and smelt very badly, but to Fryn there was nothing unpleasant about Betsy; she was all ears and loved being cuddled in the kind way Betsy cuddled her.

Though the irons were off her legs, she could not yet walk much, so she was pushed in a perambulator to her first school, a kindergarten kept by Sisters of Mercy. One day when the nun on duty was out of the room, she egged on two small brothers to help her dabble ink over the whitewashed wall. The nun gasped when she saw the havoc. As nobody confessed, she said she would have to punish everybody, whereupon the boys stood up like gentlemen and said they had done it. Fryn sat smugly and said nothing. Then 'a horrid little sneak of a girl' pointed at her. 'She made them do it,' she said, and Fryn was expelled, put into her perambulator and wheeled home. The message sent by the nuns was that she had corrupted two little boys.

She had not seen Babsie during her schooldays, but soon after this she was told that her baby sister had died. 'I can't have understood anything about it,' she wrote. 'I only remember it because my mother sorted out arum lilies on my bed. When the yellow spoke came out of one of them, she gave me the lily to play with, saying that nothing imperfect must go on Babsie's grave.' Her subsequent description of the whole South African enterprise as 'a ghastly fiasco' was precisely true, and by August Edith and Eustace agreed that they must leave the handsome granite cross, commemorating the death by meningitis on 9 February 1892 of 'our never-to-be-forgotten' baby Ermyntrude. The Bishop of Grahamstown had written: 'I regret exceedingly that means and resources are lacking which might enable us to strengthen our number of priests receiving stipends, and you have hesitated with good reason, considering the delicacy of your own and your wife's health, in accepting such posts of labour as I have been enabled to offer you up country.'

They returned to Cape Town, and Fryn remembered being driven in a rickshaw drawn by a native boy, and clapping her hands and crying: 'Faster, boy, faster!'

Edith, utterly worn out, had cabled for Nan to come out and help her, and they left the disastrous land and sailed for the Canary Islands. Nan told Fryn long afterwards that the South African adventure seemed to have wakened her up; that she had been a dull child till then. It may have been so, but Fryn believed it was the behaviour of grown-up people that had bewildered her, with their: 'How dare you say that, a little girl like you?' and its alternative: 'You ought to know better, a great girl like you!'

At Las Palmas there was a garden planted with orange-trees, set high above a ship-building yard. There Fryn sat, hearing the ring of hammers through the still air, looking down at stacks of pale yellowy planks, smelling the newly sawn timber, and listening to the sound of girls laughing. They stayed several weeks, during which Eustace took a trip to Tenerife. Then he and Edith decided to 'try France this time', and Nan took Fryn home to England.

The following spring she rejoined her parents in France, with Stella, and spent her fifth birthday at Menton. 'I think Granny had one of her moods of saying: "Edith and Eustace really ought to be able to manage their own little girl" ', she wrote. Granny and Grandpa came too, with Ethel in charge of the two children, who were both wildly excited, and Ethel was goaded into pursuing the mocking and naked Stella round the night nursery, trying to smack her botty with a hair comb.

The house they had taken in Menton was called the Villa Victorine, a long low house with a garden wall that gave onto the beach through a pointed door. In a marble basin, curved like a shell, lizards flickered with blue-green fire, and Fryn watched them entranced. She made mud-pies in the basin, mixing them till they looked so like chocolate cake that twice she took a nibble, hoping for the best, but found that mud was mud.

Among Eustace's records is a bill from the Wine Society, with the appended note: 'I had sent out to me six dozen of whisky when staying at Menton' – a generous provision of hard liquor for one clergyman in a wine country! But then it only cost him thirty-three shillings the dozen, including freight and all charges.

For the first time, Fryn was given a birthday party, and Eustace decorated her chair with garlands of evergreens. Not used to being the centre of attention, she cried and sat hunched on the little throne-chair, whiningly complaining of the prickles that stuck into her. 'No wonder I was known as Whiny Fee!' she commented. Children from round about came to the party and someone gave her a big doll. But she never cared much for dolls, and directly one got broken she ceased to love it at all, preferring no toys to imperfect ones. Then Stella disappeared again with Ethel and the grandparents, and a friendly family took Fryn to the Carnival in their carriage. She was wearing her best white frock and a leghorn hat. Everyone was throwing flowers, and bunches of soaking wet violets landed on her and her hat. She cried again, knowing too well that her mother would blame her for spoiling her expensive clothes, but they all thought her a tiresome vain child.

It was not long after this that they left for St Jean de Luz. Fryn had loved the Villa Victorine, the lizards, and the sea just outside the garden, and could not imagine why they did not stay there for ever. But Eustace has left a note in a different key: 'I nearly died at Menton from bronchitis. I made £20 by tuition; just the amount of my doctor's bill!'

It is no wonder that Eustace was driven here and there on the wings of hope; so unaccountably in his child's eyes. No appointment for him had been forthcoming, in Africa or the Canaries, in Menton or St Jean de Luz, where they stayed till full summer. In consequence, he went alone to Cambo in the Pays Basque, 'a beautiful little inland watering place,' as he wrote to Edith. He put up at a farmhouse further up the river 'where there are some trout', and while he fished and brooded there, his expectations rising and falling as he awaited a bite or a tangible reply to one of his anxious applications, Edith took Fryn in August 1893 to Holly Bowers to rejoin Stella.

At Holly Bowers the family consisted of Granny and Grandpapa; the two bachelor uncles, Somers and Squire; Auntie Margaret; and Stella. Ethel, her pink print skirt rustling, carried Fryn down the passage to the nursery so that Stella should not hear her footsteps, and called out: 'Miss Stella, I'm bringing you your big doll.' But Stella, who was playing with her dolls'-house at the far end of the room, was not deceived, and the next moment they were hugging.

Stella was wearing a frock of dark red flannel, with a thin white line in it and a frill of lace round the throat. She had on black glacé button boots and black silk stockings with white toes and heels, which struck Fryn as very superior. She was about six and a half, and her short dark hair was cut in a straight fringe. She had a round pale face, a round white chin, round dark-blue eyes, and a red mouth half-open to show the glint of her two front teeth. 'She was a regular little Merry Andrew, always on the grin,' wrote Fryn. 'She led me by the nose.'

On the whole, Fryn liked staying at Holly Bowers, though she knew she did not belong there. The food made her greedy, it was so wonderful; especially breakfast. As Grandpapa was a Cornishman, there was a dish of mashed potatoes browned on the top, and there was Cornish cream for the porridge, and kidneys, bacon, liver and fish, as well as eggs done any way the person wanted. On Sunday there was crystallized fruit to follow the mid-day dinner, and the uncles slowly turned the dish round, saying she must choose one thing. Crystallized cherries were her favourites – but one cherry was so little!

The garden was the next best thing at Chislehurst. The river Chisle ran through the bluebell wood, and there were lawns, greenhouses with peaches, a walled vegetable-garden, and bowers of holly which prickled but were good for playing hide-and-seek. There were gardeners and maids galore. The butler, Foot, struck Fryn as amazingly shambling and ancient, and she was told that he had the effrontery to propose marriage to Ethel, who had naturally scorned him.

Granny dressed in shiny silk and an endless variety of lace caps with different coloured ribbons. Her head nodded a little, her face was large and sallow, and she had truly beautiful hands with splendid rings upon them. Fryn recorded that 'her manner was always severe to me, but it did not hurt me for I did not love her. Her temper was appalling, and I remember her picking up a dish of stew once and throwing it at Foot.'

Uncle Somers was Fryn's godfather, and every Christmas he gave her one of the Andrew Lang Fairy Books illustrated by H.G. Ford, till she had them all. He worked at the Bar occasionally, but he and Uncle Squire spent most of their days riding or playing golf or squash.

Auntie Margaret was a superb rider, played tennis well, and golf. Upon her fell the burden of Granny's irascible temper, and her own temper suffered. She was always knitting scarves for the 'boys' – as they were called – and golf-stockings with fancy borders, and they expected no less.

There were wonderful stories of Grandpapa, who had come up from Stratton in Cornwall as a very young man. He had met Granny, who was helping two aunts to teach at a private school in Abingdon, had become engaged to her, and had gone to London to earn his living as an apprentice with the firm of Cory Wright the coal-merchants. As he rose in the firm, he became known as St James the Just. He had travelled all over the world and retired when he had made a quarter of a million pounds – a staggering sum in those days. He wanted to enjoy his wealth at leisure and, when not touring the Continent or crossing the Atlantic, spent every day on the golf-links of Camden House, where the Empress Eugenie had lived. He was a figure of awe to Fryn, who vaguely confused him with God the Father and was dumb-struck in his presence. The only liberty he permitted her, when he came down to breakfast each day, smelling faintly of eau-de-Cologne, was to pull out his clean handkerchief and gravely let her take a sniff at it.

There were three bathrooms, and the children bathed in the one where Ethel sewed, next to the napery cupboard. The bath had a heavy mahogany lid, and they gave themselves delicious tremors by begging her to shut the lid while they were in it. Fryn longed to bathe just once in Grandpapa's bathroom, but she never did. It had a kind of Grecian portico over the bath itself and, by pressing buttons, you could turn on a wave, a shower or a spray; very alluring to the imagination.

The rooms were sumptuous, with huge fires in winter. The walls were covered with pictures in gilt frames. In the vast drawing-room Granny used to hear the Catechism from Fryn and Stella on Sunday mornings, and Fryn was filled with a dull sense of injury that she always asked Stella the more difficult questions so that she herself never got a chance to show that they were perfectly within her scope. 'Even then, I hated not being first,' she wrote. 'I used to chafe inwardly at my timid manners which helped Granny to despise me, and I longed for Stella's *bon camaraderie*.'

In all likelihood, the frequent partings from Stella increased Fryn's admiration for 'the big sister'. Stella was her star. She tried to be like her, yet accepted that she was too little. She thought that she would surely catch up next time, but always Stella remained ahead, shining in her sky. They were almost grown-up before the awe went out of their relationship, and the competition never did. Fryn missed Stella dreadfully, while grabbing at the extra closeness to their mother which the separation fostered. She could not have told when the consciousness came to her that her mother must be placated lest she, like Stella, might be banished. The unease was constantly with her, and Babsie's too short sojourn had served to increase it, but she kept all this to herself. Only much later could she analyse the sense of threat: 'She's given one away and lost another; I thought I had to hold tight and keep mum.'

Yet, while in St Jean de Luz that same summer, a different side of Fryn had come uppermost, a less dependent quality. She was walking along the beach beside her mother when she announced: 'I want to be grown-up, and to do what I like.' Edith shook her head: 'You'll be grown-up soon enough; and you'll find that you can do far less what you like.' But Fryn persisted: 'I want to be free to choose wrong for myself rather than have right chosen for me.'

And then at last the eagerly-awaited offer did come for Eustace; he was appointed Assistant Priest at St Stephen's Church, Guernsey, and he prepared to take up his duties in October. Before leaving, there was a rare interlude of good family relations. Eustace and Edith, with Nan, Stella and Fryn, took lodgings in a farmhouse at Stock in Essex, while the Holly Bowers household rented the commodious Stock Rectory. They drove there together in the landau and shared expeditions of all sorts. The adult members, both Jesse and James, appear in a photograph of a shooting-party on Lord Petre's preserve, about to settle down to an alfresco lunch, surrounded by bottles and dogs and all looking relaxed and jovial, except the mixed bag stiff at their feet. In the centre, Eustace airily sports gun and dog-collar. Beside him, minute among the circle of guests and beaters, the slight figure topped by a feathered toque must be Edith. It is the only extant representation of her and her features are not visible, the face just a moon. The two families contrived to be on good terms throughout their stay. Even Granny, with Stella dimpling up at her big, doting face, forbore to raise a single storm. At least Eustace was not proposing to live upon Edith for ever!

While at Stock, Fryn made the stupendous discovery that you cannot be absolutely happy unless you recognize it at the time and so

'get the full juice out of it'. It was at a picnic; friends, uncles and all.
The sisters and two little cousins staying with the Rectory party were
playing hide-and-seek in a wood. The sun was setting and throwing a
gold-pink light on the tree-trunks. Suddenly Fryn stood still and let
the other children run on past her, while the thought: 'Now I am
happy!' pierced her. She let it sink in while she stood wordless, the
faint voices of the other children ringing the wood about.

Arrived at Guernsey, father, mother and Fryn went into lodgings in
the Rohais, before renting Woodlands Cottage. This had a row of
elms in front of it, and Eustace had it painted dark red. Fryn lived up
in the attics, which were made into nursery and night-nursery, with
nice low windows from which she could peer out unseen. She was in
severe pain at the time with a perforated ear-drum, having caught a
chill while watching the soldiers being marched down the Rohais after
her hair had been washed. She knew she was a dreadful coward, not
letting the patient doctor do anything for her, and she privately
determined to change herself for very shame.

Edith imported a French bonne called Marie, who was also acting-
nursemaid and was supposed to take Fryn for walks in the country.
Instead, it was to her friends in St Peter Port they went, where they
sat in a stuffy room. Then Marie would say sternly: 'Now, you must
not tell your mother where you have been, Miss Fee, or she will be
furious with you.' Fryn believed this and lived in a morass of lies and
guilt, which weighed heavily upon her conscience long after; Marie
had taught her to be a frightened, deceiving child. Later on, Fanny, a
darling nursemaid from England, with a gentle dusky face, was got
rid of promptly, because Edith must have been aware of a colour-bar,
something of which Fryn was oblivious. Sweets were another source
of a bad conscience; she was only given one acid-drop a night, which
she was allowed to take out of her mother's dressing-table drawer
when she went up to bed. She was trusted to do this by herself, but
naturally stole several. She was weighed down with morality; even
the daily inquiry as to whether she had been successfully to the
lavatory became had she been 'a good girl' that morning.

Until she was six, Fryn could not read out the letters on a black-
board and was considered slow. She was born short-sighted and
astigmatic. It occurred to nobody that both father and mother had
poor sight and 'if they ever kissed each other, which as far as I know

they did not, their pince-nez must have clashed and they must have glared at each other through them'. Eustace took a snapshot of 'Wynifried in our little greenhouse'; soft fair hair floats over her shoulders, and no mother would willingly mar such a lovely face with steel spectacles. Besides, Edith had begun to enjoy frequent compliments upon the looks of her little girl. 'And I had no idea there was anything wrong with my sight,' Fryn wrote. 'I thought that was how everybody saw, and it was only in dreams that I saw clearly. I remember dreaming a dream so vivid that for years it stayed in my mind. I was walking down to the beach at Cobo, and in a neglected cottage garden were masses of viper's bugloss in full flower, with a heart of red fire. The blue petals with flecks of flame colour looked like wood smoke. I saw the sea come rolling in over the sand. The sky was almost black, but the sun struck a great shaft at the sea, which was a clear green ridged with foam. A glassy green wave hung in suspension, and in it were the bones of an old horse. One is supposed never to see in dreams what one has not seen in life, but I am pretty sure that I had never seen the bones of an old horse, or I should have been so shocked I should never have forgotten it. My heart ached with pity for the sad bones of the old horse in the hanging wave; I knew his life had been unhappy.'

Edith had been in the habit of reading aloud, and she did it very well; had read Grimm and Hans Andersen and allegories to do with the soul. Then one morning at Woodlands Cottage Fryn had opened *Alice in Wonderland* at the page where the Queen kept saying: 'Off with his head!' and she began chanting it aloud in a sort of intoxication. The book had come alive between her hands.

Then the man who owned Woodlands Cottage cut down the row of elm trees in front of it and, in a fit of pique, Eustace moved his family to De Beauvoir Terrace next to St Stephen's Church. That was convenient for him; and convenient for Edith too, as it was next door to her new friend Miss Alice Lee. To the elder Miss Lee, her sister, Fryn had been going every day for lessons, and this was when the solemn affair of her 'bloom' had begun; a priceless quality of innocence she was supposed by her mother to have. It demanded total ignorance, particularly of anything remotely to do with sex. Edith may always have been frightened of caring physically for a man. The act of love was so repugnant to her it had to be ignored. She was able to inspire romantic feelings in women, though, and she liked that. Nan was an early conquest, but Alice Lee loved Edith with an even greater intensity and thought they were soul-mates. She was not only good but saintly, with a dry humour Fryn found disconcerting at first.

When Nan came, she took Fryn down to St Peter Port to buy cakes, and Eustace, who had been visiting at the harbour, boarded the same bus back. He caught sight of his child, but did not come to sit beside her; instead he began to talk, not to her but about her. She was wearing a white frock with a green sash. 'I knew a little monkey,' said he, warbling, 'with a pea-green tail,' and he looked at her significantly. She squirmed, hating to have attention drawn to her, but the teasing went on until her father, followed by the approving smiles of the other passengers, had to get off the bus at their corner. Nan and Fryn got off too, but Eustace – who had by then forgotten all about them – strode ahead, let himself into the house and, regardless of his little monkey with the pea-green tail, shut the door in her face. Nan, her own face red, banged sharply on the knocker: 'Showing off,' she muttered. 'That's all he does!'

Sometimes the rich relations, complete with Stella, came over. This was a great treat, because they could afford to hire wagonettes and horses and drive to Petit Bo and Moulin Huet for picnics. On one of these visits, Stella asked to see Fryn's lace collars. After looking them over she said: 'But I meant your *best* lace collars!' and Fryn took a horrid pleasure in saying meekly: 'These *are* my best', which of course Stella knew perfectly well, and knew that they had all been hers before they came down to Fryn. But how glorious the picnics were; watching the swirl of the creaming waters round the rocks while the horses munched the turf. Fryn and Stella at once forgot the affair of the collars and began playing their favourite game. This was a game Fryn had invented about two island kingdoms up above the clouds; Stella was Queen of Sylvana and Fryn was King Lionel Wildblood of Royonex. Fryn used to make maps of them with mountain ranges like woolly caterpillars, because while Stella was supposed to be 'the musical one', Fryn was 'the one who drew'. And she wrote serials of their valiant deeds and dazzling attire: 'It was an inner life, known only to me and Stella, that we lived when she came; a life many-hued, gorgeous, exciting. Like a gold thread it intertwined with the colourless one of my normal existence – the daily walk through the ugly roads, the endless seas of glass-houses – and dimmed it almost to nothingness. This was our Magic World, the Golden Secret. When the steamer bore her away, mother and father might think they saw a little girl called Stella, with bobbed hair and a round face, waving goodbye to them from the deck rail, but I knew better. She was my puissant Queen, and she was waving to me, and only to me – the World's Ruler.'

There were beds of pink and blue hydrangeas at De Beauvoir Terrace. Fryn called these calicomops, for she took pleasure in making up words and in giving her toys long imaginary names. To one of the wagonette picnics Eustace came too, and they found themselves sitting on a golden beach alone together. Fryn was carrying her brown bear, which she called Barbarossa, tucked inside the blouse of her sailor-suit. She picked up a pebble and thought of the pebble in Hans Andersen's story of 'Eliza and the Eleven Wild Swans', how it was smooth in her smooth hand. And she thought of something her mother had told her – that nothing in this world was perfect. There must therefore be an infinitesimal flaw running through this stone from end to end. Then, if it broke to bits against a rock, these would have an infinitesimal flaw running through each. She asked her father what to make of it, displaying for him the apparent pefection of the stone; and he said that she was to suppose she had an apple. It was round, it was smooth, it was red, it had a fragrant smell, a pleasant taste, but all these were only the accidents of the apple. If you took away its taste, colour, shape and so on, what would be left? Just the essence of apple. And with her stone the same things were true. Substance underlay everything. Pondering this, she took out Barbarossa and looked at him; it seemed impossible that he could be nothing but a set of accidents? Unfortunately Barbarossa immediately became the victim of what in the ordinary sense could be called an accident, for by the time she undressed to go to bed, he had escaped under the elastic of her blouse.

The gift of independent thought was Fryn's from an early age. She was out walking with her mother, hand in hand, having been told that a Channel steamer had gone down and only a few women and children had been saved. Really wanting reassurance, she said: 'Mother, which is it more important to save: women or children?' Edith answered rather sharply, as if jealous of any idea that Fryn rivalled her in importance: 'Women, of course. Children are only children.' Fryn said no more, but instinct told her that there was something wrong with the reply.

Eustace had been giving a series of lectures at the Guille–Allés Lecture Hall. He chose his Uncle Alfred, who had earned the glorious title of 'the Virgil of our time', as the subject of one of these. His deep voice in harmony with the familiar lines, he read 'The Lotus Eaters' and passages from 'The Idylls of the King', and concluded: 'His women will always rank among his best creations; a rare procession of dreamy loveliness and passionate richness.' Further lectures followed and he filled the hall to capacity every time. He was not alllowing himself to become insular, with the Continent so close at hand. In 1896 he toured by himself, visiting Tours and Bourges and on to Milan, Padua and Venice. Then in 1897, 'for the health of spouse', he took a Spanish trip with father-in-law, mother-in-law, and sister-in-law, visiting Madrid and Toledo, Cordova, Seville and Granada. Fryn was boarded with the family of a tomato-grower while they were away, and also while Edith was in hospital on two occasions for minor operations; not 'serious cutty-open ones' by Fryn's description.

'Cutty-open' or not, Edith's operations which were probably gynaecological treatments of some kind, or their cause, had a blighting effect. The mood in the house, never stable for long, swung ever more unaccountably. In her bouts of depression, pain, or the familiar but always shattering migraine, blinds were lowered, domestic sounds were banned. It was after these treatments that Fryn hit upon a plan for silent play; she would make and write a whole book, and adorn it with frontispiece, illuminated poems and chapter-headings. Nan had given her hundreds of pages of stout drawing-paper, and Fryn bound them together by hand, and covered them with grass-green linen stuck with glue and sewn with green silk thread. With pen and ink she drew the cheeky figure of Peter Pawky with a jaunty feather in his cap. At intervals throughout the book she dashed off sketches; a Prince and Princess; a little girl in a big hat; a maiden in a soap-bubble. Then she settled down to write. She worked with furious concentration for three days, and *Peter Pawky's Pheasant's Feather* is the story of a crotchety old woman, forever whining about trifles, till one day Peter Pawky dances down her lane and settles in with her in exchange for doing her chores. By degrees he brings joy into her small daily doings, but big disasters come too; her health, her finances break down, but wonder of wonders she smiles through it all. Finally he nurses her quite better and one day leaves a shower of gold-dust in her sugar-basin and vanishes. The pheasant's feather is floating up the path.

The story races along. There are no spelling mistakes, but several ink-blots and sometimes a word is left out in the haste to get on. Too excited to wait until the rest of the book was filled up, Fryn took this effort up to her mother in the darkened room, kissed her good-night and left it on the bedside table. It was two days before she heard. Edith was up; pale and languid she came into the nursery, her mouth tight. 'Am I supposed to thank you for the parable?' she sighed, and drifted away to her sofa.

Fryn was stunned. A nasty pain gnawed at her tummy and she left the book where it lay, the bubble-maiden forever to be encapsuled between bare pages. Guiltily she hung about her mother's door. At last she was called in. Edith, very matter-of-fact, sent her off to her drawing-lesson kindly, for Edith was adept at blowing hot and cold.

Not long after this wounding incident, Nan came to do the packing and the family left Guernsey. But not before Eustace had broken the back of the book he was writing. He had been accumulating material for a compendium of quotations, bearing upon the various 'Points treated of in the Twenty-second Article, for those interested in the matters at issue between England and Rome'. It must have made him extraordinarily happy to express himself in an occupation so in tune with his talents. He had used up his entitlement to leave and sick-leave, and he had received an offer to be Chaplain to the Winegrowers in Marsala, Sicily.

THREE

---·•❧❦❧•·---

Everything That You Wanted

BACK IN ENGLAND, Fryn went with her mother to Chislehurst. Holly Bowers was in a state of excitement, for Auntie Margaret was going to have her twenty-first birthday and Granny was giving a ball for her. A huge marquee was being put up, with a sprung floor for dancing. It covered the croquet lawn and was hung inside with yellow satin. Fryn looked out entranced and watched it being built, and when the night of the ball came, she and Stella stood one on each side of the entrance, handing people their programmes. 'My husband says he remembers me that night and got his programme from me, but I have no recollection of him, or anything but lights and music – and ices. I ate eleven of them that evening and many sweets as well. There was nobody to say "No" to Stella and me.'

Afterwards, while the marquee was being dismantled the next day, Fryn was put on a train, in charge of the guard, and sent for the whole summer to cousins at Torcross in Devon. They lived in a labourer's cottage, but it was a happy care-free summer, new in her experience. 'My cousin Willie Jesse, the head of the family, was a great naturalist, and spoke German and French perfectly. He was very handsome, though not in the stained-glass-window way of my father. He had married Cousin Flo, and they had a large family, of which my cousin Cicely was at the tag end and of my own age. But I must have been a bullying brute to Cicely, because although my hair was cropped that year and she had long golden curls, when we played Cavaliers and Roundheads I insisted on being the Cavalier and making her the Roundhead, and she meekly agreed. Fatty Fee not being a suitable name for a Cavalier, I borrowed my island name of Lionel Wildblood for the part, the most gallant and audacious name that a Cavalier could want. Yet I never had the least desire to share the Golden Secret with Cicely. Instead, I would assure her that I had a magic power nobody could withstand. "But you couldn't make my father and mother love you more than they love me, could you ?" she pleaded. "Oh yes, I could. They'd have to if I used my magic," said I. Poor Cicely believed me and was distraught until she confided in her parents, who told her I was only making it up. But I rather think I had a strong magic, for if to have a whole other life and world that you can step into when you like and that to you is real, is not magic, then what is?'

That was the only summer when Fryn was really a child. She and Cicely spent their days on the cliffs or on the beach, picking up cornelians or watching the fishermen drawing in their nets full of glimmering mackerel. She was sorry when the time came to be put on the train by Cousin Flo and met at Paddington by Nan.

Eustace had not yet left for Sicily. Nan put Fryn and her luggage into a cab and got in herself, and they drove to her parents' lodgings. Fryn was deeply distressed driving there, because the horse – as she had seen before getting into the cab – had a tube right in his chest! She screamed in bed that night and, when her father and mother came in, she told them through sobs about the tube in the poor horse's chest. They explained that it was to help it to breathe more freely, and at last she went to sleep again. But it had been a very ugly evening.

In November 1899, Eustace took up the Chaplaincy to the Wine-growers at Marsala, leaving Fryn and her mother in London, but it was not long before Edith decided that a wife's place was with her husband. He rowed out to meet their Orient liner in the Bay of Naples under a dapple-grey sky and, after visiting the aquarium in Naples, they went on by train and ferry-boat to Sicily.

Eustace had a dear little white-washed Parsonage and an excellent cook called Filippo. And Fryn made friends amongst the English children, sharing lessons from an Englishwoman. But while at Marsala she had a bad accident. She was taking turns with the little girl from the neighbouring *baglio*, riding a mule bare-backed. The mule suddenly picked up its heels and she landed with her right arm beneath her. She felt no pain beyond a sensation of pins and needles, but screamed with fright on seeing the arm was a mass of blood. Back at the Parsonage, a Sicilian doctor came, who brought no anaesthetic, and he set the compound fractures in her forearm by the simple method of pulling her wrist one way and her elbow the other and then grinding them both together, while her father kept repeating: 'Do look, dear. It is so interesting.' But he did have the imagination to hang a bough of tangerine oranges over the bed, to give her something more beautiful to look at.

Nan was sent for, and brought *The Red True Story Book* with her, of which Fryn wrote: 'It is impossible to say whether I was more excited over the story of Joan of Arc or any of the others, and they taught me a great deal of history as well.' The arm was kept in plaster of Paris until, at the end of Eustace's six months' appointment, they went to Biarritz, where a French doctor examined it. The bones were crossing and had to be re-broken and re-set, which the Frenchman did perfectly, and this time she was given chloroform. But the arm was much wasted, and a slight hindrance in turning the wrist proved to be permanent. They had taken rooms in a chalet, and Fryn became friends with the seven children at the villa opposite, after staring at them mournfully and alone out of her window for weeks. They were all girls, including one of over twenty known as Beauty, with immensely long brown hair on which she could sit. Beauty in a woman was important to Fryn, then and later, though she did not look for it or even like it in men, except her father.

From Biarritz they moved in the middle of June 1900 to Paris, and stayed at Passy where she went to a day-school, and she has observed: 'The general run of children must be rather unintelligent, I think, because Stella and I usually seemed to know more than others about all sorts of things. I think it was that, though my education was by fits and starts, father used to tell us such a lot of out-of-the-way things, like architecture and heraldry and astronomy. And I was curious about everything and mad on reading.'

Eustace also took her to the picture galleries, but he did not think of showing her the Impressionists. Although he knew the right terms – when to talk about gouache or aquarelle, and what pointillism meant – he only admired representational painting and never understood that the first problem of a painter is the problem of light. But they had great fun in the Louvre, whispering into the two basins and listening to each other, and she wrote of this time: 'I was not afraid of father as I was of mother, and yet it was mother that I loved the most, though I was beginning worriedly to see aspects of her which made it difficult to go on loving blindly. It took several more years for her to discourage me from this affection, and she did not even know she was doing it.'

She was getting to know her father, and he had just started to find some enjoyment in her company. 'I think,' she wrote, 'that the great difference between my father and my mother was that, though neither had much sense of responsibility, he was genuine and kind, whereas my mother was the most unreal person. In telling the story of her courtship days, for instance, she would vary between the pathetic and the noble according to the whim of the moment; ringing the changes every bit as freely as had Betsy the Hottentot. Father was not perhaps the wisest of men, but he at least was real. Mother was made of shoddy.'

During the first weeks of the family's return to England, Eustace had plenty on his mind. For his book was out, entitled: *Purgatory, Pardons, Invocations of Saints, Images, Relics*. It was generally commended, and the *Church Times* wrote: 'Mr Jesse maintains the Catholic position throughout, as against the Roman and equally against the Puritan. His comments are vigorous and to the point.' It was not a profitable publication in financial terms, but a few hundred copies sold and Eustace distributed quite a number among his friends, who all referred to it as very important and valuable.

Imagining then that the West Country with its soft airs might suit them both, Eustace and Edith took lodgings in Plymouth, where there was a well-known school at Mannamead suitable for Fryn, and for the first and only time she was sent as a boarder. She was put into a low form, but halfway through her first term she passed easily into a form with children of fourteen, although she was only twelve, the youngest and smallest. There she learned to draw from the cast, and felt this was very grand. English, history and geography interested her, and of course the French class was child's play, but arithmetic didn't convey anything to her mind, then or ever. 'This was largely my own fault,' she confessed. 'The girls soon discovered I could tell stories. I had read all the Sherlock Holmes stories, and I recited them in the first person singular as though I were Watson, as nearly word for word as makes no difference, and it was soon the accepted thing that in return for my Conan Doyle repertoire the older girls did my arithmetic for me. I apparently turned in correct sums every week.'

As she could not see the casts she was drawing, she was at last taken to an oculist, and she wrote of this: 'I have always remembered the moment when a pair of lenses of the right sort were put into the frame upon my little nose. I was looking out of the window where I had seen a blur of green, and suddenly I saw instead a myriad of ivy leaves, sharply defined, growing against the wall. It was sight such as I had had only in my dreams, and I was wonder-struck.' At the end of the second term, however, she was taken away because Plymouth didn't suit her mother, and they went to Exeter, where Eustace's cousin was Deputy Chief Constable of Devon and lived in part of the Exeter Prison. Eustace did what was called 'guinea-pigging' while at Exeter, and once he went to Powderham Castle for his guinea and preached to the servants. 'They were very nice to us, and my father too was happy, for besides having no colour-bar he had no class-sense; that is to say, he behaved the same whatever the company.' Eustace had decided to accept an offer to be Chaplain to the Forces at Colombo, Ceylon, but as this involved numerous other decisions they all three left Exeter and went back to London together.

Now, though Eustace could fairly have assured himself that he was justified in going off to do a man's job in the world, he must at the same time have been aware that he was running away, leaving Fryn to deal with her mother. But she conceded that he made some effort to see them properly settled before he went so far afield, with the result that they stopped living in lodgings. He found them a flat in a great red-brick block called Hamlet Gardens Mansions. It was decorated throughout for them, and Fryn and her father went together to choose the wall-paper for the big drawing-room, which had an all-over pattern of large flowers and stiff leaves in a mixture of indigo, buff and yellow.

Before leaving for Ceylon, he entrusted Fryn with a parcel to give to her mother when he had gone, and she presented it that evening as Edith lay on the bamboo sofa. 'Father left this for me to give you,' she said proudly, 'for you to have while he is away.' Edith tore at the paper. There was his handsome photograph, enlarged, in a brown velvet frame. Fryn admired it very much, but Edith stared at it, flung it face down, burst into tears and rushed from the room. Fryn was still sitting petrified with fright when she came back: 'But don't you like it?' she asked, to which her mother only smiled contemptuously. Of course Fryn knew that married people were supposed to love each other, and she wanted badly to believe it, but the scenes and quarrels she witnessed left her bruised and bewildered.

It was at Hamlet Gardens that religious instruction became a pressing affair, with her preparation for confirmation. It brought in a new element to Edith's emotional life and a new threat to Fryn's. Her father had been to call on the Vicar of the Holy Innocents, who had sent along Sister Mary Katherine. Edith thought her wonderful. Accustomed as she was to being adored, the boot – as Nan put it – was now on the other foot. She became still more intense, while Sister Mary Katherine began to prepare Fryn with two other children. These were a brother and sister whose father was something in the City, and when they were having tea and laughing heartily, the boy said: 'If I laugh so much I wet myself.' – 'So do I' said Fryn, but afterwards she realized that she had sinned against purity in saying so, and that any mention of the bodily functions was an offence against it. She took her preparations for Confirmation very seriously. She went to her first confession and tried to make it a full and honest one. She confessed to the lies she had told about those afternoon walks in Guernsey, and to the sweets she had stolen. She confessed to having sinned against purity. And then she had to add: 'I once was cruel to an animal.' Some months earlier, she and Stella had found a yellow butterfly on the window-sill at Holly Bowers and, quite unaware that incipient sex might have had something to do with it, they took its wings off and left it wriggling and helpless. The priest, before giving her absolution, said that there was one thing for which she must be especially remorseful, and Fryn bent her head in shame, thinking of the butterfly. But he added: 'Your sins against purity,' and in mild surprise she received her penance and went skipping out into Ravenscourt Park. It was a long walk home, but the Holy Innocents was the nearest church where her mother could get what she called 'everything that you wanted'.

Fryn was confirmed at All Saints, Kensington, and between then and First Communion Nan took tickets for a play called *Ambrose Applejohn's Adventure*, with Charles Hawtrey in it. But Edith considered that this sacred time should not be interrupted by a play, however moral, so she went to it with Nan in Fryn's place. 'My Confirmation ought to have made a great impression upon me,' Fryn lamented, 'and in my usual sycophantish way I tried to pretend to my mother that it did. The truth is that to my own disappointment I felt nothing at all. And the disappointment about Charles Hawtrey remained stronger in my memory than the laying on of the hands of the Bishop of Kensington, or my First Communion.'

Books were her outlet. She read the Brontës, and Jane Austen, and Tolstoy in Constance Garnett's translations. From the local libraries she discovered untold wonders, and never forgot the effect of truth which Somerset Maugham and Arnold Bennett stamped upon her mind. Her reading was carefully guarded, particularly at this time. She had had to learn for her first confession that it was important above all things to be pure, and had even been worried lest she had committed adultery. Without understanding what it meant, she grasped that men should be as pure as women. As her ideas of purity were exclusively connected with the lavatory, she had never asked herself: how do babies come? accepting that there were babies, there were children, there were grown-ups – two kinds of each – without wondering why. There it was, an indisputable fact, and the trouble she already had with the grown-ups she knew used up all her emotional energy, mostly in an agony of pity for Nan, to whom her mother was consistently unkind. This was one of her chief concerns and the other was to avoid having her own feelings hurt.

Nan was the source of everything pleasurable to her tastes. It was fortunate that Edith did not decree that going to the theatre would destroy her precious bloom for, having read much of Shakespeare, she was an addict, and it was Nan who took her to see Tree as Malvolio in the most glorious of the comedies; whereas *Peter Pan* left her cold – it may be because there was too much stress upon the word 'mother' in it.

It was Nan, too, who took her away every year for a holiday and, though many children would not have thought it exciting just to walk in the country or sit on a beach alone with old Nan, Fryn thought it a great treat. Occasionally Edith joined them; once at Weymouth when, after upsetting Nan, she quite enjoyed herself; and again at Southsea, when she was bad-tempered the whole time. There was no clue to her moods, except that letting fly gave her a sense of power. She allowed her bad temper to take hold of her more and more. She was still supposed to be devoted to Fryn, but Fryn was becoming most horribly afraid of her.

Fryn's life was small and poor and thin, although she did not know it. Every year the family at Chislehurst went on their travels; to Norway, to Scotland, to Bath, to Spain. And they took Stella with them, but they never took Fryn. Even when they asked Raymond, the son of Major Jack James, and collected all the other boy and girl cousins for a pantomime, Fryn was not invited, though she was living in London. She was that grievous thing, her father's daughter – the child of a failure.

*   *   *

On 15 October 1900 Eustace sailed for Colombo. The *Ceylon Observer* announced that the Cathedral work would be undertaken temporarily by the Reverend Mr Jesse, who had recently arrived in Ceylon for the benefit of his health. Almost immediately he was called upon to attend the Memorial Meeting following the death of Queen Victoria; just the sort of occasion at which he was adept. He was soon engaged upon a series of lectures, and he also applied for a licence to fish for carp in the Lakes of Newera Eliya. He had already put in his papers for the degree of Bachelor of Divinity to the University of Durham, and this was conferred *in absentia* in the first days of 1901.

When he was in due course transferred to the Garrison Church of St Peter at Fort, as Chaplain to the Troops, the Ceylon press fervently lamented the loss to the Cathedral: 'He had endeared himself greatly to the people by his gentle unassuming manners. He is a talented musician and has improved the choir very much and it will be hard indeed to fill his place.' There is no record of asthma or illness of any kind there, but hardly was he settled in at the Garrison Church than 'the morning service was interrupted by an unusual circumstance. The Chaplain, who was feeling far from well, rapidly grew worse as the service proceeded and went off in a fainting fit. He has been ordered up-country at once for rest and will leave shortly for home.'

During the first year of his absence. Fryn had entered a competition for the design of a poster, which she won. According to *The Artist* of February 1901, "There was an exceptionally interesting exhibition at the Middlesex County Council's Polytechnic at Bedford Park. The most remarkable feature was a design for a panel and frieze representing 'Water Babies', by Miss Wynifried Margaret Jesse, a girl student of twelve years of age." The following year she again won a place in the exhibition with a monochrome of St Michael and the Dragon. What was good about it was its massing of dark and light, and Edith was so struck by it that she had a photographic copy sent out to Eustace in Ceylon. He found fault with the stylized wings and wrote back a letter which upset Fryn very much, but despite his critical words he preserved the poster with apparent pride, for it stands in his scrapbook over the caption: 'Photograph of winning design by Wynifried aged 13 1901.'

On returning from Colombo, he was again in correspondence – this time with the aim of getting his Doctorate – with the Divinity Professor at Durham, who wrote: ' . . . to get the DD by the new severe system is very hard, too hard . . .' and, after going thoroughly into the difficulties presented, Eustace had to allow himself to be discouraged from that project. Meanwhile, he followed his pursuit of educating Fryn by taking her to museums and picture-galleries. The nude had an irresistible attraction for him, and he self-consciously pronounced it to be very pure.

It was not always to Hamlet Gardens that Eustace returned, for Edith's restlessness allowed her to stay nowhere very long and she had fetched up in Bedford Park, in a little house where there was scarcely room for him. She had long since given up going to church. The Holy Innocents was too far away, so the priest would come and administer the Holy Sacrament to her in her room. She explained this process by saying: 'I am afraid I can no longer go to church; church has to come to me.' Fryn would get ready the little altar, which was a prie-dieu, with a clean cloth and brass candlesticks, and it was a perpetual source of surprise to her that for the rest of the day after receiving Holy Communion her mother was in a particularly atrocious temper. In observing this phenomenon it seemed to her that it was not reaction from intense religious feeling that had this alarming result, for – as Eustace said years later with a great deal of truth – 'Your mother never had religion; what she had was religiosity.'

One of Fryn's troubles was that her mother wished her to become a nun. And in her cowardly wish to please, Fryn also said that she would like to become a nun, hoping that somehow something would intervene and prevent this ghastly fate. It had been agreed between Sister Mary Katherine and her mother that she was in spiritual danger because she was artistic. At fifteen years old, if violently attacked – as in a sort of spiritual way she was – Fryn was easily moved to tears. She wept when Sister Mary Katherine accused her of being a slave of beauty, not sufficiently devout, and no longer caring about Early Communion. But she wrote later: 'As a matter of fact, I was still very religious in a quiet way. I had great reverence and love for Christ. True, I was not as keen as my mother on a church where you could get "everything that you wanted", and had always found that my deepest religous feeling came to me when there was no pageantry. I wiped my eyes and looked at Sister Mary Katherine while I listened to her denunciations and thought "It isn't like that at all!" But I had no intention of telling her how it really was, and I wondered how mother could possibly feel romantic devotion for this silly, silly woman. I walked home and said nothing at all to mother about the interview.

Neither did I leave off going to church. It still meant something to me.'

That summer, Fryn and her mother went with Nan to Bournemouth for their holiday. The landlady kept hens and for the first time Fryn saw a hen in the act of laying an egg. Startled, she asked her mother about it, which provoked one of the worst scenes ever. She was told she had always had a nasty mind, and had now proved it by wanting to know about nasty things. This was astonishing, for her mother often had a boiled egg for breakfast – what was wrong or nasty about it? What had excited her was that the egg came out from under the hen's tail, which was a very uncleanly proceeding!

It was just after this incident that Stella again spent a day with them. 'I was seeing her off at the station when I became aware that she was bleeding in secret. My heart lurched with anxiety, for I thought her days were numbered; that she would bleed to death. My own immature body had given no warning, and not until mother saw my shocked face did she tell me drily that Stella would probably survive. "She is a mere woman at last!" she said spitefully, leaving me to find out what she meant.'

Fryn was sixteen when Edith had to have a severe internal operation. Eustace was home from Ceylon, and they went together to say goodbye to her in the nursing home. They were to spend the time of waiting at All Saints, Margaret Street, where the Sacrament was Reserved, for though they felt ravenously hungry, prayer came first. At four o'clock, after tea and a bun at some little shop, they went back to the nursing home where the matron told them all had gone well. 'But I think I can put down to that operation the insane behaviour which for the next years pursued my mother,' wrote Fryn. 'I gather she had had an ovariotomy. Little was known about the ductless glands in those days, and mother would certainly not have thought it nice to say anything about them. Father had gone abroad again. Mother and I were alone once more. And I can only say she proceeded to behave like a fiend. I had nobody to tell. I should never have been believed if I had told her family at Holly Bowers what my mother was like to me. There was only Nan, who knew but too well, and whose words would have had no more weight than mine.'

In January 1905, the final division of a Trust under the Will of his uncle, the Reverend Charles Tennyson Turner, who had died on 25

April 1879, brought Eustace a small legacy, being half his mother's portion. He left Southampton for British Guiana on 4 January, and there is this profile of him, written soon after his arrival at Georgetown, Demerara:

> 'He is at present helping at Christ Church and staying at the Vicarage, now adorned with his rubbings from Mediaeval brasses, and the loneliness of the Incumbent has been banished. His most voluminous work dealt with Prayers for the Departed, Purgatory, etc. Formerly Rector of Kirkley in Suffolk, he has travelled nearly all over Europe and has held several Chaplaincies on the Continent, South Africa and Ceylon. He is a fluent French speaker and scholar and when he resided in Guernsey was accustomed to take services and to preach in French. His erudition and accomplishments render him a very charming companion, his musical knowledge is supplemented by twenty-five years of choir training, and if only his health were more robust he would be a great acquisition to the diocese.'

Eustace's host, the new Vicar of Christ Church, wrote of him to friends in Bermuda, which he had recently left: 'I am not living alone at the Vicarage. On my arrival here I met an old acquaintance I met at Lincoln twenty-two years ago. He is a very charming man, not only cultured and well-read, but something of a theologian and canonist. When he proposed to keep me company I accepted with alacrity. Mr Jesse thinks of paying a visit to Bermuda on his way to the States, and giving a lecture or two there.'

Inevitably, Edith and Eustace were growing apart. They were learning to find companionship more congenial or more long-suffering than that of each other. If Helen James, before Fryn's eyes, once hurled a dish of stew at the old butler at Holly Bowers, her ultra-refined daughter employed other means of aggression. Edith's tongue commanded ammunition enough, and its effect could be formidable. She was singularly helpless at domestic accomplishments, yet always succeeded in finding someone willing to do anything for her. She exerted a strong fascination over certain women of simple faith, attracting devotion by the fervour with which she worshipped, and there was never a time when she lacked sympathetic support. It had to do with her look of extreme fragility, her delicate soulful face, her confidence, and her need. Yet there were times when she herself ceased to feel that need, and turned upon those about her in cold rage. It was a sort of wave motion she couldn't control; or was it that she couldn't be bothered? Consequently, half the time her humble servers were in transports and the other half in tears. Their very ministrations brought from her the sharp words: 'Your breath is vile today. Don't lean over me, for pity's sake!' or 'Please don't touch me. Why don't you take proper care of your hands? The skin is like a crocodile's.'

Some could only bear one such 'betrayal'; others came back for more, like Aunt Alice of Guernsey days. Nan too, of course; but Nan's loyalty had always spilled over on to the child she saw being caught up in the mother's complexities. Even when Edith had found a dearer friend in Sister Mary Katherine, Alice persisted in coming over as regularly as ever to take care of her; but she could say to Fryn: 'I can hardly bear to look at poor mother nowadays when she is in one of her tempers. Her little face is quite vicious.' And Fryn wrote to Nan: 'Since all the sad trouble with mother began, no one has been more miserable about it than Alice. But she is not blind – just kind. She calls her "the poor lady" and, though strong in all other things, she is straw in her hands.'

It became necessary for Edith to employ a paid attendant or companion, for Fryn grew so debilitated that she was sent for a term and a half to Gunnersbury High School nearby, where she conceived a harmless passion for the headmistress, an excellent teacher. 'This was one of the rare times that I have been "in love",' she commented. 'The curious thing is that all the time I did know that, if I met a glorious man – as of course I should one day – she would fade into the background. But the affair was real while it lasted.'

In May 1905, by then attached to St George's Cathedral, Eustace had the honour of being chosen to preach at the opening of the Synod of Guiana. The *Daily Chronicle* of Georgetown ironically reported upon the Synod sermon: 'Its unconventionality will make the discourse highly diverting reading; Mr Jesse belongs to the aggressively militant type of High Anglican clergyman who delights to essay a fall out of everybody. Even the Bishops of his own Church are not immune from his little attentions.' Pedantic and passionate in turn, the sermon showed that he had not forgotten in his middle age how to trail his coat.

Having fulfilled his engagement to the Bishop of Guiana to remain there two winters, it is evident that Eustace then paid that visit to the Windward Isles and Bermuda referred to by the Vicar of Christ Church, for he has kept a log covering over 5,000 miles from London and back, and touching Trinidad, Barbados, St Vincent, St Lucia, Dominica, Antigua, St Kitts and Bermuda. Fryn was one day to make the very same 'journey', also contriving to cover her expenses by the way.

Eustace arrived back at Bedford Park on 1 June 1906. The summer term had been interrupted for Fryn by illness, and she was away with Nan, recuperating from anaemia in the New Forest, when he reached home. He wrote her a letter there, saying how shocked he was to hear how badly she had been behaving to her mother. Fryn sat miserably silent and passed it to Nan, whose homely face went a deep red. 'As though he didn't know,' she muttered. And very soon he did know, but he had no solution, having scant means of his own, and he returned to Ceylon on 16 November, to become Acting Priest-in-Charge to the Church of St Michael and All Angels, Colombo.

The Ceylon *Churchman* published in May 1907 his sonnet: *To One Depressed by Consciousness of Life's Failures*, which opens:

> So soon began the flush of life to fade
> From glowing tone to hue of pallid tint!

His theme, taken from Dr Pusey's 'We are made up of failures', sadly recognized the plight that faced him. None knew better than he that everything was moving towards change. He was not so young that he could go on boxing the compass for trivial recompense that scarcely paid his expenses. Quite soon he would have to lie fallow more or less permanently, with all that that would mean to him in loss of freedom. And indeed his next posting to Tangier was to prove his last.

But by then Fryn too was 'dipt into the future'. She had gone to stay with her cousin Cicely Jesse again, in Torcross. For, when Stella had last come to Bedford Park, she was fresh from finishing-school in Paris, a school where she was encouraged to look most enchantingly grown-up. To Edith's mind, that settled it. 'My mother naturally disliked my dear headmistress at Gunnersbury,' Fryn observed, 'and decided there and then that, if Stella could go to finishing-school and study music and drama, I must go to art school, for was I not "the one who drew"? And thus the first great release of my life came to me.'

Conveniently, it came hand-in-hand with Cicely, who drew too, and whose mother had already made preliminary inquiries at Newlyn.

FOUR

—••₤)(₃••—

Newlyn: Her Intermittent Diary

'IN SUMMER the students are often seen dotted about the big sunshiny
garden which surrounds the classroom, making studies of the masses
of bloom as they grow under the open sky; and on fine afternoons a
ring of easels surrounds the model, posed out of doors.' That is how
Mrs Lionel Birch remembers the Newlyn School of Painting in
Cornwall.*

When Fryn went there to study under Stanhope and Elizabeth
Forbes, it had for long been a painters' colony. They had gravitated
there from the Quartier Latin, from Antwerp and Brittany and further
afield, as if a magnet drew them down the dusty road from Penzance.
The fishermen living in the huddle of grey-roofed cottages that hung
over Mount's Bay found no fault with their harmless occupation,
lodged them and fed them and sat for them as good-naturedly as the
natives of the twin Bay of Mont St Michel in Brittany.

Stanhope Forbes settled in Newlyn in 1884, at much the same time
as T.C. Gotch, Norman Garstin and 'Lamorna' Birch, and followed
by some twenty other artists, in groups of three or four. A rival
colony of painters had chosen St Ives; mostly landscape artists.
Stanhope was then in his middle twenties, and the new cult of realism
was captivating him. His square-brush technique was new, too, and
considered very French. While living at Quimperlé in Brittany he had
painted entirely in the open air, and his work, exhibited at successive
summer exhibitions at Burlington House, had excited keen attention
and had attracted disciples. Their style came to be seen as forming the
link in the development of British art between French Impressionism
and the Camden Town school of painters. Stanhope's move to the
Cornish bay facing the great turreted rock of Arthurian legend called
St Michael's Mount was scarcely a change of scene, but to a painter it
was a tremendously exhilarating change of weather mood and colour-

* In *Stanhope A. Forbes ARA and Elizabeth Stanhope Forbes, ARWS*, Cassell & Co
Ltd, 1906.

ing. A series of vibrant paintings brought fresh fame to Newlyn, and fresh faces. Elizabeth Armstrong came before the end of 1885.

She came from Canada. When her father died she – a sensitive and lonely child – and her mother had left their old wooden house in Ottawa for the riverside house of an uncle in Chelsea. From there Elizabeth had studied at the South Kensington Art School and later in Brittany, where she had heard of the independent young Englishman working at Quimperlé. Her delicate dry-point etchings had won her admission to the Royal Society of Painter Etchers, but a restlessness for greater freedom made her coax her mother to try Newlyn.

Her first studio was a net-loft, shared with the fishermen repairing their nets at the shadowy end. Life was easy and natural in the sociable little community. She met Stanhope at once, at the home of Edwin Harris with whom she had been at Pont Aven, and by the summer they were engaged. Their work was never remotely similar, apart from fidelity to nature, but each gave the other a most powerful stimulus. They married in the summer of 1889, and their son Alec was born in 1893.

Stanhope so loved flowers he could make them grow in extravagant abundance. He built a house of granite facing the sea, and they called it Higher Faugan from the Cornish word for a hiding place, and planted a protective ring of saplings, and laid their lovely wild garden within. His reputation grew, and he was made an Associate of the Royal Academy in 1891, and a year or two later was elected to the Institute of France.

Elizabeth liked to paint in a little wood of twisted trees among boulders, where she had her painting hut. She evolved her own medium of water-colour with charcoal to achieve a transparent clarity, and often chose children as her models. In 1898 she was elected an Associate of the Royal Water Colour Society for the beauty and poetry of the illustrations to her story-book, *King Arthur's Wood*.

The colony at Newlyn being a living thing, painters, metal-workers, jewellers and artists in glass and enamel came and went. But at the turn of the century it happened that there were empty studios, and Stanhope A. Forbes, ARA, and Elizabeth Stanhope Forbes, ARWS, conceived the plan to open their school. A field on the slope above the bay was bought, known as The Meadow, where an encampment of studios clustered. The cottages filled up, and a picture gallery came into being in the village street.

'Learn to draw,' urged the teachers. 'Learn to see. Have nothing to do with tricks. See that face, clear-cut as a cameo against the dark background colour; get your background true and the right shape and your face will paint itself more nearly than you can imagine.'* Visiting artists with names already famous came to supplement the teaching, and once a year Newlyn held high-jinks on The Meadow; on Show Day a great picnic was thrown, when the paintings destined for the Academy were on view to the public.

To this simple place, with its rarefied overtones, Fryn came in her nineteenth year. And how quickly its ways absorbed her! She and Cicely settled in at Myrtle Cottage, which they were to share with Mrs Shaw and her daughter Dod. Cicely was a big girl with soft fair hair, sweet small blue eyes, and a curly red mouth. She knew the Shaws already and had a romantic adoration for Dod.

Mrs Shaw 'ran' the house in a mild and unselfish way. She was no martinet and was a pupil like the rest. The redoubtable person at Myrtle Cottage was the landlady, Mrs Tregurtha, whom they called Tregaggins. She was a woman of infinite dignity. Her mother had been a de Ruffiniac – pronounced by the Cornish as Roughneck – descended from émigrés at the time of the French Revolution. Tregaggins was not as good a cook as her daughter Primrose became, and one day they were all sitting on the cobblestones of the garden, eating the pasties she had made for lunch. They called up indignantly: 'Tregaggins, Tregaggins, there's no meat in these pasties.' A stately head, crowned with red-gold hair going grey, looked out from a top window: 'Eat your good pasties, loves,' said Tregaggins firmly, 'and let me hear no more about them.'†

They had their chief meal in the middle of the day, with fruit; and a boiled egg with a cup of cocoa in the evening. At night they spent halfpennies on chocolate cream bars. Any notion of the *vie de Bohème* can be discarded; their gaiety was schoolgirlish rather than reckless. 'At Myrtle Cottage we had a trick of talking in double-inversion between ourselves, and we became so adept at it that we rarely fell into normal speech,' wrote Fryn. In no time at all, everyone had a new name derived in this fashion. Mrs Forbes became Forces

---

* *Stanhope A. Forbes ARA and Elizabeth Stanhope Forbes ARWS*, Mrs Lionel Birch
† All these details come from *Her Intermittent Diary*, FTJ, unpublished.

Mibs, and indeed she was called Mibs until the day of her death and she loved the name. And dear little Mrs Shaw became Shisis Maw, and was known as Shisis, or just Maw. Myrtle Cottage was always The Myrtage. And Wynifried slipped smoothly into Fryniwyd, as into a new skin. Only when she was in a more than usually frivolous mood was she dubbed Frilliwyd.

They used to work all day at The Meadow Studios, where the models were. The life model, whether a man or a woman, came down from London. Dod Shaw, as Dod Procter was then, was much the cleverest of the students, not only as regards drawing and painting, where she was streets ahead of anyone else except Ernest Procter whom she eventually married, but in the management of her life. 'We used sometimes to have fancy-dress dances, known as drencies, in the studios, to which the Professor – as we always called Stanhope – and his wife came with their son Alec, a lively and attractive boy being educated at Bedales. It meant hard work, getting the studios ready. Some students rubbed the floors with French chalk. Some hung draperies up behind the model thrones. Some worked on the lighting, or spread sandwiches. I used to borrow a cart and pony from a neighbouring farmer and, often with Cicely, would drive into the country and fill the cart with dog-daisies, cotton-grass and branches, and festoon them everywhere. Then we fled on to the Myrtage, had a hurried wash-down in the flat tin bath, and dressed up in whatever was our fancy-dress for that evening. Dod never cleaned or polished or drove out to pick flowers. She appeared dressed in time for the dance, looking superbly handsome.'

Many people came down to Newlyn. A.J. Munnings would sing student songs – 'He who'd kiss a pretty girl and go and tell his mother, Ought to have his lips cut off and never kiss another' – and Fryn thought she had never heard anything so dashing. Harold and Laura Knight came, she innocent-looking in flowery chintz frocks that would never date. Their brilliant painting stunned the whole colony.

In the first year or two, it was enough for Fryn to accept the discipline of charcoal, to learn to live and let live in the company of people of her own age, to laugh, dress up, and hum her tuneless songs. The Myrtage was for girls, but there were other cottages for the other sex. Norman Garstin had two sons, Dennis and Crosbie, and a daughter Alethea, all pupils at the Newlyn School. And some of the houses in the village or in Penzance took in lodgers of mature years who joined vacation courses. From one of these Fryn had her first proposal of marriage.

She also wrote *The Look Backwards*, for playing with the passing of time was a game she indulged in from her earliest days, and where it touched upon her own age she was without conscience. 'A woman,' she said, 'has not only the right but the duty to remain as young and as beautiful as possible by any means to hand.' In writing this memoir she used her new name for the first time as author:

THE BOOK OF FRYNIWYD TENNYSON JESSE

By Woden, God of Saxons
From whence comes Wednesday that is Wodensday
Truth is a thing that ever I will keep
Unto thylke day in which I creep
Into my sepulchre.

It is dedicated to 'Fryniwyd's John', who is never referred to again.

The Book has an apologia, which confides: 'I have a vague notion that some day I shall be something of importance! I suppose the feel goes for nothing and that everybody begins life with it. How terrible when the day comes on which one realizes one has been – nothing! Nevertheless it is that feel that is making me begin this book. What if I become great and want to write a novel round my life and have forgotten? It's as well to be on the safe side. I can't help thinking I am interesting; not because I am a marvellous person or anything of that sort, but because anyone, the most seemingly dull person, would interest if he wrote himself, if he wrote true. What is truth? It is, I think, a relative quality. "One man's meat is another man's poison", and one man's truth is none the less true for being another man's lie. Truth is the genuine expression of a genuine thought.'

The story of *The Look Backwards* is already told. Begun at Newlyn in the summer of 1907, it opened with Fryn's consciousness at the age of three in 1891, learning to fly from off the dingy pink dustbin in Balham. It came to an end at the beginning of 1908, with the description of the family's departure from Guernsey in 1898 when Fryn was ten. But, before it petered out, its author had a few thoughts to air on beauty; on the beauty of the body and of the dawn: 'For to this day I cannot understand why we should be ashamed of our bodies. The body is so exquisitely lovely: the pearly colour; the clear soft shadows that define the rounded planes. There is no sight so cooling to the senses, so inspiring to the mind. Truth is depicted as a naked woman, not because Truth is blunt, brutal, shocking, but because "Beauty is Truth, Truth Beauty". Mother thinks it is disgusting, she thinks it is immoral, to work from the nude model as we do down here, and with the Professor to "crit" us. But we all sit to each other at the Myrtage, and sometimes Dod and Cicely and I have birthday-suit evenings, posing on the big bed, with nothing on but a silver belt to make us feel barbaric, and a hand-glass so that we can judge the effect.'

'This summer of 1908 I hope to spend a night at Lamorna, and Dod and I will make our way to the stream that runs over the moorland, and there we will dabble naked in the running water while the miracle of dawn unfolds. For I have never seen the sun rise. Yet I know what the dawn is like, because sometimes when sitting on Trevella rocks, watching the setting of the sun and the gradual greying of the world, I have by a sustained effort of the will imagined it to be the rising of the day. At once the earth and sky have taken on a different aspect, no darkening farewell attends them but a hush of expectation, all nature holds her breath for the birth of a new day. My eyelids prick and the world swims in water. I blink. And lo! the sun is setting behind the far hills, the spell is broken, and I have never seen the dawn.'

These were the final addenda to *The Look Backwards*, and meanwhile Fryn was allowing Cornwall to cast a lasting spell upon her. The presence of the gentle, humorous Maw, calming her headaches yet stimulating her to unabashed talk, was true benison. And up at Higher Faugan was Mibs, wise, remote yet approachable, kindred in many ways. She had the same abundant store of literature and history to feed her mind upon, the same poetic vision. These two so sharply contrasted mother-figures soon began to make more sense of her confused relationship with the grown-up world and give her confidence: 'I owe to Elizabeth Stanhope Forbes my first friendship with an adult, sensible, talented human being. She helped to teach me how to express myself and not to be hide-bound. After I had had my appendix trouble and been nursed at the Myrtage by Maw, Mibs took me up to Higher Faugan and let me convalesce there, and I listened to her amazingly clear and liberating comments on life generally.'

Mibs asked her to write a play to put on at Christmas, and she wrote *The Corpse, the Coffin and the Coughdrop*, a Melodrama in Three Palpitations. The scene was laid in what she happily called 'the fastest flat in Fulham' and Fryn herself was Vivian de Rouge Coeur, the villainess dressed in scarlet silk. The plot was based round a

Marriage Bureau to which she lured young girls. It was performed twice and was a great success. The artists and the County sat on the floor of the Studio to the far wall and laughed their heads off – and Fryn began to think writing was easy.

Another suggestion Mibs made was that it would be a good thing if they produced a magazine, and that Fryn must be the editor. It was called *The Paper Chase*, and was printed at the little printing-works in the village, which was run by amateurs. But it took such a great amount of time and energy that it was all they could do to produce one annually. 'We only had two volumes of it before it died a natural death by Mibs becoming ill. I have my copies of these still and some of the drawings are very fine. Nothing I wrote for it was any good.'

The first copy appeared in March 1908, on fourteen-inch hand-cut art paper. The reproductions were by 'Lamorna' Birch, Ernest Procter and Elizabeth Stanhope Forbes and are of high quality. The letterpress included a story by Norman Garstin, and Fryn's short story 'Sans Souci', illustrated by her own lino-cut, from a series of fairy-stories to be called *My Town*. It has the rich texture of the Golden Secret life played with Stella. There is more subtlety in the telling and an ironic humour, but she plunges as straight as she ever did into the realm of magic: 'On the hill of the Longing Heart my Town is set, glowing warm and red as a ruby on a mound of green velvet; aloof as a star, alluring as a fire . . .'

As editor of *The Paper Chase*, she was given the nickname The March Hare, and Elizabeth Stanhope Forbes, in her introduction, offered a sort of portrait of her: 'Keen and clean blows the wind of the morning. Come out, you young people, and follow me! I am a merry, irresponsible little fellow, by many called Mad, but those who lift their faces to the brightness of the morning love me, and the light of heart follow where I lead. Some call me the Pathfinder, the Enthusiast; some, Imagination; some, the crack-brained March Hare, illusive, inconsequent. But to those who can catch, I toss as I run, the gift of Perpetual Youth.'

As well as her editorial matter, Fryn put in a sonnet, 'The Forbidden Vision'. So did Cicely Jesse. And so did Eustace Tennyson d'Eyncourt Jesse, DD. Not for the first time, he had slipped quietly away from London and travelled by coastal steamer to Penzance, drawn by his 'vanished dream' in the churchyard. He was there hooked by the demands of the peremptory editor of *The Paper Chase* just before leaving for his final tour of duty in Tangier.

That year, Fryn had exhibited paintings at Liverpool and Leeds, and she has acknowledged: 'As far as I was concerned, this carefree life – although I already knew I should never become a painter – might have gone on for ever, with interesting people always coming and going.' Her great friends were Crosbie Garstin and Adeodato Gilardoni, one of the printers who also made enamel jewellery. He played the viola too, and the Professor's violoncello was at the core of the musical evenings for which the Faugan became known for miles around. A girl called Maudie Palmer played the piano gloriously, and Mibs provided sandwiches and claret-cup.

Fryn began to feel so grown-up that she decided to keep a diary, and she has since said of it: 'I knew very little about life, but that did not deter me, and it was my husband's favourite reading. Slightly pompous and absurd it must have been, which is doubtless why he enjoyed it.' It was a happening on the eve of Fryn's twentieth birthday in March 1908 that had sparked off the intimate outpourings which became *Her Intermittent Diary*. The chief names bandied in it are Damit, Horse and Aunt, who had all joined Cicely and herself at the Myrtage when the Shaws moved into their own cottage at Lamorna. Damit – Sibyl Sampson – was all of twenty-three, and that seemed frightfully old to the others. She was a tiny thing, whose loyalty to Fryn was of the permanent kind. Horse was a big beauty. And Aunt of the shy childish face was Clare Collas, then Clare Waters, who became a successful illustrator and jacket-designer; she and her old cow-shed studio in St John's Wood were to figure in Fryn's first novel. Then there was Mitrat, Fryn's suitor Arthur Musgrave. And there was the fabulous Phyllis Gotch, daughter of the painters Thomas Cooper Gotch and his wife Caroline, née Burland Yates. There was also Alethea Garstin – who did the original cover for *The Tatler*, with the crinolined lady – and her two brothers, who were both *épris* with Fryn, though she did not yet know it.

Her Intermittent Diary began without preamble: '5 March 1908. I am out of my 'teens! Bring ashes and sackcloth for my head and a hairshirt for my body! My birthday I passed as usual in deep gloom, but the morning after found my sunniness unimpaired. On the eve we had a drency at the Studio. Horse in a white and pink muslin with puffed sleeves, mittens, a coral necklace, and her hair in two window-curtains tied with pink ribbons. Dod was Turkish in white butter-muslin bags, veil and tunic, real red Turkish slippers, and everybody's silver ornaments. Damit, as a brown butterfly, wore my brown lawn evening-dress, with two gold-painted wings, and on her head were wired tall gold antennae. She looked airborne. I was a Bacchante and looked better than ever before, I think, although I was rather pale. I wore a blue-green silk dress lent me by the Gotches, and my gold girdle twice round my waist and hanging down in front. Dod did my hair in a wild mass of curls all over my head, and on them a cluster of brown-gold leaves. I had borrowed a cheetah-skin, and one paw was slung over my shoulder. The effect was choice.

'A funny thing happened at the drency; Mitrat turned up and asked for a dance, and I went to sit it out with him downstairs. I suppose I oughtn't to have. Horse says that when you've refused a man five distinct times you oughtn't to get alone with him. The wretched creature grew serious all over again and bowed his head on my knee. The old theme of course: he adores me, he adores me! I can't think why I keep it up – yet I can't stop. It seems that as long as a man will make love to me, I'll let him!

'9 March 1908: This afternoon I began a big pastermiece – a dragon, and a lady in a birthday-suit – for which Dod is going to sit.

'10 March 1908: I seem to have violently upset my luckless little appendix with coughing till it aches. I was sitting on the floor with my back to the fire when Dod came in. She sat down on a low chair and I put my head on her lap and she said: "What is your cause for grief?" "It's that I'm getting so frightfully bad-tempered." "Oh no, you aren't, really Fryniwyn." "Yes, I am. Not so much to you, but to all the others. And I feel an actual antagonism to them. Yet I used to have a good livable-with temper." "It's just because you feel ill," said Dod consolingly. It is, partly, but it doesn't make it any better when there's a real cause like a growing bad temper. And why do I feel this antagonism?

'11 March 1908: Siola has come back and is lodging down at the harbour. She came round at about half-past-twelve, and she and Dod and Damit sat on my bed while I had my bath, and jeered at my skinny appearance. After supper, Bacter [as Ernest Proctor was called] came to take Dod for a walk. Oh Mrs Grundy, what a blessing it is we aren't troubled with you down here. Dod has just come in again, and says that Bacter tells her Mitrat has that portrait of me in bed, and it's in his bedroom. How *awful*!

'14 March 1908: The Students' Show Day. My brown felt hat came from Liberty's and I trimmed it with the pheasants' wings and wore it with my brown furs and a dream of a new Liberty silk coat-and-skirt. The Show was a very good one, and the Professor specially mentioned the Myrtle Cottage Class. He mentioned the magazine too, and said how much we owed to Mrs Forbes' energy, and then he said: "And for it's success we must also thank the brilliant little editor"!

'17 March 1908: I found a trying epistle from mother, suggesting my joining her at the Chiswick Convent for Easter and, at the bare idea, the memory of last year's terrible Easter crowded back on me. She says in today's letter: "About Holy Week and Easter, do exactly as you like. I thought the chance of being under the same roof as a Chapel, with Daily Mass and the Blessed Sacrament, would outweigh everything else, but it is hard to realize sometimes how far you have drifted from me." It seems impossible for her to see that it is just because I do still care for these things that I cannot bear them being made the subject of storm and fury. I dread the thought of moving into another house too. It means not only that we shan't be able to afford my staying on here, but that I shall have to live in London alone with her mother again. I'm like some little animal in a trap that allows of its running round and round, but provides no door.

'19 March 1908: In the afternoon went to Penzance to see Père Rogers. I explained how I dreaded giving up religion altogether. But I have not said my prayers since Christmas and it is now well on in Lent. All I do is to hear Mass every Sunday. I asked him if he thought it was any good my trying to go on. He was very wise and told me to try and make a fresh start now, without making my Confession, so as to have pulled up by the time I do. That gives me more to work for.

'Yesterday a very overflowing wagonette started off for the Land's End for my long-delayed birthday picnic. Fifteen of us went. Each one was presented with a penny wooden spade, and the efforts of the men to conceal theirs about their persons were peerless. Dod and Siola emerged from a sweetshop, each with three feet of liquorice ribbon hanging from her mouth – truly a low scene. Lunch was very uproarious. Siola made her noise like water coming out of a bottle, and Cicely did her gramophone act. The waiting-maid, who had eyes put in on the cross, was highly diverted. After lunch we went to the cliffs, and soon things got "werry obvious" – to use a Myrtage term: each couple went off to find a beach; each found the same and collided!

'23 March 1908: Heard from Stella to the astonishing effect that

Holly Bowers dotes upon *The Paper Chase*! Also had a letter from Mother: "I think your March Hare things are decidedly sharp and clever. If I could be sure you would care for it, I would send you the account of Father Holden's funeral and what the Bishop of London did and said".'

'25 March 1908: Show Day, and we all went down to the Gallery. The pictures were mostly splendid, and St Ives admitted we had licked them into fits. The Professor had his big portrait; Mibs her sunny oil of three children; Mrs Knight had a beautiful small oil, "Child with Toy"; and Mr Knight had a village wedding procession that was clever, but I was disappointed in it.

'26 March 1908: The day of Phil's Gypsy Beano. You looked from the pink-lit glow out into the dark garden, where a fat Chinese lantern hung against the sky. The men all looked frightful ragamuffins, with teeth blacked out. Bored with chatting to the non-dancers, I watched the lighted torch-dance. For the first three figures the processions turned in and out, just waving their lights, then all became a scene of wild confusion, each person stamping and jumping and yelling. Every now and then came a crash of broken glasses, swept down by the stampede. Little Mrs Knight was the wildest of the wild, her hair streaming and ragged skirts awhirl; even Harold unbent and was dancing and kicking with a broomstick.'

This lamp-lit scene was captured in oils by T.C. Gotch in his painting 'The Lantern Parade', which gives an eerie impression as of Walpurgis Night revels rather than the merry romp it was to start with.

'30 March 1908: Nan arrived today and I met her with a wagonette. We are giving a singsong soon to four or five of the men, so I hope they won't be paralyzed by a duenna and that dear Nan will like being here. Some of the lyrics are mine.

'5 April 1908: Nan heard from Mother: "I have had such a worrying time. I had changed from one house to another, and now both Stella and my sister Margaret think I have made a mistake. The doctor says I have nerve exhaustion, and indeed that is how I feel. But as long as I have the good gentleman and W, I shall never know peace." Poor Mother, one would really think she had taken the house for father and me!

'I went to the Faugan for lunch and walked round the garden with Mibs, and she told me I had a future before me. And I mean to have. I will.

'6 April 1908: Phil Gotch asked me to go up to supper, and she came out with a lovely plan – no less than that she and I should go away together under assumed names. I don't want dear Nan to be hurt at being left, but I will go, if only for one night. And we are going to be widows!

'3 May 1908: On Wednesday morning Phil came tearing in before I had had breakfast and I had to fly off without. Phil opened her purse and pulled out two wedding-rings we'd bought at the pawnshop. She was very noticeable in deep black with her fair hair and long creamy neck, and I was looking too startling to be true; the black hat and skirt made my hair pure golden, and my having such a colour with excitement made me painfully striking. We bought some buns and fled into the train, and every man who passed our door stared, their heads simply slewed round at us. We were choking with hysterical laughter. It was not yet mid-day when we got out at Carbis Bay. You go down a winding path through gorse and bramble till you take a sheer turn and face the sea, at which you look through the tall grey arches of the railway bridge that spans the gorge in which the hotel stands. A red clay stream runs down the gorge and across the sand into the sea, dyeing the edge of the water copper-colour, so that the bay seems girt with a ruddy shining belt, even the foam pink-tinged. The Japanesey effect of this broad red ribbon dividing the pale sands from the deep blue of the sea beyond is curious and valuable to the last degree. The hotel stands on the left of the gorge, and at the mere idea of entering this respectable-looking place under assumed names we began to stutter, but pulling down our veils we marched boldly in and secured two bedrooms on the top floor. I was acutely conscious at lunch that my wedding-ring looked a palpable sham, and all the hotel people seemed incapable of calling us anything but "Miss", which caused us to quake with panic. After wandering through the village, we wrote letters in the lounge, mine to my imaginary husband; for we had decided by now that I could do the petted young wife business, but could not get my face to assume the melancholy pallor of a widow. The lounge was beginning to thaw towards us by the time we went up to bed. Then Phil and I sat and talked in her room for ages. It is true that two girls can't be long together without getting on the subject of their future husbands and the beckoning mysteries of sex.

'We had breakfast late in solitary state and then went into the church – two pathetic black-clad figures! Phil opened the Bible at random and her finger lit on this text: "Now there came a certain widow into that city". Of course we collapsed with laughter. Then we went for a lovely walk over the moors to the monolith thing erected over the body of a man who left a sum of money yearly to maidens and matrons who would dance round the column, which they do annually to this day. We caught the express back, and for supper had fried bacon and eggs and cocoa and brown bread and butter at the Myrtage, and I liked it much more than the hotel. Indeed I had felt so married, so acutely conscious of my proprietory "husband", that it was a relief to be natural and free after all.'

Just a week after her return from Carbis Bay, following this curiously unsatisfactory escapade, Fryn left Newlyn for London with Nan, sick of the grumbling pain in her appendix. In preparation for any eventuality, she wrote to her father: 'My dearest father – Mother will give you this soon after you arrive. It is only to say I love you very much. If things have gone wrong by the time you get this, you'll be glad to be assured of it again. And if I am nearly recovered – you must be quick and come and see me! Your own Mite.'

For the fortnight before she was due to enter the Hostel of St Luke in Fitzroy Square, she had a queer sense of resting in fate. 'The strange thing was that I wasn't worrying about my soul, as poor mother wanted me to, but I was grieved that in a few days time the bright beautiful world might be blotted out for me. And I had a vision of my body lying straight and helpless underground. The thought of that smooth skin, those nervous fingers, rotting! That was my worst bogey.'

She went down to Holly Bowers late in May to spend a night. Squire was ill and, after being presented with a tepid cheek by Granny, she went to see him. There was a glazed look in his blue eyes, and she thought how horrifying it was that he might be lying there dying. 'That night I did not sleep till the birds were clamouring; I had no brandy and no means of getting it, and finally went down to breakfast dazed and exhausted. Only old Ethel remembered to wish me luck with the operation. Of course I know that I and Holly Bowers don't mix; the Philistine well-to-do air of the place chokes me.' Blind with migraine she met Edith at Harley Street and fainted while the surgeon examined her and again in the taxi home. This meant having the priest to the house to hear her confession, with her mother and Aunt Alice filing solemnly into the room for the unction – an ordeal only to be endured, untouched and dry.

That night, in a high narrow bed in the nursing home, she thought of Newlyn lying under the stars, of Myrtle Cottage with its pink walls and the sweetbriar by the black pitched fence, and the Studio garden with the larkspurs bluer than the sky, and the dear life with its freedom and warmth. And she thought: 'I've had my good time and nothing can take that from me. And yet I've not had the biggest thing of all – I've never loved. I don't want it to come yet, but feel it I must, if it spells disaster and ruin.'

The next morning, when the surgeon looked in to see her, she stuck her feet in the shapeless woollen operation-stockings out of bed and said indignantly: 'Look at those! I might have any kind of a foot and ankle inside them!' He laughed his way out, while she trotted to the lift with Matron and shot up to the theatre floor. The days that followed were miserable and shaming beyond words. 'Pain I can stand, and I'm not shy about my outside, but when it comes to insides!' On her way back from France, Mibs came to see her, simply sweet as always, bringing masses of white flowers, roses and lilies, and said: 'Goodbye, little golden-head' as she kissed her on leaving. Well aware that the evening sun would be just lighting on her coiled plaits, Fryn had not let the blind be pulled down behind her.

Almost as soon as there was no longer any danger, her mother turned against her again and for ten days didn't come near. It was a trifle as usual that tipped the precarious balance between them; on the last day at St Luke's, Edith came for her early, and Fryn suggested having a taxi and taking a spin round the Park, for which she would pay. In a moment the storm broke. Edith raged, called her a little beast, a devil, evil, unnatural, without heart. Did Fryn suppose she came to see her because she liked to? She had thought her hateful for a long time. Fryn stood, choking with tears, and tried to explain that she hadn't meant to offend or be ungrateful. She was still weak, and cried with great sobs that jarred at the scar. She begged her mother to stop, but stop she would not, till at last she went to the matron's office, actually saying quite seriously that she didn't like to see Fryn looking so ill. 'Oh, I can't bear it.' Fryn protested. 'I sometimes wonder why I have not hit out at that cold jeering face and watched it grow frightened. What on earth am I to do if I have to go back to it next summer?'

This summer, the remaining days had passed peacefully enough, in convalescing with Nan at Haslemere, just driving in a donkey-cart and reading; but when their stay was up, Fryn was still not fit to go back to Newlyn. So she had gone home, and mother and daughter had been as politely aloof as strangers in a waiting-room. Several times Stella had come to spend the day, and on one of these occasions they had egged each other on to visit an astrologer, who pronounced this opinion on 'The Horoscope of Miss Wynifried Jesse, age 20, born at Chislehurst, 1 March 1888.

'The native will be slightly above medium height and good looking. She is emotional, receptive, meditative, amiable, kind, generous, acute, clear in ideas, precise, decisive, practical, and brave. Her will is firm and rather despotic, with a love of command. At times she is rash and indiscreet and sometimes jealousy will show itself. She has a tendency to pessimism. She should possess good abilities, mental activity and intuition. There is some sensuousness and poetic inspiration, with a love of art and literature. She has a keen sense of the ludicrous and a keen eye for detail. She has a great love of pleasure and amusement, with a strong tendency to indolence. If she will practise self-restraint, she will accomplish much in the world, but indolence and dissipation are the stumbling blocks. All strong drinks are better avoided, as the Sun and the Moon are in watery signs.

'Marriage will probably be delayed. There is a probability of two marriages, or at least of two simultaneous attachments; one possibly to a foreigner or one residing abroad. There will be secrets connected with love affairs. The native is rather inclined to flirtation.

'Health will not be robust and great care must be exercised in protecting it. She is liable to accidents. She should be successful in business, or in publication, or in the practice of Art or Literature. She will experience both privation and affluence during her life. There is a possibility of some legacies being received. The native may benefit from the lower classes in some way. She will receive great benefits and much assistance from friends, some being powerful; female friends will be of much use at times. Literary and scientific people will prove of great service. Her hopes and wishes will often be realized.

'Long journeys will be fortunate. She may follow two occupations at the same time. There are signs that she may experience trouble through the opposite sex. She has a tendency to be extravagant and to waste money. The weaknesses signified in this horoscope must be restrained and controlled, otherwise the native may experience sorrow and perhaps scandal. The very powerful position of Venus in the Mid Heaven should enable her to avoid the evils and enjoy the good fortune which seems in store for her, 18.8.08'

Not displeased with the greater part of this, Fryn pooh-poohed the rest and prepared to return to Newlyn at the beginning of September, with the prospect of a Studio drency on the Saturday. Her diary records:

'6 September 1908: I arrived in a new brown frock, with long gloves and my big hat with pheasants' feathers, and they were all at Penzance to meet me. I dawdled through Friday, and for the drency I had to be the eternal Early Victorian, in yellow flowered muslin, black chiffon fishu and black mittens. I was afraid that as a non-dancer I wouldn't fill my programme. However, I went on booking serenely. Aunt was the belle of the ball in a real crinoline. She went flying round the room like a floating ball of thistledown and the men were raving over her. I had a good many bookings with A.J. Munnings, who holds the human race in scorn when it's on dancing bent, so we sat in the garden and talked books, A.J. gesticulating, talking well, and looking so odd in his horse-fair suit. He said things that would be unforgivable from anyone else, and then suddenly burst out with: "Look at 'em, Garstin – innocent little things! What do they know?" which made me gasp. Crosbie, no longer at the Newlyn School, was down for a week's holiday from his new job at Bristol, and he and I sat out three running and, metaphorically speaking, felt round tentatively for a footing, for I hadn't been answering his letters.

'7 September 1908: Dod and Cicely came over from Lamorna, and A.J. was round early, agog for us all to go out for the day in a wagonette. We sat round on the cobbles in the sun till Crosbie turned up. Then through Penzance, lustily singing, we drove, and at Gurnard's Head had lunch at the Inn, the discussion waxing so heated that the landlady was overheard to remark to some minion: "Must be all mad, I should think!"

'We sang drinking-songs all the way home, and nothing would content the men but buying brandy and rum and coming to the Myrtage to make punch. As A.J. was busy making it, and I was idly rubbing sugar on a lemon, Crosbie came and stood close behind me and told me he had loved me ever since he first saw me. And that's more than two years ago!

'14 September 1908: How can I describe that strange time before Crosbie had to go back to work? And the awful part of it is that I knew, as surely as I knew that Crosbie was leaving by the 5 o'clock train from Penzance on Sunday, that what did happen might happen. More, I was resolved to make it nearly happen anyway.

'Sunday was fine; fitfully, shyly fine. A pearly greyness veiled the sky, but the sun was merely holding his breath. And I was holding mine. We drove over the moors to Treen and ordered lunch at the pub; our conversation a light skirmishing over the surface of grave topics. Always there was that sense of waiting for something to fulfil itself. After lunch we went back to Lamorna, to Mibs' sketch-class hut, and leaving Charlie the horse to graze we lay on a bank of bracken. We had only twenty minutes before he had to mount the cart alone and speed to the station. We lay there and talked, the intensely personal thread running through it all. Then I got up, turned, and held out both hands: "Goodbye Crosbie, you've given me a stunning time," I whispered.

'I could only see his face in a blur, as his back was to the sun which was blazing into my eyes. "Fryniwyd!" It had come, just as I had been anticipating. And I hesitated, with a blind instinctive shrinking. Yet, what else was this moment for? It seemed the only natural thing, to kiss. And then his arms were round me and I was caught up close to him . . . but Oh! the blank disappointingness of that kiss! I had tilted my head back and closed my eyes, as one would to get the full glory of a kiss when one loved. And I felt nothing, absolutely nothing, in my mind. With a quick, muttered exclamation, Crosbie raced up the hill after the straying horse, and I was left, wishing I had never been born. Nothing would give me virginity of cheek again. And under that was the insistent little pang: if only it had been worth it!'

A kiss to end all kissing, evidently. It was not the end of love for Fryn, however. It was not even the end of Crosbie's love for Fryn, which ripened with the years. It was merely the end of *Her Intermittent Diary*.

Part Two

—••{ }{ }••—

Summer

FIVE

—••**)(**••—

The Descent

WHILE FRYN was at Newlyn a new relationship began to be forged
between her and her father. Trust was established in the course of
several visits which Eustace paid to Cornwall, and a trip he and Fryn
took together through Italy. It continued to prosper after Eustace
returned from his last engagement in Tangier in May 1909, but his
stay at home must have been uneasy, for he was off and away again in
October, on a tour by steamer from Southampton to Le Havre,
Caen, St Malo, Guernsey and yet again Penzance, where he stopped.

Fryn, meanwhile, had been busy bringing out the second number
of *The Paper Chase* in June 1909. The St Ives painters Thomas Millie
Dow and Julius Olsson each contributed beautiful paintings, and so
did Norman Garstin whose special number it was, the first having
been for 'Lamorna' Birch. Stanhope Forbes put in his 'Clarinet
Player', and Elizabeth Forbes her portrait of Norman Garstin. There
were three fine lithographs by Ernest Procter, a poem by Crosbie
Garstin, and Fryn wrote a comic parable and the second instalment of
her satirical fairy-story series, *My Town*. There was a wood-block by
Cicely Jesse, and two more by a young Norwegian artist, Cardale
Luck, who was courting Cicely. It was, in fact, twice the size of the
earlier number, and must have far outstripped its budget. 'Mibs is
keen on an edition of only five hundred,' Fryn had noted, 'but it is to
be very fine and big, with many aquatints, etchings and lithographs. I
think we should sell our five hundred, but even so – will Mibs not lose
on it?' But Elizabeth Stanhope Forbes clearly realized that this was
going to be its swan-song. The Christmas issue had had to be delayed
for six months, and by then Fryn's future was pressing heavily upon
her mind, though her chief preoccupation was Mibs' ill-health. The
Professor was constantly taking her up to London to see doctors.

At the beginning of the autumn term, Edith wrote and told Fryn
that she need never come home again. 'I pointed out that I should

have to make a living, and would first have to come back and pack various possessions and look for somewhere to live. And so I did. But Mother was of course perfectly right. I was of age. She was not at all well off, and had been finding my keep and allowance for dress burdensome. True, I had been augmenting that by drawing tail-pieces for *Little Folks* regularly for the past year or so. I always had a good black-and-white line. But it was plain I had to make more important money.'

In a way, Fryn had been laying the foundation for this eventuality. She had been steadily filling a portfolio with drawings and stories much in the manner she had employed for *Peter Pawky's Pheasant's Feather*. She had also got a commission to illustrate a book. This was *The Ponk and Other Perpetrations*, by H. Holmes-Tarn, 'with twenty-three illustrations by Fryniwyd Tennyson Jesse'. They are funny and charming and three of the plates which adorned the some-what whimsical verses continued to hang on the bathroom walls of her various houses for years to come. One, 'the poor girl in terrible trouble, with hardly a rag on', is a skit on the myth of Andromeda, showing a bored nude perched upon a rock in the sea, beleaguered by a dragon whose far end is menaced by a miniscule Perseus; the 'pastermiece' for which Dod Procter had obligingly modelled.

Fryn's crime, which had brought about Edith's edict, was in taking a leaf out of Eustace's book. She had on a sudden impulse set forth from Cornwall for London, at the conclusion of the summer term of 1909, not by the normal train that would bring her to her mother's doorstep at a predictable time, but by a small general-cargo steamer putting in at various ports on the way from Penzance to London River: 'I walked to the empty wharf where she would berth, and watched her as she sidled slowly towards the quay, the sunlight vivid on her vermilion lead-paint, and making her black hull a soft greenish tone like an old coat. Her masts and ropes were burnished gold against a tangle of schooner rigging that lay in shadow behind, and in the sluggishly rippled harbour water the vermilion and orange reflec-tions broke and joined again. Without warning the sea lure gripped me. "I must go aboard," I thought, my foot impatient to feel the planks on her deck.' It's all in her first novel, *The Milky Way*, together with Crosbie's kiss and an abundance of fantastical adventures which grew into what was described on publication as 'the gayest novel of the season'. But it was undoubtedly inconsiderate to Edith, who had long been in the habit of becoming nervously prostrated if anyone of her household was a few minutes late from a walk.

After this disastrous beginning to the holidays, things had never picked up. Eustace was at home, restless and unhappy. 'I did not then know,' Fryn has said, 'how sweet he was. He had often been rather irritable and not very interested in the affairs of a young girl. One day my mother murmured affectedly: "I should have been the mother of sons." In that moment I saw her clearly, and there ran through my mind the thought: "Why, if I had been a son, I would have run away to sea at the age of twelve"!' It was to be the last summer all together at the 'family' house with Edith, 'the good gentleman and W' being the bane of 'the poor lady's' life. Before it ended, Fryn was the witness of a sorry little comedy, which found its way into her penultimate novel: she walked in and discovered her father fitting a strong bolt to the inside of her mother's bedroom door. She raised an eyebrow silently. 'Your mother wants it,' he explained with a rueful little *moue*. 'I don't know why. It is fifteen years since I last disturbed her.' So they chose their separate ways in good earnest. Fryn, conscious that if her sojourn in purgatory was soon to be over, paradise could not harbour her for ever, set to with a will to stock her portfolio with merchandise, gleaning legends of Cornwall while she could. The tale of the monolith, tales of smuggling days and desperate ventures at sea, the tale of the Nineteen Merry Maidens, all were grist to her urgent mill.

When Eustace returned to Penzance in May 1910 from his steamer tour, he and Fryn left for London together, where she booked in at a YWCA. She had started to write verse of such promise that his pride in her stirred memories and youthful hopes of Tennyson glory which he had not himself been able to fulfil, and on 25 July he went to Boulogne to revisit his old boarding-school at Guines. But it was dismantled and his old school-master was dead. For a week he stayed, looking again at the ancient oil-mill and the château with its clock-tower, but that particular past having yielded him little gold, he left it to seek some other touchstone. Pursued with forks and hope, he chose Lincolnshire, where he renewed many Tennyson contacts and was warmly encouraged by Willingham Rawnsley – grandson of the Reverend T.H. Rawnsley, who had been the devoted friend of Alfred's father in his times of mental derangement – who declared 'It is quite appropriate that your daughter should have the power of writing fine verse. Your own lines are excellent.'

And Fryn? She too was on the wing. In an unassuming little book published early in the century, someone had set down the legend of the origin of the pekingese: how in Imperial China, when the world was young, a lion prowling through the shadows of the forest looked idly into a clearing where a butterfly was gyrating dizzily in and out of a ray of sunlight, and by chance she looked back at him in full flight. They looked and loved instantly, and from their rapture was conceived the first pekingese, a creature half lion, half butterfly. Such a description – as seen by the indulgent eyes of Damit – fitted Fryn then, in spite of her true antecedents. Happily she had a silly side too.

She was on her way, thanks largely to Nan. For Nan's uncle had died, leaving her his house in Church Street, Kensington, the sale of which provided her with £100 or so a year and a little spare capital. She gave Fryn enough of this to start her off in life. 'I managed to find a room in a semi-basement flat in Chelsea,' she has recorded. 'There was a bath with a geyser, and I allowed myself one meal a day, in the evening. It cost me eighteen-pence usually, and if no one was looking I slipped my roll into my bag for breakfast the next morning with the milk I had left for me daily. For luncheon I might succumb to a jam-puff from a baker's counter.

'It was from this room that I made my descent upon Fleet Street.' Fryn's 'descent' upon literary London never ceased to fill her with amazement and incredulity. 'I say that I went to Fleet Street,' went her description, 'but where I really went was to the *Daily Mail* and to *The Times*, and they both took me on. I had a distant paternal cousin in the library – what the Americans call the Morgue – at the *Daily Mail*, and she thought she could get me in to see somebody. I got to see no less a person than the editor himself, Mr Marlow, who was very deaf but very kind. I went on to Printing House Square, where I had no introduction, and spoke to the commissionaire. I had heard they were starting a women's supplement, and I thought I might get on to that, I explained. "You go in there and wait, Missie," he said, and disappeared. He soon came back for me, and thus I met Harold Child, and dramatic critic of *The Times* and editor of the ill-starred feminine supplement. Long after, he told me that the commissionaire had said: "There's a Miss Tennyson Jesse to see you, sir," and Harold Child had said: "I won't see another woman." The commissionaire had coughed: "If I were you, sir" he had said, "I should see this one." – "The devil you would," said Harold Child. "Show her up." And then – as he liked to tell his story – "the most beautiful girl he had ever seen came in".

'Now, I was not beautiful, though I gave the effect of it. The modelling of my face was bad, the spacing good. My forehead was too wide, but I had a skin that did not need powder, into which one could look even in sunlight. I had golden hair and big grey-green eyes with black lashes and eyebrows. It was only the beauty of youth and it did not last long, but I had it when I started.

'Harold Child and I talked, and he suggested a leader for the supplement. I had to go to the British Museum to read up the stuff for it, but that didn't distress me for at the reading-room a young man found me all I needed and I soon wrote my leader. After that I wrote occasional paragraphs for *The Times* itself, which made me feel very grand. Writing a paragraph is a skill which luckily came naturally to me. I remember my first paragraph was on a dress show of Lucille's with living mannequins, the first of its kind. I began it: "Since to all primitive races pictures appeal more strongly than words. . . ." and went on to describe the show. I had been offered a job as a mannequin myself, though not by Lucille, but as the pay was only ten shillings a week I did not see what I should have lived on. It was with Watteau et Cie, Pont Street, past which the van-drivers used to jog, calling out "What Ho! she bumps".'

Fryn had decided on 'F. Tennyson Jesse' as her *nom de guerre*, and when she had started working for *The Times*, she sent 'The Mask', one of the short stories in her portfolio, to *The English Review*, an important monthly. It gave her the surprisingly enormous sum of fifteen guineas for it. The story appeared in January 1912, and made the sort of hit that was possible in those days. It was by an unknown author and was startling in character and apparently also in its form of writing. Who was F. Tennyson Jesse? Rumour had it the author was Frank Harris, writing under a pseudonym. 'The editor, Austin Harrison, wrote and asked me whether I was a man or a woman and if I would come to see him. I arrived dressed in the little suit in which I had travelled up from Cornwall. It was of brown corduroy, all over pockets like a game-keeper, and with it I wore a brown suede hat like a coal-heaver's, with a pink quill across the front. Austin Harrison looked as though he couldn't quite believe what he saw. He was always a good friend of mine. And he introduced me to the Monds. Alfred Mond owned *The English Review*, and we ran into them at a restaurant when Austin was taking me out to dinner. From that moment Alfred and Violet Mond were goodness itself to me and became dear friends.'

The widening of her social horizon had very practical effects for Fryn: 'I did not always have to give myself an eighteen-penny dinner. I met a sub-editor on *The Telegraph* and we dined together most nights, very simply because he also was poor. He had two rooms up a hundred and four stairs at the top of Chancery Lane and I fell in love with them. He was so devoted that he gave his flat up to me, and I took it I fear without a qualm. I recall now that when I re-decorated, by washing it with pink all over, I pasted pictures from Newlyn on the walls. I could not live without the only roots I knew, and Herbert the dispossessed helped me to put them up. For my first murder trial in the No. 1 Court at the Old Bailey, he hired a wig and gown and escorted me as far as the door leading to the City Lands seats, which are behind the rows of barristers facing the witness-box. There he had to let me go, but, young and pretty as I was, I managed the rest by myself and attended every day of the trial. He had a good mind and wrote well, but I could not somehow see myself as Mrs Herbert Watson. I was not in the very least in love with him.'

A letter to her father, who was in Newlyn for a few weeks as locum tenens, said 'My own dearest little father, Glad you lunched at the Faugan, though sorry you broke a glass! Yes, isn't the Professor a lamb? And she's the most wonderful woman in the world. Fancy, I've had a book review to do for *The Times Literary Supplement*. A whole column I was asked for! This has struck Fleet Street rigid with surprise. Apparently my being on *The Times* at all is looked on as a miracle.'

In the spring of 1912, Fryn and her father made their leisurely tour of Tuscany together. 'The Mask' was making its sensation and, on arriving home, Fryn received a letter from someone signing himself H.M. Harwood, saying that he'd read the story. 'He thought it would make a good one-act play and would I let him do it. I wrote back, politely but unmistakably asking why H.M. Harwood thought he could write a play. He replied: "Quite right of you to question it. Come and see me and talk it over. I am at my father's flat in South Molton Street." I was asked to tea, and Herbert Watson insisted on going along with me: "I will wait downstairs," he said. "You can't tell what sort of a fellow this is." So Herbert stayed downstairs, while I went up and found my future husband waiting for me. His father was ill in the flat. His sister Maggie had just been to see him and shook hands with me on her way out. He and I conversed of this and that, and some things he said struck me, until at last I asked: "You aren't by any chance Tottie Harwood, are you?" for, all my life, I had heard this strange name of my Uncle Squire's great friend at Cambridge. "Yes, I am," said Tottie, "but you can't be – you can't be" – eyeing me, for I only weighed seven stone – "you aren't Fatty Fee?" – "Yes, I am," I said.'

This meeting of Tottie and Fryn was seen with quite other eyes by the Harwood family in residence at the flat. Ruth, Tottie's youngest half-sister, remembers: 'From our viewpoint, so I as a little girl heard, that courtship began unfortunately. Our father was dying. He was lying in his room along the corridor, dying of pernicious anaemia, and mother was with him, when Tottie asked Fryn home. Hearing their laughter, we assumed that it was just another of his love affairs, and we thought it was in the most appalling taste. All that was visible of her from the hallway was a pair of long slim legs under the edge of the tablecoth, clad in shining black silk stockings.'

But, to the owner of the legs, in ignorance of any dark portent; 'Here was another man to take me out; another escort to give me dinner. He had a Napier car, which made going to Richmond and such places very easy and pleasant. I liked him from the beginning, and we set to work on "The Mask" and did it together. We have often collaborated since, and with never one word of dispute.'

She found that Tottie was not only a would-be playwright; he was a doctor. This, he explained, was because at Marlborough he had been unable to do Greek iambics, and so had had to switch to 'stinks'. Thence he had gone to Cambridge and to St Thomas' Hospital for his MB. He had had a quiet little practice in the City at one time, and had spent his days vaccinating ABC girls and his evenings writing plays. He told her that the surgeon he was working under at St Thomas' used always to don a frock-coat stiff with blood when he came into the operating theatre to demonstrate. 'But this was all before I knew him; he was not practising when I met him.

'The story of the next few years is, I suppose, the story of my gradually getting to know Tottie better. Although he was always interested in me, it was not a *coup de foudre*. Why he was called Tottie is lost in the mists of antiquity. He told me that the name was given him at Cambridge and he had forgotten what or who began it. I thought it was certainly better than Harold, which was his Christian name.'

Tottie's grandfather, Richard Harwood, had begun as a cabinet-maker, making coffins, but had later graduated from coffins to cotton

and founded the family firm Richard Harwood and Sons, Cotton
Spinners, of Brownlow Fold Mills, Bolton. Tottie was proud of
having a mortician, as he called him, for an ancestor, in the same way
as Fryn was proud of having a poisoner. It tickled their silly side; one
of the qualities they shared.

Tottie's father, George Harwood, as well as running the family
firm, had been Liberal MP for Bolton for many years. His election
address to potential voters had been unusual. He had said: 'I have a
cotton business of which I am very proud, and I shall always put that
first. And I am a family man who loves his family, and I shall always
put that second. What time and energy I have left, I shall be happy to
put at your disposal.'* He had got in with a tremendous majority. But
George Harwood never spoke of himself as a Member of Parliament,
a clergyman, a barrister, all of which he was; he thought and spoke of
himself as a cotton-spinner. That was his pride. In Bolton he *was*
Bolton. In his prime he was a great oak of a man, with a splendid
head, a generous mouth, and an air of abounding vitality. He had
great charm, as Tottie had. And he had a fine mind, as Tottie had.

Busy as she was, Fryn had not forgotten Elizabeth Stanhope Forbes,
who was then undergoing further medical examinations in London:
'Presently it was established that she was tubercular and she was
moved to the South of France, where she stayed in a little hotel at
Vence, with a hospital nurse to look after her, and she was able to go
out and paint. I wanted to be near her and decided to give up my flat in
Chancery Lane. It was thus that I met May King, who has had the
greatest influence on my life of anyone with the exception of my
husband. She has been an integral part of my household even longer
than he.'

May was the younger sister of a well-known model called Winnie,
who had posed for Fryn's Newlyn friend Clare Waters for the cover
design of a novel by Henry James. Having given up her flat, Fryn
took a temporary room in their Maida Vale flat in Queen's Grove –
the neighbouring YWCA being full up – for a night or two. On the
last evening, Fryn had an impromptu invitation to dine and dance,
and May was the greatest help, ironing frills and heating the curling
tongs. Throughout this activity the two girls chattered away, May

* Ruth Harris, in conversation with JC

sharing her ministrations between Fryn and her sister's little boy, who she was supposed to be putting to bed. May had been amazed at Fryn's insouciant way of hopping into bed at night, leaving her little garments as she stepped out of them, and now she suddenly dived like a cormorant, fished a twist of paper out of the grate, and growled: 'What you need is a keeper!' It was a five-pound note, hard-earned by the pen, which Fryn had plucked from her hand-bag to cool the tongs, and when they both began to laugh there was fright in Fryn's laughter and laughter in May's scorn. Fairy tales had had no part in May's upbringing, but she would hardly have been surprised if a pumpkin-coach had drawn up at the door for this lodger. Her feeling of wonder, however, was pleasingly leavened by contempt for such helplessness, and before the oddly assorted pair parted the next morning, there was an unspoken pact between them.

When Fryn reached Vence, she lodged in a convent Mibs knew of. She wrote of this time 'At the convent I had a little north room for four francs a day. The food was good and there was *vin compris*. On fast days we only had a boiled egg with a Huntley & Palmer ice-wafer, but on ordinary days I fared excellently. Sometimes they gave me a roll with meat in it and a half-bottle of wine, and I used to take it out into the olive-groves and lie and write, and Mibs painted me there.'

It was while she was at the convent that Harold Child wrote and told her he was being sent to Grasse to do a series of articles for *The Times*. He hired a car and called for her every day and took her out. 'He made what I may call very literary love to me. That he was old enough to be my father meant nothing to my mind. He never attempted to make love to me in the physical sense, which would have alarmed me, but he did lay deliberate siege to my heart. He took up a lot of my thoughts and emotions and prevented my being interested in anyone else for a long time, which was a pity. He had his own life, which he meant to continue. His letters I used in a short story called "A Garden Enclosed", which made quite a hit. I think he deserved that I should use them and I have never felt remorse about it. It will be seen by anyone who reads that story how religious I still was and how I had not lost my faith. The ending of it means nothing to me on reading it now, but it did when I wrote it.' The story tells of a girl's fear and pain of barrenness when her love affair turns to ashes, and of the dual vision she shares with dead Santa Beata, a sixteen-year-old virgin: 'With that she knew, as Beata had known, that this was the reward of virginity, that each virgin could mother the Christ-child afresh.'

Mibs became less well and had to go back to England. Fryn went on to join two ladies whom she always called 'Auntie' – friends from Newlyn who were then living in Florence. 'I grew to know and love Florence, and I put the setting of "A Garden Enclosed" in Tuscany instead of in Provence. Finally I left the "Aunties" to go back to London with a new batch of short stories.'

She put up at a club in Hay Hill, and William Heinemann wrote to her at the office of *The English Review* and asked her if she would come and see him. He asked if she was writing a book, and she told him she had two in her head, a serious one and a light one, which latter she thought she could write comparatively quickly. He suggested she should begin with that and let him have it. 'That is how I came to write *The Milky Way*, a very bad book. The only excuse I had was that, though I knew it was bad, I had to make a living, and *Secret Bread*, the other book, would take me much longer.

'William Heinemann was to become a good friend of mine, and for years I dined with him once a week whenever I was in London. He gave me Precious, my little Willoughby pug. I had never before had a pet of my very own. Preshie, as I called him, was the dearest little dog imaginable, fawn-coloured with black points, and a one-man dog if ever there was one. I had him for years. I need hardly say that literary London was agog. I ran into Ivy Low – later Madame Litvinov – at a party, and she said: "I hear that William Heinemann had given you a black pug!" She had written a book called *Growing Pains*, which had been the young girl's success book before I wrote *The Milky Way*, and Heinemann had published it as well. But he had not given her a pug. A little taken aback by this remark *coram publico*, all I could think of to say was: "Oh, but he isn't black".'

'The Mask' appeared as a play with the title of *The Black Mask* at the Royalty Theatre, Shaftesbury Avenue, in December 1912, with two other one-act plays. It was a considerable success, was also shown in New York, and was on the permanent programme of the Grand Guignol in Paris. The play was published by Ernest Benn, translated into French and Italian, and there have been radio, television and music-hall versions as well as a film. The *Pall Mall Gazette* wrote of 'Mr F. Tennyson Jesse's exceedingly well-written story, the remorseless story of Vashti Bath's division of the heart between the stalwart cousins, James Glasson and Willie Strick; the affrighting part played by the surgical mask worn by Glasson after his pit accident need not be here revealed.'

Mibs was back in a nursing-home, 'already greatly changed from the Mibs who had painted me sitting under an olive tree in Provence,' and the decision was made to bring her home to Newlyn. She was taken down with her nurse, and the next thing Fryn heard was that she had died. 'Stella went with me to the funeral, and we stayed with Tregaggins at Myrtle Cottage. I had lost the best friend I had and I knew it.' She wrote to her father:

> 'I don't know what to say. I have more work than I can do and my brain refuses to budge. I can't believe it yet, but I know that some night soon I shall wake up and know it is true. For all these years she has never once failed me in the smallest thing when I wanted sympathy or advice. The Professor sent a cab for me to come straight up. It wasn't her. I never saw anything look so unutterably dead. Everyone was very good, and Norman Garstin and Lionel Birch were at the station to see us off. I do nothing but sleep all day; I suppose it's the shock. I don't even cry now, what's the good? It can't make it not true.'

As time went on, the Professor grew more and more to depend on Maudie Palmer, who was one of the older students and had been the massière at The Meadow Studio. She had been good to Mibs, and fond of her too. Tongues of course began to wag. 'The Professor, knowing my affection for Mibs, was afraid of what I might say, but when he told me he had grown to love Maudie and wanted to marry her, saying "otherwise I should lose my little friend," I was delighted. Mibs might, I think, have been glad too. Maudie loved the Professor, and was undoubtedly less alarming as a wife than Mibs had sometimes been, and her musical talent was a joy to him. His son Alec had been home for the holidays. He was going to be an architect and had begun brilliantly, winning a travelling studentship of the Architectual Association. He and Maudie had always liked each other and had been thrown much together, and he too welcomed the marriage.'

Just to be working, and surviving, in London, was something of a marvel to Fryn. In those exhilarating days: 'I loved the human race and – to misquote – I loved its silly face.' She had met Tottie's sister Maggie again during the collaboration on 'The Mask' and, when Maggie said she was going to Madeira for the winter and invited her to join her, Fryn happily accepted. When Tottie said that he was coming too, she was not altogether surprised and rather pleased. She stayed the best part of a month. They played roulette in the evenings and she won enough to pay the bill for Preshie, left at home at the vet's.

There were two ways of getting about in Madeira, in a sledge or on horseback, and when Tottie asked her if she would like to ride she said certainly. 'But my horse was very spirited, and I got lost by myself on the mountainside. It must have known perfectly well that it had someone on its back who could not tell one end from the other and preferred boats, but I was indignant that Tottie did not take me riding again. He took me sailing though, and that was the beginning of another partnership.

'He and I left Madeira before Maggie. I had to get back, to journalism and to Preshie. And Tottie said he had work to do too. So we spent two days in Paris together on our way home. By this time he was very excited by me. I allowed him to come into my room to see my dress, before he took me out to dinner. I was wearing an opalescent dress with a zigzag hemline, made of layers of chiffon in blues and greens edged with brighter beads of the same colours. I loved that dress and I spun round to show it off properly. He slid his broad hand on to the nape of my neck under my whirling hair and brought me to an abrupt stop, holding me there while he looked down at me slowly and the dress settled back into its separate variegated petals. And I remember him tilting the hand, so that my feet in their green-dyed satin slippers almost left the ground. I seemed to swing like a puppet for an instant, before he dropped his hold to my shoulders and swept me out of the door saying: "Oh, you foolish virgin! You foolish, foolish little virgin"!'

Fryn had been working well in Madeira and her light novel was finished, but she had some difficulty finding a title for it, till she decided that *The Milky Way* would suit it admirably. Unfortunately, that title had nothing whatever to do with the book. 'I therefore had inscribed upon the title-page: "He who is light of heart and heels can wander in the Milky Way – Provençal proverb." It gave me some pleasure to read in the notices: "Miss Tennyson Jesse takes her title from the well-known Provençal proverb . . ." for I had invented it myself. *The Milky Way* was a very light-hearted affair and amazingly successful.'

Indeed it was. This 'very bad book', as she was later to call it, was the first of a score of her works to be published under the Heinemann imprint, and it received a generous share of praise from the serious and frivolous alike. It appeared in October 1913, with a frontispiece in colour painted by herself of two young things walking under a wide sky, and with a curious little device engraved on the front cover – a piping boy, half Pan, half cupid, winged and with a scorpion's body and tail, which was to become her 'mark'. Early in the writing, she had dedicated it to Elizabeth Stanhope Forbes, just in time to tell her so: 'Dearest, At first I thought this too light and slight a book to give to you, but then I remembered it is to you anything of good in it, as in its author, is so largely due, that both are yours already. F.'

'A book of youth and high spirits,' the *Daily Mail* called it. 'In this altogether delightful *Milky Way*, all the characters are young, full of the zest of life, penniless idealists careless of poverty . . . Seldom does one come across so fresh and blithe a fantasy. The story is of Vivian Lovel, art student. Stranded in Cornwall, she books a passage in a small steamer bound for London. On board, she encounters a strange pipe-playing youth, Peter Whymperis. The steamer is run into by a brig and at the height of the catastrophe a baby is flung into Viv's arms. She cheerfully mothers it and dubs it "Littlejohn". Wherever they go, this wholly enchanting heroine adds to her entourage and makes them all as gay as herself. Miss Tennyson Jesse is very young, and that is why she has given us so blithe a book, but she has great gifts.'

Rebecca West, reviewing it in *The Daily News and Leader* in November 1913, wrote:

'Certainly it is a delight in the technique of life for its own sake that makes Miss Tennyson Jesse's *The Milky Way* so vivid a book. Miss Jesse's talent is not suited to the picaresque form she has chosen, for she has only a slight faculty for invention, and though she can put her characters into a fantastic situation she cannot develop it into an episode. But her faculty of vision is marvellously intense. "Oh! the way things look and feel!" her heroine cries as she stands at the furnace door of her steamer's stokehold. "I'd go anywhere to see how a thing looked or do anything to know how it felt." It never matters much what Vivie and her Peter say or do in the penny gaff or wax-works or any other queer place where their vagrancy brings them. It matters tremendously when Miss Jesse describes the queer places themselves. She describes a thunderstorm at sea, with pearl-hued Dover and her cliffs seen from afar by rose-coloured lightning; she describes Covent Garden wrought to magic between the yellow glare of the paraffin flares and the ice-blue dawn light; she describes the dawn coming over the brightening sea, up the misty valleys, to a ruined manor-house; and she describes Provençe in glittering English that gives one not only the lights and shadows of that land, but its winds and its silences. Miss Jesse cannot be quickly forgiven for a self-conscious heroine who, when kissed by her lover, regrets that "nothing could ever give me virginity of cheek again". But she has shown herself a master of descriptive prose, a kind of Stephen Crane. English writing, which has latterly lost the visual in the psychological, will be the better for her. Her style is strong enough to be an inspiration.'

'Miss Jesse is evidently a poet,' said *The Queen*: '. . . Evidently a poet,' said *The Times*. There were to be many new impressions in the next six years, and a popular edition in 1930. Fryn must have been pleased by the fanfares, but they did not turn her head. Her comment was: 'It is difficult to take one's own book seriously, especially when it isn't a serious book.' She was earning her daily bread by writing reviews for *The English Review* as well as for *The Times Literary Supplement*. She was giving interviews for women's pages on love, of which she freely admitted she knew little or nothing. She had sent stories to New York for the *Metropolitan Magazine*, and *The Milky Way* had appeared there in serial form under the title *Viv's Adventures*. Young men there were in plenty, 'like cabs on a rank' as Crosbie once said; Crosbie among them, urging her in poetry or balder terms to accept him. Weekends with the Monds alternated with weekends at Holly Bowers with Stella.

Stella had always wanted to go on the stage, but she was a girl who fitted into her environment. It would have been impossible for Fryn to have lived at Holly Bowers; Stella made the very best of it. 'They did all love her, so on the whole she had led a happy life. At amateur theatricals she had been given good parts, and the stammer which afflicted her in private life had not worried her upon the stage. She had stammered from a tiny child. Our mother used to tell how, when Stella had cried pitilessly, she had taken her up by the back of her little nightgown and shaken her, and the crying had stopped. Whether this could have caused the stammer I cannot say, but the fact remains that when she first began to talk, even before she was sent away to the grandparents, Stella stammered.'

Fryn was seeing more of Stella and more of Holly Bowers than she had for years. The uncles were rather struck by the fact that she was earning a living. 'On one occasion, Somers said he thought I had done very well, and he gave me a cheque for five pounds just to spend. I was thrilled, and bought a purple leather bag with it; my first real handbag. With my brilliant colouring then I could wear purples and mauves and often did.

'One weekend while I was there, my mother came down. Her animosity towards me showed so much that Squire was shocked: "I can't understand why you never answer her back!" he said. I do not know how the myth had persisted in the family of mother's and my devotion to each other. I suppose because it had once been true; because she hadn't given me away; because we were always together. But could we be anything else? My only defence against her spite was to remain calmly polite.'

Had Edith, then, no virtue in her? Some implacable quality in Fryn, which could not excuse treachery, cruelty or injustice, be they in large or small matters, maintained forever that she had none. Yet only the stern judgment of one whose idol had toppled, instinctively aware of something menacing to her own stability, could have denied some pity to Edith in one of her schizoid moods. Her poor strained face was pastily white, as etiolated as a blanched almond; her appetite so small that on this visit she ate her jelly-dessert with a knife and fork, and ate nothing else, for which even the easy-going Somers had to chaff her. Yet she had her devoted slaves. And she was the mother of girls of unusual intelligence, spirit, talent and looks.

Fryn's earning her own living made the notion of Stella going on the stage seem not impossible, and both uncles were in favour of it. Stella had already been attending the Royal Academy of Music, but she would not have amounted to anything special there and she knew it. So she asked to go to what was then the ADA, and here she amounted to something almost at once. She had great personality on the stage and a naturally good technique. And she too had begun to be very pretty. 'She had not been a patch upon me at one period, for she was very pale by nature, but now she began to put on make-up, and she did it so well and it made such a difference to her that we tacitly accepted the fact that she should; I had priggishly looked down on people who so much as used powder, and called it "painting oneself". I remember my surprise when one day at the ADA, where I used to go for lunch sometimes with Stella and the other students, a girl-student said to me: "Oh, you've come to see your pretty sister." I had been the pretty sister, and I realized with pleasure how lovely Stella looked nowadays.'

It is a fact that Fryn and Stella almost never quarrelled. The bond between them, accentuated by separation, precluded jealousy. In looks, talents and temperament they were complementary; Stella extrovert, Fryn introvert. They acted on each other like champagne, and whereas both liked to sparkle, they liked specially to sparkle in the other's eyes. It was long years ahead before a bubble or two began to burst.

Fryn had never entirely forgotten her longing to fly, since those childish efforts to launch herself from the pink dustbin, and now there was an aeroplane taking people up over Windermere on joy-rides. 'Tottie had invited me, with a girl-friend as chaperone, to stay at a hotel nearby, and he had promised me that I should go up.' The friend who accompanied Fryn was Clare, 'Aunt' of Myrtage days. She was living then in the old cow-shed studio in Cochrane Street, behind St John's Wood High Street, which had figured in *The Milky Way*, and she had put Fryn in the way of doing a jacket for Henry James's short novel *Daisy Miller*. It was a gala occasion on the lake, and Tottie drove over from Bolton and collected the two girls in his yellow Napier.

'It was a lovely sunny day,' Fryn observed, 'and I got in hopefully and sat behind the pilot. It was an old "pusher" machine, with the propellor just behind the passenger's shoulder-blades. It only carried one passenger at a time and I was to go up first. No one warned me of the dangers of that propellor, and I naturally knew nothing about it; the wretched thing was quite invisible to me when it was whirling round. We took off. I peeped round and down and put out my right hand to wave – and it got struck. It didn't really hurt. I pulled the hand back into my lap, and watched fascinated as a pool of blood reached to my knees. My pretty new pleated skirt had formed a basin for it. I leant forward and tapped the pilot softly on the shoulder: "Look," I said, "you'd better turn back". He took one glance and did so. As we approached the quay at the lakeside I called out: "Take any children away; there's a lot of blood." I was taken back to the hotel and doctors were sent for. My hand was very badly smashed.

'Looking back, I can see I made heavy weather of the whole thing. But I had had beautiful hands – really beautiful, not like my illusion of a face – and I felt it deeply. I thought no one would ever be in love with me again. And I felt most horribly mutilated.'

Tottie took her to his house at Bolton, and Stella joined them there and looked after her while she was patched up more or less, and installed her in lodgings in London when she was well enough. 'There I was looked after by Mibs' old nurse Susan, who had always been fond of me. She had only one failing, and this I did not know at the time – she drank. But she was a good nurse, and gradually I began to work again and taught myself to type with my left hand. I had six operations in the course of the year, losing more of my hand each time, but still it would not heal. Then my grandmother, for all her bad temper, came forward with a present of £100, and with it I determined to go to New York.'

Before she left for America, the short story which grew out of her wooing by Harold Child was published, and the *Daily Telegraph* wrote: 'There is nothing better in *The English Review* than Mr F. Tennyson Jesse's striking little story "A Garden Enclosed".' To keep the home fires burning, Fryn deposited with *The English Review* two more stories from her portfolio of hard rations: 'The Greatest Gift' and 'The Man with Two Mouths'. Then, primed with a nest-egg in one pocket and an understanding with the *Daily Mail* in the other; with an introduction to the New York surgeon who would operate, and a trained nurse by her side, she sailed away to the West. A burden of pain lay behind her and before.

Fryn was to speak and write of the period following her accident as 'my lost years.' Never, then or later, did she mention her medical, as distinct from surgical, treatment more specifically. But her 'world', comprised of intimates, acquaintances and that portion of literary London which had recognized her promise and appropriated her as their own, has been more forthcoming. It has been affirmed that, in order to enable her to bear the intense pain and strain of incessant operations, she was put on morphia and became an addict, eventually a registered addict; no doubt has been left about the nature of the injections Susan was required to administer. It was supposed by some that she may have fallen into the hands of a doctor fashionable at the time who was reputed to prescribe drugs with utter recklessness. It was known positively that Dr Armando Child treated her for the addiction; he did not introduce her to the drug. He is said to have been a charming man, possibly not able to cure her because the drug problem was too little understood in those days.

'I was very fond of Fryn,' Rebecca West has declared, 'and I admired her. Her tragedy was that she was put on drugs almost at the start. I have always understood that it was the hand, the pain and shock of that, that began it all. The wonder is that she achieved so much. She must have fought and fought to go on working as she did. Such courage! I am only perturbed that anyone should feel that she has been portrayed as too ideally beautiful when young. For she *was* ideally beautiful. I have never seen a lovelier girl. The three great beauties of our time were to my mind all writers: Susan Ertz, Rosamond Lehmann and Fryn. Her hideous voice – and that improved as she grew older – was her only handicap. Its harshness seemed not to belong to her and was startling in one so young and lovely.'

SIX

—••€)(Ʒ••—

Roses and Desolation

FOR ONE OF somewhat impulsive decisions, Fryn was surprisingly well prepared with introductions for her journey: 'I had friends in New York whom I had never met; the editor and sub-editor of the *Metropolitan Magazine*, for which I had been writing. They were Carl Hovey and Sonya Levien, later to marry each other and always my dear friends. They met me on arrival, arranged for Susan and me to be put up in a little hotel, and took me to the exceptional surgeon I had heard about. He performed the successful operation, cutting out all the nerve-ends in the stumps of the first two fingers so that I could wear artificial fingers and a finger-stall and use my right hand more or less normally.' The thumb had remained intact, and the third finger had apparently contrived to lengthen itself a trifle as its bones knitted, and to curve gently towards the thumb as if to encourage the grasping of a pen. A plaster cast was taken of the left hand and presently the new fingers, slender and jointed, matched it perfectly to all appearances.

'The Mask' had already been published in New York's *The Forum*, and the *Detroit Journal* gave a column to the story. Of the writer it said with admirable inventiveness: 'On her mother's side she traces back unbroken Cornish blood to the eleventh century, so she is well qualified to interpret the people of the Royal Duchy.' During Fryn's stay in New York, *The Black Mask* was put on at the Princess Theatre where, according to *The New Plays*: 'The story is simple; you might work it out yourself in any nightmare.' It was described in *Music and the Drama* as 'much more than a thriller; it is singularly imaginative and a very haunting tragedy.'

The day came when Fryn had not enough money left either to pay her hotel bill or to leave. 'So I sat down and wrote two short stories, sold them for what was to me the mighty sum of £200 in dollars and, taking Susan with me, sailed for the West Indies. I had had two proposals of marriage on the ship going out; the oldest man who ever proposed to me and the youngest man who ever proposed to me. The oldest-man-who-ever-proposed-to-me remained a friend of mine until he died, long after my marriage. We went along the Canal together; it was before the water was let in and it was intensely interesting.' Her description of the building of the Panama Canal is brilliantly clear. And she had the temerity to add: 'It sets me longing for an aeroplane from which to see at one breathless moment the entire maze of sun and shadow, land and water, steel and concrete and gleaming rails and, thus seeing, understanding it as a whole.'

The Italian ship on which she and Susan took passage to the West Indies was a freighter, putting in at Caracas and at innumerable islands, and in this way Fryn saw most of the Windward and Leeward Islands, finally disembarking at Barbados, where she presented a letter of introduction from Austin Harrison to the Governor. He and his wife asked her to stay with them, which she did, and 'that was my first taste of a Government House. From St Vincent I decided I wanted to go to St Lucia, whence my Uncle Jack James's beautiful French Creole wife had come. But there were no ships sailing, so I hired a sailing-boat. I afterwards discovered it was called a *Maman Prends Deuil* because, when the men go to sea in it, the mother of the family goes into mourning. These boats always carry a dog as watchdog, and a pig in case they are becalmed and have to kill and eat it. I hired a couple of mattresses, and spread them on the deck with my pillows for Susan and me. At first the dog growled and would not let me touch him, but when we ran into a storm and the sea came over us, he crept up beside me on one side, and the pig's sharp little hooves prodded me as it crept up on the other side, and I lay between the two of them all night.' The distantly-related in-laws were welcoming, and when she returned to New York the George H. Doran Co. had just published *The Milky Way*.

The New York City *Sun* sent an interviewer round to her hotel, puzzled by her choice of subject-matter: 'for *The Milky Way* is about as different from *The Black Mask* as a chocolate éclair is from corn beef hash,' said the interviewer. 'Tell me, didn't you write *The Milky Way* as a protest against the over-sexed fiction of today?' – 'I did not,' was her reply, 'I wrote it to make money.' – 'Is there not a deep and brooding soul behind this pretty young face of yours, taking revenge against the poetic Tennyson tradition with elementary power in *The Black Mask*?' – 'No, I don't think so,' said Fryn firmly. 'I wrote that because it amused me.' Then the *Evening Sun* reported: 'She has come to New York by way of the Panama Canal and the West Indies, being fond of getting to places by way of Robin Hood's Barn. She sits demurely, gowned in a débutante frock, twirling a purple steamer-hat in her artistically moulded fingers, and you can't help thinking she must have interesting love-affairs to record. But she tells you only of adventure!'

On 28 July 1914 she was off again, with a special visa for Haiti from the Consul General in New York, and bound for Jamaica and Cuba as well. But, by the time she reached Havana, war was declared and all steamers running between Cuba and Haiti had stopped. German cruisers were hanging about the island, and thousands of cigar-makers, thrown out of work by the war, were indignantly parading the streets. Fretting at the delay, she went shark-fishing, and caught one considerably larger than herself. 'There were English, French, German and Dutch ships outside the habour,' she wrote, 'but not one would put her nose out.' 'Eventually I got myself and Susan on an English ship, going with all lights out on a dash to New York. She was packed from stem to stern and we slept in the saloon. We must have been allowed to send marconigrams, for Sonya Levien was there to meet us when we docked, and she and Carl saw us on to another strange little English vessel. On board I made friends with a young man who travelled in ladies' underclothes. He told me he had been educated in Germany and France for the sake of his father's lingerie business, and certainly he spoke both languages well. When we arrived at Liverpool, my luggage had gone astray, except the jaw of the shark I had caught off Havana which – stinking to high heaven – I had in a biscuit-tin. My kind young man gave me all his models of ladies' underclothes, so at least I was able to go to London feeling fresh and clean.'

In London, Fryn stayed again at the club in Hay Hill. Her object was to get to the war, and she went to the *Daily Mail* to see Mr Marlow. He shook his head and doubted if he would be able to send a girl out, but he said he would hold a meeting. It was unanimously agreed that if anything were to happen to her they would be howled down as sensation-mongers, to which she replied indignantly that she was going all the same, and in much less safety than with their backing: 'For I had contrived to present myself in front of three gentlemen, to whom I told that I was a sociologist. They believed me and I got my permits, and to the war I went with £40 in sovereigns and hugging a large hold-all.'

Using Ostend as a base for her first sallies to Ghent and Termonde, she bombarded the *Daily Mail* with words. The directness and visual appeal of these despatches made a strong impact on readers, and the paper made haste to claim and proclaim her as a star War Correspondent of its very own. Throughout that September of 1914, the headlines given her from Ostend, Ghent, Antwerp, were: 'Girl in the Firing Line – The Advantage of Being Small' and 'A Woman Among the War Ruins – Roses and Desolation,' and so on. 'I went to the town of Termonde,' she wrote in the early days, 'where a little time ago ten thousand people were living. Half the bridge had been blown up and so, arrived at the river's edge, I embarked in a boat which was plying back and forth, returning refugees to their ruined homes. Termonde against a livid sky looked like a cardboard scene in a theatre. Up a swaying plank slippery with mud, to the ankle-deep black ooze of the bank, along a street strewn with splintered glass I went, clambering over mounds of fallen brick, and suddenly I was sniffing the air. It was a medley of brick-dust and plaster-dust and charred wood, above all a burnt-out smell, subtle and penetrating. The smell of something utterly scorched and destroyed, it pervaded the air and filled it with the sense of death. Through the arcade formed by the shattered rooms of a house, I saw hanging on the wall a plaster plaque of a mother suckling her child; a cheap little fancy plaque, yet it attained a wonderful dignity there in the midst of so much havoc. The remains of the Academy of Fine Arts drew me down a long passage piled high with stones, between two sagging walls. To right and left, through gaps, hung pieces of sculpture: a Venus with her triumphant half-smile contemplated a Piéta; gigantic heads stared up at me from the floor; a torso strode perpetually over the rubble; and high above, a Donatello Madonna smiled serenely over the uninjured head of her child. Everywhere the swifts were wheeling. From a tavern came the sounds of singing and laughter. And the most ironic thing of all was the great bronze statue amid the chestnuts outside the Church of Notre Dame. It represented De Snedt the Jesuit Missionary, with uplifted crucifix and a face of strength and tenderness, who brought the heathen "out of barbarism into religion and civilization". He stood holding his crucifix out over a town which was as much an example of religion and civilization wrecked by barbarism as any wreck by those forbears – the Huns.'

She talked to a priest whose vicarage had been razed to the ground, and to a peasant whose three school-boy sons had been marched away in front of the German columns. 'My first experience of war,' she was to recall, 'was in Belgium, and I conceived an unfaltering liking for the Belgians. My landlady and her husband at Antwerp were good and kindly people. She was a big gentle Flamande with a new baby, by trade a dress-maker and, when the Germans were approaching, I helped her pack away her yards of lace and embroidery into a tin box, and peppered it against moths, and buried it and the black cotton-covered busts for making frocks upon under the floor of her sewing-room. And I remember standing at a corner and seeing the sky lit up with the flames of Malines burning.

'I was unprepared for the endless waiting for passes or transport. American correspondents would sometimes give me lifts if I stuck to them like a burr, and thus I got into the Battle of Alost. I was turned out of the car at the place where the Guides and the Lanciers in their beautiful Napoleonic uniforms were deploying across the road. I explained that I wanted to go up into the battle. "Well, Mademoiselle," said the Colonel of the Lanciers, "you are undoubtedly very small. And if you were to walk along on the far side I do not suppose we should see you." So I took his advice, and arrived in time to see a cavalry charge across a field of sugar-beet. I heard queer pinging noises going past me, and saw seasoned correspondents flattening themselves behind trees. And that was the only time that I heard bullets actually going past my ear.

'I left Antwerp the day before the Germans came in, by the last boat leaving for England. It was crammed, and we arrived at Tilbury in the dark and were told no one would be allowed on shore till morning. But I made friends with the pilot, who said that if I dropped down the chute into the pilot's boat he would take me ashore. On reaching London I went straight to the *Daily Mail*. It was about eleven o'clock, and they broke a stick for me while I wrote about the imminent fall of Antwerp, and they gave me a cup of cocoa and a slice of cake. I was glad to be back; away from the dreadful tedium of war.'

The *Pall Mall Gazette* took up her articles. The *Daily Citizen* wrote: 'To my mind, quite the most brilliant of these young people is Miss F. Tennyson Jesse, who has been doing splendid work in Belgium. Not only has she an infallible nose for news, but she has unlimited courage. Best of all, she can write.'

In January she was in Holland, where the chimes of Rotterdam had learned to play Tipperary. She was the guest of the Commission for Relief in Belgium, and Stella wrote to their father, from Holly Bowers:

'Darling Paw: Fryn told me to let you know she and her nurse have gone to Holland. She has been sent by the Minister to write a pamphlet for the Belgian Commission, to encourage American sympathy and help. The Commission is paying all hers and nurse's expenses. She told me I was to send you her dearest love. She didn't write and tell you, for fear you tried to stop her going. You can't write to her as she has no address; she will let you know when she gets back. Your very loving – Pet.'

On her return, Fryn made a passionate appeal for funds and specific help, pointing to where it was most urgent, for the two hundred thousand tragic Belgian refugees, and she ended: 'It is the need that makes the claim, and it is no good giving unless you keep on giving.'

Reports from her appeared also in *The English Review*, *The Tatler* and other periodicals, and it is not surprising that official use began to be made of her fighting words. Fryn went four times altogether to the war in France. She was sent in December 1915 by the Croix Rouge Française in Knightsbridge to inquire into their hospitals, and wrote a series of articles on their work, published in the *Daily Mail*. She also took the opportunity of seeing her own *Le Masque* performed in Montmartre, where she was seen and described in the Sunday Chronicle of 23.4.1916 as 'exquisitely feminine, slim and soft-voiced, pirouetting to let her gown be seen with all the pleasure of a *debutante*.'

She was also sent by the Ministry of Information to write about what was then called The Women's Army, commenting later: 'During the weeks I was in France, I never slept twice in the same bed, which means that I practically did not sleep at all, and arrived back in London tired out. Tottie had gone back to St Thomas' when war broke out, and he took the first fleet of ambulances out to Ypres and Mons as a Captain in the RAMC. He was at this time living in at St Thomas', so I asked him if I could have a bed for the night at his Adelphi Terrace flat, and he took me there. Before he left for the hospital, I begged him to give me something that would certainly make me sleep. It woke me up so completely that I spent hours walking up and down, enraged and exhausted, and when he came home to breakfast the next morning I accused him of having done it deliberately. He had given me three Dovers Powders, an old-fashioned remedy even then! However, I forgave him.'

That was about the time when Fryn began her lifelong practice of speaking up for women, wherever she thought they were being unfairly used. Her letters and articles were outspoken, verging on the outrageous, and as time went on her books took up the cudgels ever more strongly. The very idea that a woman should remain married, or submit to bearing children, to a man she did not love, was shocking and repugnant to her; divorce should be at least as easy for a wife as for a husband; abortion should be at her discretion and made safe. Yet she loved men, and many of her most fervent pleas were quite as much for their sake; that for the right to die, whether by suicide or euthanasia, for example.

Heinemann had been pressing her for a new book, and as Fryn was too occupied with the war to tackle the long novel, they compromised on a collection of eight short stories, including those which had already appeared in *The English Review*. Called *Beggars on Horseback*, this was published in August 1915, and Fryn had again painted the frontispiece, showing a baby satyr holding in one hand a tragic and in the other a comic mask. It had her piping Cupid with the scorpion's sting embossed on the front cover, and she dedicated it: 'With love and gratitude to Miss Hannah Mercy Roberts (Nan), as a small acknowledgement of a large debt.' The book was widely reviewed and met with enthusiasm except from the *Observer*, which complained: 'Miss Jesse has all a young author's passion for grim, ugly, speciously passionate subjects. Murder, lust, treachery are revelled in with that deliberate abandon which so rarely brings with it artistic conviction.'

Conversely, the *New Statesman* thought well enough of it to analyse each story at length, saying:

'The outstanding merits of *Beggars on Horseback* are range of theme and maturity of treatment . . . The effect depends on a large sureness and wisdom which underlies them. They are not strained after or painfully fashioned; they seem the inevitable products of creative power. I should like to quote more from "The Greatest Gift", but must keep to this one illuminating sentence: "The naked plane-trees made a silvery network against the cold pure blue of the winter sky; into a raised wash-house across the square the sun shone obliquely, and the many-hued skirts of the stooping women made vivid blotches of colour that harmonized with the rhythmic splash of the water as only music of sight can with music of sound." In "The Coffin Ship", last and strongest, the body and soul, not merely of skipper and mate and engineer, but primarily of the ship herself, are realized with extraordinary exactitude. Through storm, mutiny and disease the telling is at once breathless and steady; the total effect wonderful.'

All the stories have reappeared in anthologies, and they have been compared with the work of Poe, of Conrad, of W.W. Jacobs – all as male as could be. A favourite comment on them, particularly in the American notices, was: 'there is a mystical element, a touch of the supernatural, and a frankness of expression that seems more masculine than feminine.' *The Nation* of New York City found 'at least half of these very unpleasant stories have for their theme some abnormal strain of feminine eroticism.'

When it happened that the maleness of her writing was remarked on, Fryn would smile wryly at the implied compliment, knowing that emotion and sentiment were supposed to constitute the acceptable stock-in-trade of a woman writer, and that she had given them short shrift; knowing too that the reviewers were inevitably men.

At this time, Fryn was naturally concerned with thoughts of death, which she expressed in a poem of sweet comfort; published in *Country Life* in 1915*:

A LITTLE DIRGE FOR ANY SOUL

Scatter sad-leaved cypress here,
Hope lies rigid on this bier.
Bring the berries of the yew,
All of bitterness is due
When the joy of life is fled
Ere the body's life is sped.
He who goes with deadened heart
Is set from living men apart.

But where a body quiet lies
With the death-coins on its eyes,
Shed no tear and make no moan
Body's end is there alone,

* It also appeared in her collection, *The Happy Bride*, Heinemann, 1920.

And the unloosed soul hath breath
With its weary master's death.
Death in life's a heavy thing —
Life through death doth freedom bring.

Death hovered at everyone's shoulder then; it was not safe to turn the head. One day it was Dennis Garstin, Crosbie's brother, killed in France.

Early in 1915, Fryn had rented a house on Campden Hill. It was small and very charming, one of a double-row facing each other across a footpath in a leafy *cul-de-sac* called Gordon Place, where the houses had been built for the émigrés at the time of the French Revolution. They all had gardens in front of them, with trees and flowering shrubs. They still have; wistarias stretch mighty arms across three frontages and honeysuckle festoons the low fences. Fryn went there with Susan, soon after she got back from Antwerp. It was run something like another Myrtage, and like the Myrtage it was usually full to bursting. Girls came and went, it might be for a meal, a night, a month. An atmosphere of open-handed, open-hearted hospitality permeated the place. Stella was free as a bird to come when she wanted, and took to spending several nights a week, bringing with her a friend or two from the ADA and, when the time came, fellow-actresses on pre-matinée nights.

There were other promising young women-about-town too. Among the writers there was Rose Macaulay and Virginia Woolf; Rebecca West, Ivy Compton-Burnett and G.B. Stern; Elizabeth Bowen, Enid Bagnold and Sheila Kaye-Smith; Ethel Mannin and Ivy Low; Dodie Smith, Dot Allan and Noel Streatfield. On a more intimate level, the Newlyn contingent was always dropping in, though Cicely was in Norway, married to Cardale Luck. Then, just as Susan's drinking became so excessive that Fryn could no longer countenance it, Eustace unexpectedly became an extramural member of the establishment.

'My father had had an accident,' explained Fryn. 'He had been run over in Kensington High Street and taken to the hospital at Hammersmith. When he was well enough, Stella and I took him down to Bognor and pushed him out in a bath-chair till he looked more robust than we had ever seen him. He had long since ceased to earn a living, even sporadically. Seeing his quiet face, I decided I must continue to look after him. As there was not room for him to sleep at number 46, I took a bedroom for him in a house opposite, with the idea that he should have his meals with me. Almost by chance I got into touch with May King again, and she came to take care of me and my father.'

The step Fryn had taken 'almost by chance' had involved more deliberation than she knew from the other party to it; for a crisis had arrived in the life of May King.

George King, May's father, had been born at Burton-on-Trent, the eldest of four sons whose mother was widowed when he was eight. Schooling was not compulsory then, and if a boy of nine had to go to work to enable his mother to keep his three younger brothers, he was not in the way of getting his reading and writing. George got work with a farmer, and rose at four to fetch the cows up from the fields for milking. The farmer did not give him much money for his labour, but he gave him the best of advice: 'If you're afraid,' he bawled out to the little figure trudging among the beasts, 'Shout!'*

When George grew older he got work, like everybody else in Burton, in the breweries, and stayed with them all his life with never a day off. Though he was a frail-looking wisp of a man, beneath his timid front lay an adamantine will, and his otherwise untutored mind was never at a loss for a text from the Bible. May was the daughter of his second wife, Elizabeth, who had also been married before. Her husband had died in an influenza epidemic, and she had become a matron to the 'young gentlemen' at Repton School. George's three sons were already full grown, and they and his three brothers were all quiet, dour men with a gallows humour, which May somehow contrived to absorb or inherit.

This lugubrious heritage may not have come from her father's family alone. Elizabeth was a harsh and handsome woman, who 'went to bed mistress and got up master', in the local phrase. Winnie was the first born to them, in 1882 when Elizabeth was in her later thirties, and Madeline and May followed in 1884 and 1886, Cyril coming later when all hope of a boy was past. Elizabeth ruled the children as she had the 'young gentlemen' at Repton. She expected to rule George too, but in spite of her superior background, he could always turn the tables on her with one of his apt texts. Countless times his exasperated Betty would fire a strident volley at him. His

* Descriptions of May King's background: conversations with JC.

soft answer might silence her, but did not turn aside the wrath that filled her. To cock a snook at his retreating back became a habit with her, and the children expected no less.

Their life was not unhappy and they were never hungry, though money was short. 'There,' she would say, plunking the pot of good stew down on the table in front of them, and sharing it out evenly with the help of a thumb against the wooden spoon, 'you couldn't be served quicker in a cook-shop.'

Winnie was the odd one out among the four children. The others all grew up to be hard-working and conscientious, like their father. Madeline became a nurse and Cyril followed his father's footsteps at Bass the brewery, but Winnie was something of a freebooter. She encountered art students when she was working as a waitress in a restaurant, and they asked her to sit for them: she had a beautiful statuesque body, a spiritual face and an acquisitive nature. Later she moved to London armed with introductions and became a professional life model, sitting regularly for Alma-Tadema and MacWhirter. She married an artist who turned out to be addicted to drugs, and they had one son, who was a year old when his father went away to take a cure. Winnie then sent for May to take care of the child while she continued modelling. Only six weeks after the end of his cure, her husband died of an overdose, and during that interlude Winnie had again become pregnant.

May was not strong and was given to fainting. She had won a scholarship which had gained her two extra years at secondary school in Burton. She was fourteen when she got her first job, with the Worthingtons, going directly 'upstairs' to the nurseries in spite of having 'hair as straight as a yard of pump-water'. She went to three different families, all resident posts in brewers' country houses, and it was slavery. She had no confidence in herself and the children knew it. She did not like children anyway, and she came to fear them.

When May came to live with Winnie at Queen's Grove, Maida Vale, 1911, she'd never had money in her hand and Winnie gave her none. They were desperately poor in the months while Winnie was expecting her second child. Bloater paste on bread-and-scrape served for lunch, and they were often without food in the house. After a weekend feeling wobbly with hunger, for the first and last time May had to go to a pawnbroker. All she could find to take was a pair of embroidered French knickers, given her by a guest of the Worthingtons one Christmas. Suspicious of their frivolity, she hadn't even

ventured to unfold them. Colouring up painfully, she produced them
for the pawnbroker, who entered them in his book as 'Oh-be-joyfuls'
and gave her the florin that meant food for all. But by the time the
doctor came to deliver the baby girl, there was neither money to pay
him nor gas to heat the water. He put his own coin in the slot, and
Winnie rewarded him with a painting. May had to help him with the
accouchement and, hating it all, she muttered: 'I'll never, never get
married!' He looked round and said: 'My dear child, have a cup of tea
and you'll feel quite different.'

By the middle of 1915, when she made her regular trundle along the
pavements with pram and toddler, May's legs were shaking beneath
her. It seemed to her that every girl she knew was going off to serve.
Daily she anticipated being drafted as a land-girl, and she dreaded it as
any slave dreaded the plantations. She knew she had neither the
strength nor the courage. Remembering that felicitous visit of two
years before, she appealed to Fryn in a letter addressed to her at
Heinemann. It asked point-blank if Fryn would save her. The reply,
by wire, was: 'Certainly. Come at once.' And then began the unravel-
ling of ways and means. Fryn was known, she was valuable, she was
disabled, and she had friends in influential places. She achieved the
necessary permit. Also – and this was a far more difficult thing for her
to do, involving the conscious dismissal of a trusted hand on the
syringe – she told Susan at last that she and her bottles must go. No
other motive was given out; Fryn kept her own counsel as usual. But
everything points to her having made up her mind to break the drug
addiction this way. For the next ten years, the work she was putting
out, and the zest she was putting into life, must be the measure of her
victory.

Thankfully then, May delivered herself 'in seizin'. She left the flat
in Queen's Grove, and her young charges, and Winnie whom she had
come unhappily to resent. She had too often been made aware that,
though others might go short, Winnie seldom did.

On looking about her new abode with scared eyes, she saw that
blind instinct had led her to a fair place; a place moreover with no
horrid men; not at least what she would call 'men'. She made no
stipulations about the salary Fryn should pay her; as things panned
out, she took over the house-keeping purse itself. If she came to need
a suit or a dress, Fryn was the first to see and to take her on a shopping
spree. For the rest, she basked in Fryn's glow; content to shelter from
the intimidating outside world; to have her bony knees under some-

one else's table, and to work. For May was a work-horse, cast in the image of her father.

Despite the good doctor's admonition, Man remained vile in her judgment. With a few familiar exceptions, the creature alarmed and disgusted her. Of course she was teased mercilessly by Fryn's young household. When Crosbie was going back to the trenches, and May came in moist-eyed to say goodbye, girls' voices broke into bubbles of laughter: 'Oh, do look at May's expression! Let's dare him to kiss her!' On such occasions she would run out of the room. Yet, to everyone's astonishment, she proved to be the lightest of dancers. Dancing was all the rage; *thé dansants* in particular. Fryn and May took lessons in the basement of Canuto's restaurant in Baker Street, and Fryn paid for both courses. When she withdrew half-way, she bequeathed the remainder of hers to May, who thus became very good indeed. There were plenty of partners and it was always tremendous fun. In May's words: 'Gordon Place was a lovely time!'

SEVEN

—•t)(3•—

Girlfriends

NUMBER 46 Gordon Place had a small dining-room on the ground-floor in front, with a tiny kitchen behind where it was usually May who did the cooking. Above the dining-room was the drawing-room, which was also Fryn's bedroom unless Stella or her actress friend, Mira Kenham, was staying there. May had the bedroom behind that. And then there was another floor, with a bedroom in front and Fryn's study behind, where she often slept when all the rest was full of visitors. Beyond the kitchen, in an outhouse decorated like the Pied Piper in red and yellow, she had a bath put in.

Stella had gone straight from Sir Herbert Tree's Dramatic School – the ADA – to play in *The Man Who Stayed at Home* with Edith Evans and Mary Jerrold, and the *Sunday Times* wrote of her 'nothing could be more charming.' Then, with Marie Lohr and Dennis Eadie, she had played in Edward Knoblock's *Home on Leave* and was described as 'a bright winsome girl, making a decided hit' and 'so natural that she filled the stage with sunshine'. 'Dennis Eadie,' said Fryn, 'had been struck by Stella at the end-of-term performance at the ADA, and gave her a part at once at the Royalty Theatre with him. Stella looked years younger than I did. Her face was round, her eyes big and of a deep and beautiful blue and with the blessing of good sight. Her hair was dark, her skin not transparent like mine but of the white kid-glove variety that lasts so well. Her smile was very lovely and she lifted her upper lip just as she had as a child. She was not slim as I was, and it was at a time when slimness was *de rigueur*, but her slight fullness was that of a girl. She became a success as an *ingénue* straight away. She carried an impression of the country into her dressing-room, with her photographs of the uncles and their guns and their dogs. She knew quite well what she was doing. Once she asked me what was the difference between ingeniousness and ingenuity and

I answered: "Darling, ingenious is what you are for succeeding in making everyone think you are ingenuous." '

Almost at the beginning of Stella's success, sorrow had come upon her when her Uncle Squire died of a pulmonary embolism. He had been going to Bagnolles, because of a tendency to a clotting of the blood. Stella had loved Squire, and so had his sister Margaret. His death had the odd result of bringing aunt and niece together. 'For,' commented Fryn, 'my aunt could love only one person at a time, and had centred her affections on this brother and shown indifference to Stella. But when Squire died, she transferred to her the whole of her power of loving. She had not liked me. She could see what Stella and I meant to each other; that we were as much one person as two sisters could be; that every success Stella had delighted me and every success I had delighted Stella. But she could not help resenting any successes of mine, because she wanted Stella to have everything. Somers never took Squire's place in her heart, strong as her affection for him was.' And nobody took Squire's place in Stella's heart 'till the only pretty ring time' had been left far behind.

Once only did May go to Holly Bowers. She was invited for a weekend by Auntie Margaret, for Stella's sake, and Stella was there to do the honours. The grandfather was already dead; the grandmother subject to increasing tantrums, and bed-ridden since her widowhood. Fryn had not been greatly affected by the death of Henry James, but it was a bitter blow to her when Granny died, for then Holly Bowers was sold. 'Somers, Margaret and Stella moved to a large flat at Albert Hall Mansions. Stella no longer had any excuse to spend her nights with me and I missed her dreadfully.'

To Fryn's logical way of thinking, the joy of having a place of her own to which her father and sister had been able to come seemed only natural and decent. But to her mother and her aunt it had appeared quite otherwise. To Edith it seemed that Fryn had deliberately exposed the break-up of the marriage. To Margaret, she had slyly enticed her darling Stella from home. 'And I think my Aunt detested Papa by then; partly for his chiselled features and his unworldliness, but most of all for no longer even pretending to live with her sister, my mother.

'Now, though my mother did not like to be so openly deserted, she had no love left for my father. It was not without satisfaction that she had made her own life with various friends. She referred to these as "my dear nurse friend" and "my friend who paints blossom in the spring-time". She had a car and a chauffeur, following the death of my grandfather, and could have afforded to live in pleasant places, but she had a genius for choosing not only places but people who were in some way second-rate.'

But Eustace was happy at last, living under Fryn's wing. 'His manners to May and me were perfect. He would stand up when we came in, and open the door for us to go out. There was little or nothing else for him to do, and this suited him.' Delightedly he added cuttings to his Fryniana and Stellana scrap-books, and he never went off again in search of the sun. 'He walked in Kensington Gardens when it was fine, and he used to tell me how he loved seeing the little girls running about with their long black legs. I never said: "But you had two little girls of your own with long black legs, and you took no interest in them, and one you gave away!" It would only have hurt him, for by then everything I did was perfection in his eyes.

'One day, William Heinemann asked me if I would like to become their reader. I willingly accepted, and read some dozen manuscripts a week. I was paid £120 a year, and I found it magnificent to have this steady sum pouring in.. It exactly paid the rent and my share of an allowance for Papa which Stella and I contributed jointly. Also I had the pleasure of discovering Geoffrey Dennis, E.M. Delafield, Clemence Dane, Margaret Lane, and others. I took a taxi, with my typescripts and my pug-dog, from Campden Hill to Heinemann, and dictated all my précis. I used to think the secretary must like taking down my dictation for, unlike William Heinemann who corrected himself continually, I just went straight ahead. I learned later that I was known as "the horror". After dictating, I would discuss outstanding manuscripts with Heinemann and then go to lunch with him at Romano's. Then Precious and I would walk home through St James's Park, the Green Park, Hyde Park and Kensington Gardens.'

As often as not, to save Fryn wear and tear, May used to be popped into a taxi instead, with Fryn's précis on each book, and in this way she met C.S. Evans. Long before William Heinemann died in 1920, C.S. Evans had joined the firm as Managing Editor, and then became a Director, and eventually took over as Chairman. Fryn, and May too, liked him immensely, and he treated Fryn's books very beautifully.

It was not only William Heinemann who was captivated by Fryn and called her his 'golden lass'; Alfred Mond had a fatherly passion for her and loved to do generous things. When she gave a wedding-party at Gordon Place for a girlfriend, it was he who insisted on providing the breakfast meats and the car with chauffeur to make things easier for her. Lady Meyer too, a well-known hostess proud to entertain talent, couldn't do enough for her; sent her garden-produce and baskets of rabbits. A divinely craggy Australian Group Captain wanted to marry her, and so did Robert Holland Martin the banker, one of four brothers of that naval family. To thank her many hosts, she threw a return party in a hired hall, and the accompanist and dancing-master from the Baker Street Dancing School played and gave demonstrations. The Monds and the Meyers came and every-body loved it.

Sir Alfred Mond was the son of Ludwig Mond, a gifted Jew who had come to England from Germany in 1862 and had been one of the founders of Imperial Chemical Industries. Sir Alfred became the first Chairman. He was a Liberal MP, a Zionist, and a genuine lover of art and music. He had acquired *The English Review* and from his first meeting with Fryn in the company of Austin Harrison she had been a constant visitor to Melchett Court, the home of Alfred and his wife Violet, of whom he was known to say fondly: 'Such a stupid woman but a wonderful mother to my children.' Fryn had an open invitation to come down whenever she could, and Sir Alfred, later Lord Melchett, would pay her fare first class, as though she were indeed a child of theirs – an indulgence Fryn adored. They were very amused by her and very good to her. There were four children in the family. Eva, the eldest, was a few years younger than Fryn and about to marry Gerald Isaacs, only son of Rufus Isaacs, the first Lord Reading. She and Fryn were good friends always, and Gerald became the second Marquess and Minister of State for Foreign Affairs. He served in both wars, and it was an incident in their war-time lives that prompted Fryn to start writing her first full-length comedy, again in conjunction with Tottie Harwood.

What was it about Fryn that caught and held the attention of distinguished people? Was it the thing poor Edith saw as the precious 'bloom', or that Fryn herself called 'the spark of youth', or was it what Noël Coward was to define as 'star quality'? To the eyes of Joan O'Connor, currently writing and adapting plays for radio, then a drama student aspiring towards her first career on the stage, Fryn was a living torch, an incandescence. 'I used to meet her, or rather to see her,' she relates, 'at parties at people's houses; quite often at my cousin Gwen Otter's house, where promising young men and women were invited and expected to show their paces. I used to sit there, just looking and dreaming, for I was very young and hopeful, full of admiration for those who had "arrived", and rather awed. And I can only say this of Fryn: when she came into a room, she brought with her a golden ambience. She glowed. It was not only the whorl of gleaming hair, or the warmth of her resonant voice, or the flashing humour that lit her words. A visible aura clothed her and it was golden.'*

She wore her aureola unconsciously, or she might have spared herself many an ordeal. 'It was never easy for me,' she has said, 'to come into a room full of people. I went through agonies of fright because I could not *see* who was there. I always had to put out all my antennae.'

Now, a golden aura for all to see is a glorious attribute. And a basket of rabbits to augment short rations is a useful tribute. 'But they won't buy the baby a new dress,' as May succinctly put it. A radical change had to be made in Fryn's way of life, if she were to get her teeth into *Secret Bread*. What she needed was peace, and Cornwall: a need she voiced in these lines, published in *Country Life*, 1917, and included in *The Happy Bride*, 1920.

ET IN ARCADIA EGO

When may I come again to the Western moors,
Dappled with cloud-shadows and chequered with fields
That grudging the wild earth yields?
My heart is sick for the blown pallor of mists,
For the young-curled bracken and budding heather
And the soft grey weather.
Shall I hear again the wail of the peewits,
Listen once more while the pale-lipped sea of the West
Sings the song that is best?
Wind-swept land whose soul is known to your children,
Spacious sky where clouds from the ocean pack,
How would you welcome me back?

'If your heart be sick I will teach it calm,

* Joan O'Connor (Mrs Osiakovski), in conversation with JC.

My soul is a grave for the sorrows with heavy feet,
My mist is their winding sheet.
Again you shall see the blur of blue in the hedge
That tells of the first dog-violets, see the new gold
Of catkins on hazels old.
But never again with a careless heart shall you lie
Where young love once gave shining veils to folly
In that stream-threaded valley.
Dust are the birds whose song seemed of half-shy kissing,
The leaves that embowered you away on the winds are blown
. . . First love also is flown.

In the company of May and Precious, Fryn made for Land's End and rented The Red House at Paul early in 1916, and Damit joined them. Damit had married a chartered accountant called Percy Bell, with a practice in Ceylon, and had gone out with him. But something was not suiting her there; whether the climate, or the marriage, she wasn't yet sure. Back on leave alone, she had been staying with Dod and Ernest Procter at Newlyn till she heard of Fryn's proximity. To fly from Dod's cool presence into Fryn's open arms was to outstrip the wind. Soon their days slipped into a simple pattern: in the mornings they worked; in the afternoons they walked, and worked again till dusk; and then early or late to bed as the mood took them, after a Myrtage-style meal.

The Red House was surrounded by boulders and in a clearing among them was a little hut, and there Fryn sat alone doing her stint. Subconsciously she may have been emulating Elizabeth Stanhope Forbes and her painting-hut in the wood. As the summer advanced she decided to move closer to that enchanted place and took a house at Lamorna for a month. Laura and Harold Knight lived near, and A.J. Munnings, whose young wife had committed suicide leaving him in a lonely and neglected state. May used to darn his socks, and he gave Fryn some hunting sketches which hung in the hall in all her houses.

She was writing one morning when the son of a Newlyn painter arrived on a bicycle. 'May was making blackberry jelly, and I shall always link the smell of blackberry jelly in warm sunshine with the news I was given: Alec Stanhope Forbes had been killed and the Professor wanted me to go over at once. Alec had been unable to get into a fighting Regiment until he underwent an operation for, I think, glands in the neck. Afterwards he was able to pass into the Duke of Cornwall's Light Infantry. He was sent to France, drafted into the First Battalion, and within three weeks was shot through the head in a charge from the trenches.

'I borrowed a trap from a nearby farmer, and drove to the Faugan. Maudie, in tears, took me up to the bedroom where Stan was lying in the big double bed. He was distraught, grieving for Mibs all over again as well as for Alec. What he wanted me to do was to take all the flowers that Maudie and I could pick to Sancreed churchyard, and put great bunches on Mibs' grave in memory of Alec.'

Fryn wrote to her father on 14 September 1916: 'Darlingest – I am rather dead after five awful days with poor Stan. I have never seen such agony of grief. It has been enough to tear one's heart out to be with him. What he would have done without Maudie I don't know. He asked me to write an appreciation of dear Alec for the local papers; the most difficult thing I have ever done.'

When Stan was able to talk about Alec, Fryn went back to Lamorna, where she saw many old friends, and Alethea Garstin painted a portrait of Precious. Myrtle Cottage had been let, but Tregaggins came out and said gently: 'Well love, pain has come to you again. But to do all the good you can, and to all the people you can, that is the way to live nobly. I talk to you very often at night in bed alone, and although we are separated by time and distance, yet there is a cord more swift and fine than the electric wire that death itself cannot sever. May God bless you, my dear one.'

Then Fryn went with May and Damit, Precious and Blackie the cat, to a house on a narrow strip of land outside Newquay. It was primitive and the wind blew in from the sea on both sides of the peninsula. It had no road to it, and they only had a tin tub by the fire to bath in. Knitting was in high favour then, and by lamplight even Fryn made heroic efforts to be a knitter, impelling May to write her opus:

LEARNING TO KNIT

Though I'm sure you won't believe me,
Listen while I tell a
Story of these handsome slippers
Made for little Stella.

Fryniwyd led a lazy life
In a cottage by the sea;
Two kind friends were there as well
To keep her companee.

These friends were always knitting.
Gracious!! How they 'knat'!
Fryn among the cushions sitting,
On her knee — the cat.

'I should like to knit,' said she
With a pensive sigh;
'Wool and needles bring to me.
Sure, I can but try.'

Oh, the trials that beset her
While she learned to knit
Bedroom slippers for her sister
That would never fit.

Nobly she began each day
As soon as it was light,
And her friends could hardly stop her
From sitting up all night.

When at length the work was finished,
Thin and feeble she had got;
The result was very special
When the slippers had been 'knot'.

Her friends had thought her wonderful
And very clever — but
When they first beheld the glory
Of the slippers she had 'knut',

They simply fell down swooning
And have not recovered yet,
At the thought of future slippers
That she still may wish to 'knet'.

May King, 1917

May had become indispensable. She shopped, she cooked, she
cleaned, she mended. She it was who groomed and walked the pug,

and fed 'the cat that killed the rat that ate the malt that lay in the house' where Fryn was; she who changed the linen, washed the lingerie, knitted Fryn's innumerable flesh-tinted finger-stalls, dyeing the gossamer thread. She changed Fryn's library books, cut out her notices, and fetched her medicine prescriptions. Fryn has described her: 'She has without exception the greatest genius for a home of any human being that I have come across. She is neatness and tidiness itself; everything in fact that I am not. As a house-keeper she is perfection and nothing is ever forgotten. She knows all the books that I have ever read, whether or not she has had time to read them herself. She remembers all the people that I have ever met, and where, and when, and how. She can choose what I will eat better than I can. She can buy my clothes and they don't have to be altered. She is a master at packing, and at the making of inventories and lists; lists of presents, of guests, of Christmas cards. I owe the fact that I have been free to write entirely to May. She has cleared my life around me.'

Tottie came down on short leave. He put up at the best hotel, and treated them all to a night there so that they could have a real bath. They knocked up the proud total of twelve baths between them.

Secret Bread appeared in April 1917, eight years after the idea was conceived under the original impact of Cornwall. It was published by Heinemann, by George H. Doran of New York, and by Nelson's Continental Library in the same year. Fryn dedicated it to 'Eustace d'Eyncourt Tennyson Jesse, my father and friend.'

The Times Literary Supplement called it 'a long, ambitious, strong and thoughtful book.' 'It grew gradually in my mind,' said Fryn. 'It was a Cornish story of the whole life of a man, from the day before his birth to the day after his death at the age of seventy. Taking the text in the Book of Proverbs about "bread eaten in secret", I developed the idea that every man has some secret bread of the soul by which he lives, that nourishes and sustains him. It may be a different thing for each man alive . . . For myself I know that by taking risks one lives, and every danger faced brings fresh grace.'

Ishmael is the youngest and only legitimate son of the Squire of Cloom who, dying, married the mother of all his children for a whim, so that a child of his name might inherit the estate and live to breed hatred and malice with every hand of his own flesh and blood against him. And Ishmael's inheritance does indeed arouse the jealousy of his eldest brother, Archelaus, a fiercely magnificent creature with the vindictive nature of their father. One phase of his vendetta takes the form of preying upon the weakness and confusion of soft little Phoebe, Ishmael's first wife, who dies in childbirth. Not until both men are old, and the young heir is himself the father of a son, does Archelaus exultantly confess to Phoebe's seduction, and only on realizing that the inheritance has passed through the blood of Archelaus and not his own, does Ishmael discover the true nature of his secret bread, the knowledge of death that rounds all.

'Suddenly,' wrote the *Westminster Gazette* of 6 June 1917, 'this brilliant, delightful girl, this amusing blender of Turgenev and O'Henry, has become a serious novelist. Like all her work, *Secret Bread* has a strong pictorial quality: it returns to the mind as a large richly-filled canvas.' – 'Some of the episodes,' said the *New Statesman*, 'have that painful intensity which made Miss Tennyson Jesse's short stories so memorable. There is something painful and terrible in her genius. She is preoccupied with pain – not morbidly, but as the sane and sensitive must be preoccupied with it in this world of pain.'

Enthusiastic notices were still tumbling over each other when *Billeted* opened at the Royalty Theatre on 21 August 1917. It ran for over two hundred performances there, was produced at the New York Playhouse on Christmas Day, and was made into a silent film by Paramount. 'It was a very light comedy,' according to Fryn. 'I had been to stay with Gerald and Eve Isaacs in the country for the weekend, and Gerald, in the Army, had been billeted upon Eva, which struck Tottie and me as making the basis for a play, so we worked on it whenever we could meet that winter. It was very successful, in London and New York. In London, Iris Hoey played the wife, Stella the ingénue, and Dennis Eadie the hero. Stella's part was more attractive than that of Iris, who was generosity itself over Stella's success. It was a happy production.' *The Tatler* described Stella as 'sweet and sane and fresh as the morning, this lady bids fair to becoming a raging popular favourite.'

The journal *Woman at Home* featured 'Two Clever Sisters', their genuine lack of vanity, and the earnestness with which they put their success down to 'Luck, extraordinary luck'. It contrasted the way in which each managed to convey in her art an unusual *joie de vivre*; Stella in every look and gesture, Fryn from a deeper and more secret level. Of Fryn's blinding bouts of migraine not one whisper escaped, nor of Stella's struggle to control her stammer; such things being out of place in a success story. But the *Observer* warned:

> 'Miss Tennyson Jesse seems to have a various talent; she can write grim and horrible stories, subtle little studies of love, long serious novels packed with ambitions, passions and the "tone" of a whole period. And now here is this smart comedy, written as smartly and brilliantly as if she had devoted a lifetime to polishing dialogue. We nurse a private hope that she is not going to desert her other fields for this. To our thinking, any one of her stories in *The English Review*, any one chapter of *Secret Bread*, is worth all three acts of *Billeted*. After all, Captain Harwood can write such plays as this unaided. But, putting that aside, *Billeted* is excellent light entertainment for a summer evening in London. Here is good talk, talk which does not contort itself or try to be profound, and between them our two authors have had a good many happy thoughts.'

As to the co-author, Captain H.M. Harwood was reported to be 'in hospital with a damaged hand and unable to attend the first night.' His only comment was 'Of course I was in hospital. I was always in hospital.' Certainly he was always hard to find on first nights.

The *Observer* was in a position to know what he could do alone, for, since *The Black Mask*, he had had several other successful London productions to his credit. A one-act play, *Honour Thy Father*, had been followed by *The Interlopers* at the Royalty Theatre with Miles Malleson and Dennis Eadie. And, in January 1916, *Please Help Emily*, a Flirtation in Three Acts, opened at the Playhouse Theatre, produced by Charles Hawtrey and dedicated to FTJ. It featured Precious and his absurdly naive mistress – a teasing compliment to Fryn – and was played by Gladys Cooper, Nigel Playfair and Charles Hawtrey. It appeared in Paris under the title of *Moune*. In addition, Tottie had collaborated with George Grossmith on the libretto for a musical comedy *Theodore and Co*, which had a long run at the Gaiety. Fryn at her loftiest could no longer ask why he thought he could write plays.

Established once more in London, with the consciousness that *Billeted* was set to run for months, she wrote some articles for *Vogue*, on women serving in France; one on the First Aid Nursing Yeomanry, or FANYs; the second on the Voluntary Aid Detachment, or VADs. The Ministry of Information thereupon asked her to undertake a full study on these lines, and she prepared to make another tour of the war zone.

The faces to be seen about were changing all the time, and Fryn was constantly adding new friends to old. Girls were marrying at a great rate. Mira Kenham, originally Stella's beautiful friend, was offered a contract by Williamsons to go to Australia with a touring company, and when she had left Australia and reached Auckland she married Hugh Crosse, who had come from his remote sheep farm and seen every performance. Ivy Low, whose uncle Sir Sidney Low was literary editor of the *St James's Gazette* and Atticus of the *Sunday Times*, was living and writing in a whitewashed cottage in the Grove in Hampstead when she met and married Maxim Litvinov and had their first baby in 1917. During Fryn's absence in the West country, she had arranged for her father to occupy number 46 and be taken care of by an aunt of May's, her mother's sister, a widow with four daughters. He had made the acquaintance of a fashion journalist on the *Daily Mirror*, a tough little Scot with a mane of blazing red hair, who had moved into the house next door and was about to marry Alfred Settle, invalided out of the Army. The upshot was that Fryn and Alison Settle became good neighbours and friends ever after. For Fryn accumulated dear and lasting friends as some people accumulate money and others go for bottle-tops or the Impressionists. At the end of her life she had no richer treasure.

At this stage it was, in the nature of things, mostly young females that came into her orbit; later the sphere widened to include all ages and sexes. For she loved people. She adored making matches, so that she was nicknamed after Jane Austen's Emma. Her instinct was to give, and there was no greed in her. For those she took to her heart, there was nothing she would not try to do, though it might cost time, strength or money.

When the money had started coming in, on account of royalties for *Secret Bread* and *Billeted*, it had had to cross a yawning gap; the long novel having caused her to walk a financial tightrope for years. On the one hand she was ashamed to be 'in the red', liking to write light-hearted *billets-doux* to her bank manager fan. On the other hand, she was – like Viv in *The Milky Way* – never without an entourage to support. Where Viv had acquired a troubadour, a baby, its simpleton nursemaid, a monstrous cat and a cadaver, Fryn had Papa and May, Precious and Blackie, her house, her string of guests, and semi-dependents such as Nan. For she and Nan had gradually changed roles as Nan grew old and blind. No wonder that, when a distracted Damit telephoned confiding her panic-terror, Fryn's balance was shaken.

Damit had had to go into a nursing-home, and had cabled her husband in Ceylon to come to her. But when Percy had arrived and tried to start up in business again, his new clients had let him down, he had had to borrow, gamble and lose, and suddenly there was a hideous discrepancy – a cash shortage. Unless he could produce a thousand pounds he was ruined. Horrified, Fryn drew out everything she had, and when she saw that it was not enough she wept. But not for long. She had never borrowed for herself, but now she raised three hundred pounds on her expectations and took a cab, with the thousand pounds complete, to darling Damit's bedside. To Fryn, cash meant cash.

In the pursuit of her précis-writing for Heinemann, she had suggested that Winnie, May's sister, should sit for Arthur Rackham for the frontispiece of *Cinderella as Retold by C.S. Evans*. C.S. was dedicating his book to Fryn, and this involvement led to an introduction to Jean de Bosschère. He had written and illustrated a collection of Flemish folk-tales, and was planning a further book for children, *The City Curious*, which Heinemann was to publish. Fryn's French was good and so was her fairy-lore. She was invited to undertake the work of adapting the story. The adventures were preposterous and the characters grotesque, except for Fritilla and her lovely sisters Laptitza and Kisika, but Fryn liked the idea. When Jean de Bosschère saw his proposed collaborator he liked the idea too. He asked her if she would not only write the English version but sit for him, and he came to Gordon Place to paint her as 'Fritilla and the Red Flying Fish' for the frontispiece. A year later, William Heinemann, and Dod Mead and Company of New York, duly published *The City Curious* by Jean de Bosschère, illustrated by the Author and Retold in English by F. Tennyson Jesse.

Fryn left for France in the early days of 1918, and she wrote her book *The Sword of Deborah*: First Hand Impressions of the British Women's Army in France, as she went along. On the fly leaf is a verse by Thomas Dunn English:

> *Women are timid, cower and shrink*
> *At show of anger, some folk think;*
> *But men there are who for their lives*
> *Dare not so far asperse their wives.*
> *We let that pass — so much is clear,*
> *Though little dangers they may fear,*

When greater dangers men environ,
Then women show a front of iron;
And, gentle in their manners, they
Do bold things in a quiet way.

The book, published in 1919 by Heinemann, and by George H. Doran in New York, gives a scrupulous picture of the lives, at work and at play, of the WAACs, the FANYs and the VADs, without false glamour or heroics, but not without flashes of beauty and of deep insight. It was not released by the Ministry of Information till the war was over, and Fryn was to say of it ruefully: 'The little book I wrote on the Women's Services looks very old-fashioned now', but *The Times Literary Supplement* assured her that 'she need not be perturbed. Her book has life in it. It will remain a record worth reading long after peace is signed.' On the jacket flap Fryn commented: 'It appears to me that people should still be told about the women workers of the war and what they did, even now when we are all struggling back into our chiffons – perhaps more now than ever. For we should not forget, and how should we remember if we have never known.'

EIGHT

The Happy Bride

SOMETHING MORE MOMENTOUS than the delay in publication of a new book had taken place. On 9 September 1918, in St Martin's, London, Harold Marsh Harwood, bachelor, Captain RAMC, living at Adelphi WC, son of George Harwood, Cotton Spinner, MP, wedded Fryniwyd Tennyson Jesse, spinster, novelist, of 46 Gordon Place W, daughter of Eustace Tennyson d'Eyncourt Jesse, Clerk in Holy Orders. The bride wore black: a short, straight, silk frock with a boat neck and with tier upon tier of white silk fringe from throat to hem. Fryn had designed it herself.

Though adept at drawing a veil over the passing of the years, Fryn was then thirty years old and Tottie was forty-four. She had rejected a number of proposals of marriage from ardent and persistent wooers. For six years she and Tottie had known each other and relished each other's company; had worked, triumphed and holidayed together and had survived the traumatic shock of her accident. Against a powerful determination to remain free, Tottie had been ceaselessly drawn to her, and now he was being posted to Syria. No doubt it was this impending separation which compelled them to acknowledge a reciprocal attraction surpassing and dwarfing all others.

Theirs was a marriage made in secret, with strangers as witnesses, and Fryn was to say: 'In a way it was a casual thing, in that I had not yet grasped the importance of what we were doing. At the last moment I said to Tottie "Look, don't let's do it. You want to marry me but don't particularly want to be married. I should like to be married but don't particularly want to marry you." His answer "But we must! I've bought the licence," sounded unarguable. And I was very attracted to him, though not what is called "in love". Love came with marriage. It came almost at once. We lived on our letters; long, long letters to each other. But I was not afraid of never seeing him again, even when he had a kind of breakdown in Beirut. He was moved to the hospital at Alexandria and eventually he came home. I was out, visiting a friend, but as I got off the bus and walked to my house, I was certain I was going to see him there. May came to the door as I opened it, and I said: "Tottie's here!" Then I saw his military cap, upside-down on the hall table. After that, as he got better, he came to see me every day, or I went out with him, until people took to asking us together everywhere.

'I told May at last, for she was getting worried. Stella knew, of course. It is impossible to describe how happy that time was, when we were secretly married, seeing each other at least five times a week and going away together for the weekends. So many people stay away in hotels and pretend they are married when they are not. It was the greatest fun to stay away and pretend we were not married when we were.'

Immediately after the appearance of *The Sword of Deborah* Fryn and Tottie had their first unofficial honeymoon, spending the summer on a barge yacht chartered by Tottie called *Thoma II*. Starting from Essex, they went to Falmouth and Helford. May went with them, and was prostrate until Southampton, where she came to energetic life and brought out a skipping-rope. Scandalized by this disturbance of the peace, Tottie betted her she could not skip to a hundred – he was always thinking of new methods of what she called 'torture' and she always fell for them – but she was so exhausted by the time she won her moral victory that she scornfully refused her due reward.

When Fryn came to describe the man her *alter ego*, Ginnie, married in her novel *The Alabaster Cup* of thirty years later, she was describing very much the kind of man she had chosen for herself: 'In some ways a strange creature, a strongly political animal, a strongly sexual animal, with much humour and a great love for his pretty Ginnie.' A good deal older than his wife, he was 'important in a far different field than that she knew, though she never felt his unknown world made a barrier between them.'

Tottie was born to George Harwood and his first wife Alice Marsh on 29 March 1874, at Eccles in Lancashire, and was educated at Marlborough and at Trinity College, Cambridge. He came between two sisters, Alice and Margaret. Alice was clever and rather hard. She married Graham Spence, and they adopted a son, Dermot. Fryn liked

Alice, but earned a black mark from her on her first visit by spending a morning in bed with a headache, thus heinously deflecting the house-maids from their duties. Margaret, called Maggie, was less intelligent but had more heart. She had experienced a failed marriage, over by the time Fryn came on the scene, and never mentioned, and after it she had reverted to her maiden name and bought herself a lovely house in Kent, which was run to perfection by her housekeeper-for-life, Clara Parker. In the early days she was quite fond of Fryn and had enjoyed her company at Madeira, but she rashly tried to dissuade Tottie from marrying her, saying 'She can't even cook!'; to which Tottie retorted flatly 'But I don't want her as a cook, you fool! I want her as a pet!'

The family house of the Harwoods was on Lake Windermere, and there is an anecdote of Tottie's about his childhood there, less appeal-ing than the man became. Playing in the nursery with his sisters, and assuming the authority of a sheriff with two horse thieves, he hanged little Maggie by the neck with a leather strap from the coat-hook behind the door, and set out into the orchard with a toy gun to deal with Alice. He never recalled how Maggie was retrieved and resusci-tated, but was satisfied that she must have been. At this point in the memory a wondering smile would irradiate his whole face.

George Harwood loved all his children, but his favourite was Tottie, as a child and later. They were both big men, vital men, Tottie was even flamboyant: in town he wore a greatcoat with a wide astrakhan collar, and gave his top-hat a jaunty tilt. He had a pugna-cious jaw belied by a merry eye, and had inherited his father's excellent brain and originality of thought. He was very athletic, a good Rugby player as well as excelling at golf, tennis and squash rackets. Whereas the father was strong in his religion, the son was agnostic. They were the best of companions, travelling far and wide together to buy cotton in Egypt and sell their product in Italy, Germany and even Russia. Both were attracted and attractive to women – it was said that nobody had ever refused Tottie.

On returning through the Mediterranean after one of their cotton enterprises, George and his son encountered, as a fellow traveller, a woman who was to have a disturbing effect on both their lives, and on Fryn's. Her distinguished husband was with her, but he had work to do and she was restless and bored. Her way of walking was graceful, she was elegantly turned out and stimulating to talk to. At first both men sought her company – George being by then a widower – but when her behaviour became explicitly inviting the father retreated, deeply shocked. Not so the son. Amused, he pressed his attentions, and so their long *affaire de coeur* began.

Knowing its history as he did, George deplored his son's attachment from the very first. That is not to say that he himself had done with women. In 1904, when he was fifty-eight, he took as his second wife a girl of twenty-four, Ellen Hopkinson, whom he called Nellie. Her mother was a great friend of his and of his first wife Alice. The marriage was extraordinarily happy, and they had three children, Georgina, George and Ruth.

Of this younger branch of the family, Georgina was educated at an Anglican convent school and at Lady Margaret Hall, and has written biographies of Charlotte Mary Yonge, Mrs Gladstone, John Keble, Queen Alexandra, Lord Shaftesbury, Elizabeth Wordsworth and Christina Rossetti. Her father, grandfather, step-father and three uncles had been Members of Parliament, and she was thinking of standing herself when she married Christopher Battiscombe, then Librarian at Durham and living in the Cathedral Square. She began writing instead, and used to send her books to Fryn for comment, and she wrote of her: 'This made a very great deal of difference to me, the vivid interest she took in my writing. She was such a good writer, so gifted and so painstaking at the same time; you felt she would never tolerate in herself or any other writer work that was less than the very best they were capable of. That intolerance of lazy work is in itself a very rare gift.'

George made his home in Johannesburg. He used to visit Fryn whenever he was over. They were fond of each other, though she would pretend to wax indignant about him: 'That Georgery' – as she called him – 'never stopped having children. He has a lot of money too – as they all have, under their father's Trust – and he has "made his million" from what he has described as "hat-hooks and coat-hooks".' He is quoted by Ruth as saying: 'Oh no, I'm not wich; I'm vewy vewy wich,' for he had a slight speech impediment. To Fryn's delight he once mused, glancing down at her long legs stretched out on the sofa: 'You know, Fwyn, I wegard the toes as the embwoidewy of the feet.'

Ruth, too, was convent educated, she spent some time at a famous ballet dancing school, and went on to Lady Margaret Hall and then to the Courtauld Institute. She has said that her sister and brother were of a radiant fairness, and when their mother introduced them all as: 'Here are my two beauties and this is my plain treasure' it was precisely true. 'But I did mind,' she added ruefully. She married Christopher Harris, who was in the Forestry Commission, brother of the actor Robert Harris. As a child she worshippped Tottie, regarding him with romantic veneration for his wicked ways. Not that the two families of George Harwood saw much of each other: the gap was too great, Tottie's step-mother being several years younger than he.

After the birth of Ruth, George began to suffer from the pernicious anaemia which was to kill him at the age of sixty-seven. When the illness became evident, Tottie left St Thomas' Hospital where he had been house physician, and returned to the family business of Richard Harwood and Sons, of which he later became managing director and chairman. Meanwhile he had begun writing his plays. In November 1912, only a few months after Tottie and Fryn met and the misunderstanding arose in the family about the nature of their relationship, his father died.

George left an ample share of his estate outright to his widow, who bought a great house near Oxford called Ewelme. There she lived, bringing up her three children alone, for some ten years. Then she married again, retaining the name of Harwood and becoming Mrs Harwood-Murray. Before George died, however, he had formed the Harwood Trust. His purpose in this was to prevent any of his large fortune from leaving the family, and in particular to guard against any possible claims against Tottie from his mistress – claims which, in the event, were never made.

From copious notes she assembled for a potential sequel to her semi-autobiographical novel of thirty years later, Fryn had evidently intended to call Tottie's mistress Leila Fladbury. It must serve hereafter, but it was not her name. Nor was Benjamin the name of her son. And the sequel was never written, though numerous drafts were begun, abandoned and destroyed as 'too near the bone'. Had it been possible for George to get to know Fryn, had they ever met and learned to appreciate each other, she believed he would have welcomed her as a daughter-in-law, and what she called 'the dead-hand-will' need never have been devised. But the timing was disastrous, and the effect, direct and indirect, of excluding a man's seed from inheritance can never be assessed.

How and when a loving relationship began between Fryn and
Tottie who can tell, since they did not? During the long years from
1912 when he had read 'The Mask', to 1918 when they married in
secret, and after, she was under public scrutiny and some obloquy
because of this association. Friends and aquaintances naturally
wondered; it was a favourite topic of the day at one time. Since Tottie
had volunteered for the Red Cross before Fryn got back from New
York, and had then crossed to France with the RAMC, they met only
at intervals during the war years, and they met openly to work on the
plays. The attraction between them was not initially, and not primarily, a physical one. But, to the family at Ewelme, Tottie had long
ago branded himself as a philanderer, and though they believed they
were tolerant as well as affectionate, they could see that he had these
two strings to his bow, apart from the perennial garland of actresses
round his neck. 'He gets letters from the same two women every
morning,' they marvelled, and did not credit that he could be faithful
to either.*

Tottie had always got on well with his step-mother and she with
him. He bore no grudge against her for the frustrating effect of the
Trust, and she never forgot his sweetness to her when his father died.
But, for Fryn, as for Nellie, there was a built-in tendency to see the
other in a false light. 'In those days it was important to act like a lady,
and Fryn did not,' was Nellie's verdict; a verdict hotly denied by
everyone close to Fryn. But there were some who maintained with
Nellie that Fryn used her broken hand as a means of binding Tottie to
her. Why she should have coveted him they could not tell, these
people said, for he was nearer the gorilla in appearance than most
maidens pray for – but covet him she did. Others refuted this and
accorded the greatest respect to Fryn's behaviour, protesting that the
shoe was entirely on the other foot. But Nellie could see only the
adventuress, who had not scrupled to employ her hand as bait.

Inevitably the hand did play a part, for it was inescapably there
between them almost from the beginning. But, once the initial shock
was past, Fryn had become reticent about it, treating it with such
grace that others could and did forget it. She had provided for herself
and her dependents in spite of it. It was not by her clinging to him that
she and Tottie came together, for the man who had written *Please*

* Detaills of the Harwood family's reaction to Fryn: Ruth Harris in conversation
with JC.

Help Emily did not need to be coerced. But none of this is important, or can ever be proved. The important thing was the growth of their enduring love. Yet it is strange that a woman so inviolable, so heedless of mercenary values, should ever have been seen in parasitic guise. Fryn's dear ones at Gordon Place saw her as a radiantly happy girl, at her best; nicer than in Newlyn days, when an uneasy conscience about her faith and about her mother gnawed at her, or when a grumbling appendix made her fretful; nicer than later in the marriage, when anxious craving for a child began. They remember her as a darling and a honey-pot.

Tottie was no misogynist, and indeed he had always found women irresistible. But the tragic outcome of an early and disastrous love affair with a morbidly possessive woman had made him resolve never to be so caught again. Hence he had allowed himself to be solaced by a married woman; one, moreover, who fully intended to remain so, since she had a position, a husband and a daughter she valued. When Leila Fladbury bore Tottie's son, her husband had not repudiated her or the child. The family had remained together and apparently serene. Tottie was godfather to the boy, and continued to escort the mother on various established occasions even after his marriage to Fryn. As Ruth has said: 'The Harwood Trust was conceived before Fryn came on the scene, purely to safeguard Harwood money from going to the mother of Tottie's son. His relationship with her overlapped with his courtship of Fryn by several years. It must have been maddening for him to be unable to provide properly for Fryn. And maddening for Fryn too. I do so wish I had known her! But it did not happen.'

Rebecca West, who had got to know Fryn the moment she appeared on Fleet Street, has protested:

'Why did Tottie make it all so difficult for her? Why the secret marriage at all? And why let it go on so long? It was cruel and pointless. There was nothing blatant about his existing liaison. Few people knew of its existence. His mistress was protected from scandal by her position in life, and Fryn had enough to contend with already. There had been talk, which I knew to be baseless, about her friendship with dear Alfred Mond. When she and Tottie began going away together, naturally nobody knew what to make of it, and Fryn's reputation must have suffered. When at last it was announced as a war-time marriage, nobody wanted to believe such an unlikely tale! I only knew myself because I happened to be with them on the day they married. What was it all for?'*

Well, those who shared this attitude knew nothing of the son. And it was never what people might say that moved Tottie. He wanted Fryn, and he wanted his son. He thought that, given care and time, he could have both. He was wrong.

The fact is, Tottie had not been in the habit of denying himself until he met Fryn. But he had recognized that here was something different; and he wanted it to be different. When he had decided to marry, it was because he had accepted that he was utterly bound up with her; had indeed been so from the beginning. The idea of the secret was simply to give him the chance to make the break with the minimum of unnecessary pain and damage. He would not treat the existing bonds as of small account, and Fryn understood that. He had said to her: 'I have responsibilities which you would be the last person to make me wish to evade,' and she had answered: 'I know.' Hugging their secret, she had prepared to wait.

She waited a long time, and it wasn't easy. She was happy as she had never imagined being, yet there were arrows in the flesh. Doubts, which she strove to subdue and to keep to herself, show through the poetry she was writing then:

LOVER'S CRY:

I have hated
Every moment of the sun by day,
Every moment of the moon at night;
Eating my own heart.
For since you never write me words to ease my hunger
My love unto my love is fain to be phrasemonger.

I have scorned
Myself for my own pain each day,
For every aching nerve at night,
Yet, eager waited
Lest my too-anxious thoughts or pulses' drumming
Should drown the first faint noises of your coming.

---

* Dame Rebecca West in conversation with JC.

I have despised
You more; because I knew each day
And every golden-houred night
You would but want
Easy companioning and easier passion,
Naught keener to disturb and trouble your soul's fashion.

And I have known
When once you came, that in the day
And while I held you through the night,
Again I should forget . . .
Forget just in the nearness of you all my sorrow,
That I ached with it yesterday and will to-morrow. *

Delicate and highly-strung, Fryn was subject to terrible headaches and crushing fatigue. She had then to lie fallow until the vital spark was mysteriously renewed. Yet she was tough in parts; could work round the clock if the work made progress. Many tastes and qualities she shared with Tottie. It was not that they thought alike, far from it. They were alike in that their views were their own. Some were alarmed at Fryn's brilliance in argument, at her apodictical conclusions; not Tottie. It was a duel of wits between them, immensely enjoyable. That was what gave excitement to their talk, for them as for their listeners. And that was what made the dialogue in their plays come to life.

They were living apart and coming together, and with each coming together and each parting their pleasure in each other increased. What more could lovers want? And yet, time was passing and Fryn had had a miscarriage. She kept it from him, because she didn't want to put pressure on him. She knew what a price he put upon his freedom; that he had had enough of feeling caught. All the same, she had not expected that, with physical ecstasy, hunger for a child would take so powerful a hold upon her. She was always torn, her body wanting to conceive, her mind commanding with cruel logic – not yet!

Tottie had taken a lease of the Ambassadors Theatre, to produce his own and other plays. He was going into theatrical management and

* *The Happy Bride*, Heinemann, 1920.

had formed a company called Regency Productions, with Leo S. Daintree as Company Secretary. In April 1920, he produced his serio-comedy *The Grain of Mustard Seed*, with Cathleen Nesbitt and Norman McKennell. It was his first entirely independent venture and it firmly established him in the volatile affections of the West End theatre-going public. The theme was politics, with an idealist pitted against the cynics. James Agate wrote of 'this admirable play's wit, savour and sanity. A play of its period . . . yet without Ibsen, Shaw, Galsworthy, Granville Barker and the rest, this play would never have been written.'

Lord Dunsany wrote from County Meath: 'The dialogue is the most masterly thing I have read in modern drama and every one of the curtains is a joy.' Although it was less immediately popular than *Please Help Emily*, with its French-farce air, or than the sparkling *Billeted*, *The Grain of Mustard Seed* was revived successfully several times, and earned a place in the Anthology of Great British Modern Plays. A BBC version was produced, and Cathleen Nesbitt joined the circle of greatly beloved friends.

Also in 1920, *The Happy Bride*, a collection of twenty-four poems, beautifully presented on hand-cut paper and with Fryn's 'mark' etched between each of the four parts, was published by Heinemann. She dedicated it to 'B', who was Badger, her newest name for her husband, and she added: *Mihi Dolores Tui – Tibi Gaudia Mea*. Some of the verses had appeared previously in periodicals and many, including the hymn of 'The Happy Bride,' had Cornish themes. It was prefaced with the explanation: 'In Cornwall, when an unmarried girl dies, she is borne through the streets followed by her girl friends dressed in white and singing a hymn of which the refrain is "O Happy Bride".'

THE HAPPY BRIDE

Along the lane where I passed the faded sorrel shows rusty,
Naked the wind-wilted thorns crouch by the granite boulders;
On the day that I buried you, lass, the June sun was lusty,
Made the new-varnished coffin gleam upon the black shoulders.
Lie you warmly, my lass, with your head on your lonely pillow,
You that I was to wed when the pilchard huer's first 'Heva!'
Told that the harvest of fishers made dark the long rippled billow,
You who'll wed never?

Dead before you were mine! As they jolted you up the steep street
Meaning wedded to Heaven, they hymned you as 'O Happy Bride'
. . .
Bridal shift was not sewn nor the bridal wreath twisted, my sweet,
Until you had died.

Lass, I cannot forget you — the one soft curl in the hollow
Dimpling the nape of your neck; the way that the curve of pink ear
Was half-hid by your hair when you turned to see if I'd follow,
Then the smile that narrowed your lids when you found I was near
. . .
But — there's Nan to the mill who would have me, come fair days
come wet;
Must I get me no sons for the sake of my pledges to you?
When my hands are too feeble for drawing and tucking the net,
Then what shall I do?

When the tiller will wrench at my grip and send the boom swinging
And the white eye of dawn looks vainly to find me afloat,
Then I'll want of my own flesh and blood to set the sails winging
In my own boat.

'Lad, you need have no fear that my dead hand will pluck at the sheet,
Sleep without recking of me and get you children about you;
Thicker than gulls at a haul come flocking the troubles you'll meet,
For sons grown to manhood will quarrel and daughters when fair will
flout you.'

What better folk have you here, my lass, grass betwixt you and the
bay,
With the church tower pricking one ear across to the morn?
'Children I would have brought to you; babes of the spirit are they
Who never are born.'

May I take Nan and wed with her, never think her your debtor,
Nor see her cheek pale from the envious breath of the dead?
'Have her and be glad, for the Happy Bride sleeps with a better,
Nan you may wed.

'Tis the man that I thought you lies closer to me than a wraith,
Dreaming with him and his babes I'll covet no live woman's morrow.
Take my wish — that till women forget or till men can keep faith,
You may miss sorrow.

That summer, Fryn and Tottie spent at sea again, and she said of it: 'Tottie had bought a yawl of about eleven tons. He had always thought that Stella and I had come to London like the two beautiful Miss Gunnings, but unfortunately he got their name wrong and said: "the two beautiful Miss Gudgeons". So Stella and I took to calling each other Gudgeon – Gudge for short – and he called his yawl *Gudgeon* after us. She was a good sea-worthy little boat, and we went through the Crinan and the Bowling Canals in her, and up the West Coast of Scotland to Skye and Eig and Rum and Mull. As we weaved between the islands, the image of a little old mill-house hung like a mirage in the mists that enclosed us. For it will be seen that with us marriage had not meant having a home. And yet we did get a home in spite of everything. In July, we had sailed up Chichester harbour in *Gudgeon*, and I fell in love with Cut Mill at the top of Bosham Creek, and Tottie bought it for me as a wedding present.'

In February 1921, Tottie produced his play *A Social Convenience* at the Royalty Theatre, with Hilda Moore, Nigel Playfair, Dennis Eadie, and Stella Jesse again. It was produced in France and Italy the same year. Bright, light and witty, it toured the United Kingdom in 1922, and Austria, Hungary, Czecho-Slovakia and Germany in 1924. A Scandinavian adaptation was made in 1951 and repeated in 1958. The *Daily Express* wrote of its London production: 'Among the very good plays that have been written in the last twenty years is *A Social Convenience*. If I said it was among the best plays in the last two or three hundred years it would sound exaggerated, but I would still believe it to be true. I would much sooner read a new comedy by Mr Shaw, Mr Harwood or Mr Somerset Maugham than any of the great English "classics" – even Congreve himself.'

Fryn had been working on *The White Riband*. In it, Loveday, an illegitimate orphan girl with a passionate longing to dance 'The Flora' through the houses and streets of Helford, is driven to steal the silken sash from the wreath on a maiden's grave, and is shamed into hanging herself by it. The book was published in the autumn of 1921 by Heinemann and by George H. Doran of New York under the title of *The White Riband* or *A Young Female's Folly*. The scarlet and white end-papers and frontispiece were drawn by Fryn, and it was inscribed: 'To Stella; a Young Female: I dedicate this tale in the hope that it will encourage her to persevere in that indifference to personal adornment for which she is conspicuous at present. Should it fail in this high endeavour, nevertheless this book is hers in all sisterly love.'

'The flavour of the story is in the telling,' commented the *Birming-ham Post*. 'Pity, irony and poetry are the artist's weapons. We congratulate her most sincerely upon her work – on its fine, polished and unwrinkled surface, with the fierce heart-beats beneath.' Joseph Conrad was enchanted with it, calling it 'this jewel in a casket.' And St John Ervine wrote: 'There are not many tales that will stand a second reading. Yours do. The fact is, Fryn, you are a genius insufficiently recognized.'

On the evening of the same day in October 1921, *The Hotel Mouse* was produced at the Queen's Theatre, adapted from the French of Paul Armont and Marcel Gerbidon by Fryn and Tottie in collabora-tion, with Henry Kendall and Dorothy Minto leading. It didn't quite come off, being too long though 'full of witty passages', according to the *Observer*. The *Daily Telegraph* called it 'quite amusing; a little closer knit and it might have been very amusing indeed.'

It was on the first of December, at Devonshire House, that Nigel Playfair put on a charity performance by amateurs, in which Ivor Novello was the success of the evening. The play was Sir Edward Bulwer Lytton's *Not So Bad As We Seem*, which had first been produced in 1851, at Devonshire House, for a charity, by amateurs – Charles Dickens and his circle. This time it was fortunately cut from five hours to two-and-a-half. *The Times* said it was a brilliant social gathering. Fryn and Tottie were both in the cast, and it was also their first public appearance in the guise of married blessedness. As Fryn said: 'My husband and I had decided to make our marriage public and go to Italy. We had been married over three years then, and Tottie told me he would like everyone to know it. I had left it to him. It had to be his wish, and it was his wish.'

Yes, so it was. There is surely no doubt that Tottie would finally have come to the decision that he had been treating his mistress as wife, and his wife as mistress, too long. Yet, perhaps unknown to herself, it was a crisis in Fryn's inner being that had brought matters to a head. For a shadow had fallen across their happiness – and passed on. Only Fryn and Tottie were there to hear the words that were spoken, to mark those that were not, and their memories became so criss-crossed in after years by the passions that were stirred and the scars these left that, of all the many people who heard her story, none could pinpoint the cause of the obsession that was to haunt Fryn at intervals for the remainder of her life.

They had met at Lymington, at a little house rented for September near the yacht-harbour. May was there, and Fryn's cousin Hebe Andrews. It was the eve of their wedding anniversary, and the two had walked down from the house to the quay after supper, and boarded *Gudgeon* together as usual. He obviously did commemorate their day, for when she came back to the house the next evening, ill and alone, she left a jewel-box on her dressing-table.

Tottie had gone back to London. Telegrams came from him every day, but Fryn was out of her mind, like a thing possessed, her eyes blank. She hadn't got back to the house till dark, and had been in a state of exhaustion. It seems clear that on that morning Tottie had given her his present of a pair of jade ear-rings. She had tried them on, excited, anticipating some sort of proposition for the future, and it had not come. He had taken it for granted that she knew the time was ripe for the open acknowledgement of their joint life to begin, and that there was no need for him to say so. He had earlier given her to understand that his own public school had accepted Benjamin, his son, and that discreet financial arrangements had been made to secure his education. But whatever reassuring words Fryn looked for had either not been spoken at all, or they had not been specific enough for her peace of mind. Instead, he had warned her hurriedly that she simply must run along now or they would be caught by guests he was expecting. Of course she had divined instantly who the 'guests' were; such near-misses had occurred before, though never on the yacht. He had continued to attend certain functions with Leila Fladbury and until all his cards had been played this could not be helped. He was satisfied that there was no question of broken faith. And it was his own integrity alone that had always guided him.

Stunned and shamed, Fryn had left in a daze, feeling she never wanted to see the pokey little saloon again. Everything was spoilt! How could he do this to her? And even while she hated him, and suffered the pain of jealousy, she knew that she couldn't bear to lose him. That was the most shameful fact of all.

Did she then go to Adelphi Terrace – as she sometimes seemed to say – and let herself in? Did she stare round the room where they had made love, and see on the walls and on the mantelpiece those photographs and drawings of other women he had known, a photograph of himself, his son and the mother of his son among them? Did she tear them down and stamp them under her heel before going back to Lymington, there to creep into bed feeling deadly ill? Or did she annihilate them in her mind's eye only, while she lay on her bed in a fever, and the storm broke over her frantic thoughts for days and nights on end?

The household treated her illness as a peculiarly severe migraine; combined as it often was with her monthly period, also a peculiarly severe one. May bathed and warmed her, then pulled the curtains close and gave her the usual relief of eye-shades and sleeping-pills. The doctor came each day to give an injection, and gradually the signs of distress abated, her hands ceased fluttering, the power of thought came back, and she could open her eyes without agony.

The etiology behind the brain-fever was not established at the time. it may have been a migraine, a virus or a second miscarriage – which last Fryn affirmed later. Whatever the cause, it left apprehension in its wake and, each time it came again, happiness flew out of the window. Yet it would pass, and afterwards her spirits rose spontaneously and it was almost as if the whole episode had never been. It was always to be like that. She lived through it time and again, as if it were a recurring dream; and like the ancient mariner she had to hold someone, sometimes almost a stranger, by her 'glittering and fevered eye', till the pathetic tale of the wrong that Tottie had done to her had been told once more and sweet reason could return.

This first time, tired out but with her mind again unclouded, she submitted gently to Tottie's suggestion that they should tell the world they were married and spend six months in Italy. He had taken a lease of the Castello at Portofino from the first of January. He would put an announcement in *The Times*. And he would send Maggie a telegram: 'Happy Christmas! Married Fryn three years ago.'

When Tottie had decided to make the marriage known and to take Fryn away on a long honeymoon, it went without saying that May should accompany them; or rather, she should go ahead. But first Fryn had to consider what was to be done about her mother. She decided she must present the reluctant Tottie, and Edith rose to the occasion. Indeed, she rose to heights greater than even Fryn had envisaged. She was lying back on her *chaise-longue* to receive them, her still beautiful legs crossed, and her ringed hands supporting the slightly trembling head on its piled cushions. Then came the virtuoso bit. She leant forward and her arms wavered out, to clasp Fryn and the ermine cape Tottie had given her, and thus forcibly to prolong their usual duty kiss, while she murmured wistfully: 'Oh, my dear one, my baby!' After this seal of approval, Fryn staggered up from the unaccustomed crouch to which she had been subdued, with a light-headed feeling compounded of relief and hysteria, and the rest of their brief visit went off very well indeed. 'I had written the news to all my friends,' Fryn has told, 'and it was amusing meeting the people who had still been nice to me when they thought I was not married, and who now discovered I had been fit to know the whole time. So we departed in the odour of sanctity; an odour we had not enjoyed for a considerable time.'

She did not give up the house on Campden Hill. 'When we went to Portofino,' she explained, 'my father remained in it, and so did the wonderful old aunt of May's, Aunt Jennie, known to everyone as Auntie. She ran the house and looked after Papa far better than I could ever have done. Strangers must have been puzzled on hearing these two old people speaking to each other as "Auntie dear" and "Papa love", but no one bothered to explain.' Eustace wrote to Fryn before her departure: 'Your love made my short visit one of great happiness. To be so close to you, and to cuddle, and to talk so seriously yet so lovingly! No wonder that I think this intimacy between father and daughter is the greatest pleasure in the world. Perhaps it ought to have been in another quarter, but you have done your best to give me the happiness which should have come from elsewhere; and with the greatest success. The purity of that happiness is equalled only by its depth. You are going away for a long time, and I am old and rickety, but in the years to come you can now and then think that your father's idea of beautiful love is that which you have given him. God bless you, my daughter of the sweet heart.'

The Castello was owned by a man called Yeats-Brown, and was often called the Castello Brun. Tottie had taken it until 31 March 1922, and accordingly May left London in the last days of December, with Tottie's valet-butler Johnson and his sharp little wife Agnes, known as Hagnes, escorting twenty-four pieces of luggage. May was petrified of them both, for they were a pushing pair, but they travelled together perforce by train and boat, Johnson warning the inexperienced May: 'Don't you pay no hattention to those hawful hurinals!' He did not suggest, however, what else she should do to be saved. At Genoa the odd threesome spent that night, then on by train to

Rapallo, and by carriage to the tiny harbour at Portofino, whence the luggage was wafted up the goat-track by the many and eager hands of Italian youths. At the Castello, up on the crest, Teresa and Angelina, who went with the house and spoke only Italian, stood to greet them and offer refreshment. The staff was complete.

May wandered about the rooms and the terraced gardens. She picked the bedroom Fryn should have, and the one for Tottie, and the one for herself. Next day, after she'd unpacked the trunks, she climbed down to the harbour and started walking along the Rapallo road till she met the ancient Victoria. Fryn and Tottie were sitting in it, proudly clutching one small piece of hand-luggage each, having come the direct route by sea. With surprising speed Fryn, wrapped in her new serenity, was up the goat-track, having made friends with half the natives and several of the visitors inhabiting the rock as well. These were few enough, for only a handful of English people lived above Portofino then. There was young Edward Terry and his new wife, and there was Eric Kennington the sculptor. 'Luckily, in those days it did not matter to us that you could not drive up to the Castello,' Fryn wrote. 'It used to take twenty minutes then, from the pastel-coloured fisherman's village. Later, a contraption on the pulley system was rigged up. Now a tunnel has been bored through the rock.

'Harley Granville Barker, who was married to Helen Huntington, used to come and see us, and I don't think Helen cared much for the goat-track. She was his second wife, a sophisticated American, beautifully dressed, and she came up in high-heeled slippers, a little black dress, and the most gorgeous ermine coat. They had never seemed to me very human, either of them, but when we nearly got drowned taking a cat-boat out from Portofino and sailing her across the bay, they were infinitely kind and comforting to us. It was a glorious day, the wind was right aft, and we did that tempting thing – running. Suddenly we noticed that all the fishing boats had disappeared. We tried to go about, but it was impossible. Half a gale was blowing by then, so we had to keep straight on. I crawled forward and got the jibsails off her, Tottie got the mainsail down and, under the bare pole, we went hell for leather for the gulf of Spezia. We heard the roar of a train going through the tunnel on the other side. There was just one place where there was a sandy beach, and we managed to head for it. We struck the beach and rolled right over, and some men working in a timber-yard rushed down into the sea and pulled us out.

We left the cat-boat pulled up on the beach, hired a car, and drove home through Rapallo where the Granville Barkers were living. Helen dressed me in her beautiful woollen clothes, and Harley produced the money to pay off the car at the bottom of the goat-track. We arrived home after dark, to find May anxiously pacing the Castello floor, having thought we had drowned where Shelley had drowned.

'We had one glorious trip to Genoa with Harley and Helen, to see Eleanora Duse in *The Lady of the Sea*. She was perfection and her movements were wonderful. We stayed the night at Genoa, and were sitting at table, before a delicious cold roast beef after the theatre, when Helen got up and said: "Come Harley, let us leave the carnivores." I am afraid Harley was enjoying his beef, and did not appreciate her invitation in the least.'

It appears that the only other Fryn was the Greek courtesan Phryne of extraordinary beauty, who lived in Athens in the fourth century BC. The name meant a toad and was not her own, but was one commonly given to courtesans. Phryne sat for the painter Apelles for his great picture 'Aphrodite Anadyomene', whereas Fryn had no extraordinary beauty, and had modelled as a sylph instead of a goddess. But Max Beerbohm remembered her as 'quite extraordinarily pretty' when she and Tottie came to visit him in his house at Rapallo. 'Sometimes Max and his wife came to lunch at the Castello, and he was as charming as his writings,' wrote Fryn. 'And he, who by all accounts had been a cynical bachelor, was devoted to his wife and only lived in the light of her eyes.

'We loved being at the Castello, and we used to eat out on fine days in a sort of bay in the fortifications. We used to climb the steep hillsides exploring, or walk miles over the mountains to San Fruttuoso, have a picnic lunch lying under a tree, and then hire a sailing-boat back in the cool of the evening. Tottie's nice sister Alice, whom we called Fat Alice, and her husband Graham, came to stay. Also the great J.O.P. Bland, "Chinese Bland" of *The Times*. And sometimes we went to Rapallo to have a little gamble in the Casino.' But the three months at Portofino came to an end, and Lady Russell – Elizabeth von Arnim, married to Bertrand Russell's elder brother – took over the Castello, using it as the backdrop for her novel *The Enchanted April*. Johnson and his Hagnes went back to Adelphi Terrace, while Fryn and Tottie and May set off for Venice, for the Grand Hotel on the Grand Canal, and Tottie roared despairingly 'I will not travel with twenty-four pieces of luggage!'

At dinner on their first night, the *maitre d'hôtel* swooped low before Tottie, displaying the dish containing the *chef d'oeuvre*; and then before May, whom he took for the first lady. She stared at him blankly, and he remained swooped there until Tottie gave her a nudge and grunted: 'Bow, you fool!' – 'But how could I know?' wailed May, when the dish had been wafted away. 'I've never bowed to a plate of food before.'

They got back from Venice in the early summer of 1922 and fitted out *Gudgeon* again. While spending a few weeks with friends on the Riviera, they handed the yacht over to E. Phillips Oppenheim, who recalled in his memoirs, *The Pool of Memory* 'I received the offer of a friendly charter of a small motor yacht from Tottie Harwood; large, genial, expansive, with a perpetual smile and never an ill word to say of anyone.' Of that second year with *Gudgeon* Fryn has written: 'We went foreign, first on the Riviera, and later up to Holland and through the canals to the Dollard Sea. That was the hottest summer imaginable, and we used to lie next to a barge laden with Gouda cheeses, through nights without a breath of air. It was very lovely though, and the Zuider Zee before the harbour was filled in at Volendam was well worth sailing.

'I had been working on my novel *Tom Fool*, a story of the sea, while we were at the Castello. I had always had a feeling for the sea and sailing. I was a perfect sailor and I thought it was bliss. In September we made the London River cruise and came home to Cut Mill, anchoring off Bosham that autumn.'

Part Three

—◦◦⟨⟩◦◦—

Autumn

NINE

—••€)(3••—

Cut Mill

IN AN ARTICLE called 'London River', published in December 1922 by *Blackwood's Magazine*, Fryn charted the pilgrimage she made in *Gudgeon* that summer. The eleven-ton yawl, white with a green bottom, 'seemed like a silver birch amid blasted oaks as she lay with her elegant spoon bow curving up towards the overhanging sterns of three bluff black hoppers filled with thousands of tons of Thames mud.' With a pilot whose father had been First Officer of the *Cutty Sark* she sailed up the mouth of the estuary, from Tilbury tidal basin, past Dartford Creek, to Greenwich on an evening flooded with sunlight, and so to Limehouse and the entrance into the cloister that is St Katherine's Dock. 'Hushed as a church was this little bronze-coloured pool of a dock, hemmed in by tall pillared ware-houses. Only the pigeons filled the air with the soundless sense of wings.'

The Pool of London glowed like a lake of topaz; Tower Bridge was etched dark against a luminous sky, as *Gudgeon* slipped through the dock gates. After a supper of fried steak and onions, they slept that last night in the shadow of the Tower, lapped in calm.

By the time Fryn and Tottie anchored off Bosham in the autumn of 1922, the fifteenth century Cut Mill had been occupied for months by May and Stella, an army of workmen, and a menagerie of pets. There was May's black cat, Bootiful Sing; Stella's Persian cat, the Luverlee Boyee; Somers' retriever, Sweep; Stella's spaniel, John; and of course Precious, Fryn's pug.

After the house was bought, plans had to be put in hand for a new wing. Work was at its height when May got back from Fryn's honeymoon and Stella arrived with the animals, so they all camped in the attics. There was nowhere to sit, so they spent their days knee-deep in the verges of the stream they were trying to clear of weeds. On

24 July, jointly they wrote Fryn a twenty-two page letter describing
their tribulations, harried by the thirty-three workmen, the animals,
the Council officials and admiring motorists, all asking questions
they had been given no authority to answer. To this anguished letter,
they received a wire from Tottie and Fryn, just saying: 'You poor
things', which made their blood boil. May had written:

> 'Your clothes are original, beautiful, costly and becoming, but to carry a
> parcel, open a door, or strap-hang in a bus, they are of no use at all. Your
> house is the same. You cannot open the doors because of the elaborate
> fastenings. You cannot hang up a dressing-gown in the bathrooms, which
> are far too beautiful to mar with a hook. Our heads have been banged on
> your ancient beams till we are cross-eyed. Stella says how like you it is to
> buy a kitchen-table because you admired its legs; the top is perfectly
> rotten, with slits full of the dirt of ages, through which the scrubbing-
> water flows straight into the silver-drawer beneath. How bitter it is that
> you should be so happy and we so miserable!'

They ought to have been glad Fryn and Tottie were out of their
way, for when Fryn next wrote, kindly advising them which table to
put her favourite amber figures on, there was as yet no furniture at all
in the drawing-room, as the floor was only just down, so they
solemnly placed two deck-chairs for them in the middle of the empty
room. When the work was really finished, however, Fryn gave a
grand farewell dinner to the builders and the nurserymen, in the
workmen's shed in the garden, and all the toasts in praise of the house
and its gardens were published in the local paper.

'Cut Mill was a perfect house,' she wrote, 'except during Goodwood Week when the traffic was so noisy we couldn't hear the birds
singing or the fountain playing. But then, during Goodwood Week
we lived like idle rich and went to the races every day ourselves. It was
a beautiful house architecturally. Darcy Braddell, whom I had made
friends with when he did Melchett Court for the Monds, turned it
from a mill-house into something really swagger. We kept the mill
wheel, though it was too old to work. And I must say that, out of
rough fields, I made a most lovely garden, with a water garden and an
orchard, rose gardens and a lavender walk. There were pigeon-cotes
too, and the mill-dam I turned into a swimming-pool. We had a punt
on the stream, and we used to have a tennis tournament every year,
with the house full of guests. It seems to me to have been always full
of guests, but of course it wasn't. In that first year, Edna Best, the

Cassons and the Monds came, and in the following spring the Nigel Playfairs and Alfred Sutro and Madge Titheradge. Violet and Alfred Mond came again, and C.S. Evans of Heinemann, and the Phillips Oppenheim, and though none of these people can be said to have been strong at tennis, they were the most delightful guests.'

Since the reign of Henry VII the house had been a water-mill, and it is mentioned in the Domesday Book. After the new wing was added for Fryn, Cut Mill could hold seventeen at full stretch, including three men in the garage block. Margaret and Stella and their two servants occupied the guest cottage. And Fryn's clever young cook, Mrs Williams, had the attics with the two kitchen-maids. When Gerald Kelly and his wife Jane came, May gave up her room and made up a bed for herself in the drawing-room after everyone had retired. There is a photograph of the house in this full-to-bursting state, with heads framed in every window. It looks like Stanley Spencer's painting in the Tate Gallery, of the multitude of angelic heads thrust through windows to watch Christ carrying the Cross.

That is how it always was in Goodwood Week, and most summer weekends too. May took care of the shopping and Tottie's new Alsatian puppy Bisto, and all the other dogs and cats, their grooming and their feeding. She re-arranged the ever-changing beds, ordered the meals, and provided for everyone's foibles. She was sitting one afternoon, embroidering H-for-Harwood on the borders of sheets and towels, when someone suggested drily that she might put Hs all over a bedspread when she had nothing better to do. This she did, in multi-coloured patchwork, and a many-splendoured thing it made.

Cut Mill is not a grand house; it is an intimate one. Above the linen-fold front door, 'the little man' and 'the little woman' hover half-in and half-out of a stone weather-house, and carved on the tablet beneath are George Herbert's words: 'Building is a sweet impoverishing, HMH and FTJ 1922'. Within, the doors of solid oak are supported and adorned by steel hinges, shaped like a sea-horse embodying the letters FTJ. This was Fryn's very own cherished abode, and even the gutter pipes are embossed with her initials. The furnishing, though unusual, was not extravagant. What Fryn cared about was atmosphere; open windows and lighted fires. She liked the soft tone of a pigeon's breast for walls and carpet, with a spectacular outline or a splash of brilliant colour against it. Apart from comfortable, specially-made mattresses, the beamed guest-rooms were fitted out with simplicity; chairs, shapely chests and roomy old cupboards, collected on her travels round the Mediterranean coasts, had been sent down by train to her friend of Newlyn days, Dato Gilardoni. He had them stripped in his workshops behind the printing-press which had produced *The Paper Chase*, and then enamelled with sprays of flowers and fruits. In Fryn's workroom, lined with book-shelves, the old-rose curtains and cushions were hand-embroidered with cottage flowers in wool and silk; the work of her Cousin Hebe, who also made a fine tapestry of Cut Mill in *petit point* for the wall above the mantelpiece, and several rugs designed by Fryn of sea and sky and ships in full sail, surrounded by *gros point* borders of flowers and butterflies.

In the long drawing-room, the white plaster ceiling with its striking Italianate design of birds, cast a flood of light upon the black-and-white chessboard parquet. Pale gold curtains framed the leaded windows, and lacquer cabinets on slender legs stood before the panelled sycamore walls. A painted head of Nefertiti was enshrined in an alcove; Stella had fallen love with Akhnaton's queen, the 'Beautiful One', and bought it for Fryn. A photograph shows Fryn and Stella sitting back-to-back on the floor, beneath the wood-cut by Brang-wyn of a galleon, in front of the wide hearth. They are wearing the knee-length frocks of the twenties, which broke into pleats at the hip and were called 'boyish'. Their heads are in profile, tilted dreamily back against each other, the hair short-bobbed and sculpted into waves. In a postscript to May's 'tribulations' letter, after such a barrage of straight talk as can rarely have hit Fryn, had come a softening of tone:

> 'Your house is going to be absolutely beautiful. Thank you darling for your kindness; I shall indeed be grateful for the extra money, but won't start it till September, when I shall have "served seven years for Rachel", so to speak. I hope you aren't tired of me, pet. And I do love you as much as anyone so cold and hard-hearted as I am can love.'

Every morning there was bathing in the pool, and every evening there was dancing to the gramophone. May wound it and changed the records and danced 'The Cobbler's Dance', shooting out her legs in Magyar fashion. Everyone else tried, but usually fell over with laughter, so then they played games and the men did tricks. Margaret and Stella came every summer. So did the Monds, the Meyers and Sybil and Lewis Casson. Fryn invited all these guests and many more, but Tottie loved the house-parties just as much, and the guests never wanted to leave. Nobody minded the impromptu sleeping arrangements. They always came back because it was such fun. 'If ever Stella and I were missing,' Fryn recalled, 'Tottie would say: "Oh, they'll be lying in their bath, creaming their faces and talking about their mother".'

At the making of a garden, Fryn was in her element. She had turned the housing of the water-wheel into a fernery, and was busy one day planning a back-water for the punt when a man from the Surveyor's Office arrived. In spite of a warning she had had by telephone to expect a visitor, the two of them became immersed in the problem down by the water's edge, and when he had gone she hurried guiltily up to the house, bleating: 'Oh, what a time the dear man took! I haven't missed the Countess of Ayr, have I?' 'But darling,' was the answer, 'that *was* the County Surveyor.'

It fascinated Tottie to observe the similarities and contrasts between Fryn and Stella. He found their natures were very different, but their minds so alike that if you coralled them apart and asked each her opinion on any matter, social or sexual, political, religious or artistic, they could be depended upon to give the same answer. Brought up almost entirely apart, they thought the same way, though Fryn had the more analytical brain.

Alan Bott, who was at that time the editor of *The Tatler*, stayed often at Cut Mill. He was busy taking photographs of the house-party, when Fryn made herself small as she liked to do, but Alan commanded: 'Forward, God!' She was always right, he said, so he had to call her God. And she deserved it, but she didn't like it. She didn't like to hear God mocked, she said. True, she no longer went to Sunday Mass, but her beliefs had not yet changed, only the church observance of them.

Between guests, Fryn found the old house ideal for working in, and she was making her first serious study of murder when a letter arrived from Alice and Rufus Reading. The first Marquess of Reading had always been fond of her, since she used to stay at Melchett Court with the Monds and he was Lord Chief Justice. He used to instruct her in law then, and he had more recently given her passes to the City Lands at the Old Bailey. Now he had become Viceroy of India, and he was inviting her and Tottie out to stay. 'We may never have the luck to know another Viceroy. Let's go!' she said.

They arrived at Bombay to find a letter of introduction to every Resident Governor and native Prince, and also one inviting them to

Viceregal Lodge later on. They had made friends on board the steamer with a Brigadier who had a coffee plantation in the hills of Hyderabad, so first they all three went down through India in a train, and the Brigadier and his neighbours took them out shooting in the jungle. The lowest branches of the trees began forty feet up, but – rather to Fryn's relief – there was no game stirring and the most lethal creature the Brigadier shot was a cobra, coiled up and sunning itself.

When they left there, a car was supposed to meet them and take them to Madras, but it failed to turn up and eventually they went to an abandoned *dak* bungalow, where Tottie spent the night huddled on a planter's chair and Fryn stretched out on the table. 'I was eaten alive by bugs all night,' she wrote. 'They never touched Tottie, and I am convinced that the insect world prefers blondes. We had nothing to eat except one square of turtle soup, which we boiled in a brass chatty of river water. But we had acquired the most excellent servants, a bearer called Pema and an *ayah* called Lackshmi, supplied by Thomas Cook, and when we went on to Burma they came there with us. To see Pema advancing on us through the jungle, whatever disaster had occurred, was to receive a lesson in imperturbability.'

The car turned up the next day and they piled into it and started to go over the mountain range. At each turning it fetched up against a low wall of loose stones overhanging a precipice, but at length they came to a village where there was a railway station, and Fryn bought a dozen tiny eggs. They boiled them, dipped them into coarse salt, shared them out three for each, and ate them thankfully. Then a train came in and they went to Madras, to the best hotel. Fryn sent along the Viceroy's letter to Lord Willingdon the Governor, and that night they dined at Government House. 'Lady Willingdon always dined with a Bee Clock on the table beside her,' wrote Fryn, 'and I am a slow eater. My feelings when each course had been swept off before I had begun it were expressed in a low wail. Lord Willingdon was all sympathy and had the main course brought back, but my nerve was broken.'

During the days that followed they drove out to the Seven Pagodas and to Congeeverum, the Holy City of the South. A holy festival was in progress, and they had to share a room at the *dak* bungalow with a Collector of Taxes, who had fallen ill as he made his rounds. They were afraid he was going to die, but Pema found a guide who took Tottie to a shop stacked with liquor, and there he bought a bottle of pre-war Usher's whisky as mild as milk. 'That night we drank it all, except what we gave to the Collector of Taxes, whose life it saved,' Fryn wrote. 'I have often wondered what a bottle-shop was doing there, in a city given over entirely to Hindus.'

From Madras they went all the way up India again to Delhi and spent a fortnight with the Readings in the Viceregal Lodge: 'It was a treat to be with them and to listen to his talk. They were as unspoilt as ever, and Alice arranged the flowers in my room herself.' After leaving Delhi and staying in a house-boat on the Dul Lake in Kashmir, where the thatched wooden houses had their roofs covered with wild tulips, Fryn and Tottie followed up an invitation from Sir Spencer Harcourt Butler. He was then Governor of the United Provinces of Agra and Oudh, and this turned out to be Fryn's most vital meeting. His imminent appointment as Governor of Burma fostered the happy idea that they should go on to Burma. While there, Fryn made the acquaintance of Rodway Swinhoe, known as 'The Father of the Mandalay Bar', and he it was who told her the true story behind the annexation of Upper Burma in 1885, on which she based her novel, *The Lacquer Lady*. At once she was hot on the scent to find anyone still living from the reign of Thibaw, whose wife Supaya-lat included Europeans among her Maids of Honour. 'I was only just in time,' wrote Fryn later. 'Long since, everyone has died. The Sawbwa of the Northern Shan States, with whom we stayed first, had been a little hostage Prince in Thibaw's Court, and had played as a page in those beautiful gardens of the Gem Palace at Mandalay. Dear Harcourt Butler was the kindest of hosts, and he liked us and asked us to come out the following winter too. And I needed that other winter to talk to all the incredibly old people who still remembered that brutal reign.'

Hosannah Manook, whose Burmese name was Mai Mya meaning Miss Emerald, was married to an Armenian. She had an Armenian father and a Burmese mother. Her father had been page to good King Mindoon, and she was one of the European Maids of Honour to Supaya-lat. Little Fanny, whose real name was Mattie Calogreedy, was the other – the Lacquer Lady. Her father was a Greek, her mother half English and half Burmese, and she had been married to an Englishman employed on the Irrawaddy flotilla. Fryn met both Maids that second winter, and had long conversations with them and with Mademoiselle Denigré, the blind French silk-weaver of the Royal *tameins*. Captain Archie Batty, an ADC to the Governor, was deputed to help Fryn in this, and he worked miracles: she met Sir

George Scott, the authority on Burmese life and literature, who vetted every line of her novel, and Godfrey Harvey, the historian, who had been twenty years in the Indian Civil Service in Burma and wrote *A History of Burma*.

Having harvested a rich crop, Fryn carried it all home and allowed it to mature in the recesses of her mind like wine in the cask.

For the early part of 1923, *Gudgeon* lay in the creek at Bosham, but on returning from Burma the first time Tottie decided to sell her. In her place he bought *Moby Dick*, an eighty ton ketch. 'I prefer a ketch to a yawl,' Fryn wrote, 'because in case of dirt – and Heaven knows we came up against a lot of dirt! – I prefer to have everything inboard. She was thirty years old when we bought her. She had a straight stem, with the result that she hove herself to after being pooped, like a bird, instead of yawing about as a spoon-bowed vessel might. She was a good ship and I cannot imagine a better.'

Between the two Burmese winters, Tottie kept his finger on the pulse at Brownlow Fold Mills in Bolton as well as at the Ambassadors, while Fryn turned her attention to interior decoration, designing a new curtain and refurbishing the boxes and foyer of the theatre. She also wrote the airily entertaining *Quarantine*, her first full-length single-handed play, though it was not staged till a dozen years later. Her work programme had never been under greater pressure, for her entry into the lists of crime, *Murder and its Motives*, was running neck and neck with *Tom Fool*. Quantities of Burmese notes and statements had accompanied her from Mandalay. And yet another tragic theme was germinating, based on the trial of Edith Thompson and her lover for the murder of her husband. The harsh verdict had shocked Fryn, and everything said in Parliament, in Court and in the press had been saved and stacked in piles on her workroom floor.

The atmosphere of leisure that pervaded Cut Mill and its charmed guests was achieved the hard way, and one thing had become obvious to Fryn; a secretary was essential. The first of many shortly made her appearance. She was a daughter of Canon Guy, who had about ten other children, the sons all either in or going into the Church, and Fryn called her Guylet. She was lodged in a room in the village of Bosham, propelling herself to work daily, so she used to say, 'dressed in her mack, bearing her gamp, and riding her bike.' The way of Fryn with a secretary was charmingly thoughtful. Her employee was absorbed into the bosom of the family, shared lunch and tea, morning coffee and apéritifs, with the rest of the house-party. She was wheedled into doing her hair more becomingly and into accepting a pet-name that would carry down the garden. After tossing off any correspondence while dressing or in the bath, Fryn's style of dictating her 'work' was neither fraught nor hesitant. With a few scrawled words in pencil as guide, she knew precisely what she had to say, and seldom changed a word during an hour or so of steady delivery. Remembering Edith's fits of fury, she had a maxim never to indulge in bad temper to her helpers, and at that stage she lived by it faithfully. Her memory was prodigious and a great deal of writing was done in her head, while she lay awake through the night.

One short story, from an actual dream of hers at Cut Mill, was first published in *McCalls Magazine* in the Spring of 1924 under the title of 'Thirty Pieces of Silver'. She wrote it down straight out of sleep and found nothing to alter. In it, two farm-hands plough up a hoard of battered silver coins from a strip of wasteland. The coins bear the faint outline of a Caesar's head. Possession of them stirs up strange passions between the friends, and only at the point of murder are the thirty treacherous pieces of silver recognized for what they are. The story has appeared in anthologies as 'Treasure Trove'. It has also been broadcast in the USA and Canada and televised in the USA several times.

From Cut Mill, Fryn wrote to Tottie at Adelphi Terrace:

'My own heart – I've written a short story and done lots of letters, and am now going to lie down in the courtyard and be read to by Kitty – [Kitty Roseo, her Paris cousin].
'My own heart – It is better than ever, isn't it? For you, too? There's been something I wanted to say to you. You know the letter you're leaving me, so that I can do what you want me to do about the money? Well, it has occurred to me that you probably want *her* to have some little personal things. Will you tell me what they are, so that she shall have them? I *do* thank you for taking the *name* completely out of your Will. I couldn't have borne that, especially as any little personal bits of Wills of people at all well known are always in the papers. But I want them to have *everything* you want them to, and I shan't be a bit hurt. You have, this last two years, armoured me in happiness and confidence as never before and I want them not to suffer. So you will tell me what you want, won't you, darling? and love your – Me.'

The ketch *Moby Dick* had been fitted out and equipped with a master – Captain Rice – and crew, and was lying at Malta on 2 March

1924, when Fryn's birthday was celebrated by Tottie in verse – and no doubt 'some little thing' in addition:

2 March 1924 *Yacht Moby Dick R.Sn.Y.C.* MALTA

My name is Fryn
T'would be a sin
If it were Win-
i-fred — or any common thing — like that

I'm very sweet
It's a fair treat
To see me eat —
or drink — or talk — or try on a new hat

Birthday today!
I always say
That people may
Often forget a little thing like that

Not that I want
An elephant
Indeed I can't
Accept a present quite so large as that

Still, if you can
Think of a plan
To make some han —
dsome recognition of my natal day

T'would be so nice;
Don't mind the price.
Dear Captain Rice
Will lend you all it's necessary to pay.

Some people think
You ought to shrink
— as from a drink —
From mentioning the day when you were born.

I don't agree;
Unless I see
Some gift for me
It makes me feel most curiously forlorn.

Tuesday's the day
— so people say —
On which you may
Expect — with confidence — some slight attention.

Or am I wrong?
Some old wive's song
Running along
A line of country that I mustn't mention.

In any case
I'm sure you'll race
To see my face
On March the second — that's when I was laid.

And p'raps you'll bring
Some little thing
A diamond ring
Pearls — or some coral — tortoiseshell — or jade.

Then you will see
How pleased I'll be
Because to me
It's all the same — whether it's 'plain or pearl'

It's just that I
Should surely cry
To be passed by — (and why?)
Because I'm such a very little girl. 'B.'

Among the guests at Cut Mill in the summer of 1924 were the Harold Deardens, the Dennis Eadies, Fay Compton and Leon Quartermayne; also Captain Archie Batty, home from Burma and working with Tottie at the Ambassadors Theatre. When they had all departed and Tottie was back in the North, Fryn wrote to him:

'My dearest heart – I have about written myself out on *Tom Fool* for a few days. No, leaving you is not an event, it is a break in events; a break I have the sense to be thankful for because of the rapture of meeting again; which, though not a deeper, truer rapture than being together, yet, in the nature of humanity, is bound to be a more thrilling one. Being together is such a quiet, deep, passionately *aware* event that I cannot, sometimes, bear it – it is like a strain of music that at once soothes and hurts.

'You will never be made into a house-holder by me, neither shall I become one myself, if by a house-holder you mean what I think you do – one whom a house holds. This place stands to me for a beautiful thing which it is a keen pleasure to make more beautiful, but it doesn't stand as a master. If you find yourself hard up and want to sell it, or feel it will save our souls alive to do so, I shall be able to let it go without regret. Not because I don't appreciate it, or your thought for me of which it is the symbol, but because for your love I would be happy to do *anything*. That's a bit of what I mean when I say that I so bitterly mind not having been poor with you. Don't think for a moment I'm what you call "divided in mind" about you and this place. Nothing in earthly life counts with me compared with you and your love. If you ceased to love me, only work would count. So houses don't count anyway. The only thing in life I am "divided" about is having a baby. I fear to lose you. And by "losing" you I don't mean the obvious interpretation. I mean tying you down – snaring the thing in you that is like the thing in me – making it captive. But don't spoil my pleasure in beautifying this place, by letting me feel you fear I am trying to "make a house-holder" of you or of myself. The test is whether one could chuck it all up tomorrow or not. I am very lightly tied to everything except to our relationship. I have always kept myself clear of wrapping my heart up in anything except singleness of soul – until you. You remain the only exception, and it is an exception to which I would not hold either of us a moment after it was better not. Keep this letter. It is my gospel of you and me – and you will never be able to produce it at a time I am not prepared to stand by it. Only yours, Fryn.'

Murder and its Motives had come out, dedicated to the memory of William Heinemann. It was published by Heinemann and by Alfred A. Knopf, USA, in July 1924. 'It was my first book on crime,' Fryn recalled, 'and Harry Hodge, the publisher of the Notable British Trials series, wrote to me at once from Edinburgh, addressing me as "Dear Mr Jesse", and asked if I would consider becoming one of his editors. I became a friend of the whole Hodge family, and some of my most exciting memories are connected with editing trials for them.'

'This is an informative, provocative and masterly study,' said the *Police Review*. 'The author has great insight and her conclusions will not be acceptable to those who tend to sympathize with the criminal rather than the victim.' – 'It is a fascinating piece of work,' wrote *The Sketch*. 'The author names six motives for murder and gives an example of each. There is murder for gain, with the poisoner William Palmer as its odious exponent; murder for revenge, citing the celebrated Constance Kent; the Querangel family exemplify the murder for elimination; and the astonishing Mrs Pearcey, who slew her lover's wife and baby, is chosen as the murder for jealousy; the habits of Thomas Neill Cream demonstrate the lust to kill; and the last case, that of Orsini, gives the murder from conviction.'

The spell-binding introduction included Thoreau's epigram: 'Some circumstantial evidence is very strong, as when you find a trout in the milk.' But Fryn's own comment, when dealing with domestic boredom, is incontrovertible: 'It is impossible for the outsider to judge how grindingly the mere presence of one human being in a house may crush down another.' Her observations are often wickedly funny as she traces the devious path of the female mind to the conclusion that an unwanted husband would be much better dead; the word 'murderee', much used since by others, is of her mintage; and she confesses that she would not expect to find a 'nice' girl in a trunk.

On 20 October 1924 *The Pelican* opened at the Ambassadors Theatre. Written in collaboration again, for the first time as husband and wife, it was produced by Tottie and dedicated to Stella. Herbert Marshall, Josephine Victor and Nicholas Hannen appeared in it, and it was a serious play, based on the Russell baby case of 1921; the famous paternity suit between the Hon John Hugo Russell, later third Baron Ampthill of Ampthill, and Christabel his wife, in which the Court declared her son Geoffrey to be the legitimate heir, though his father denied it and got his divorce. Fifty years later, this decision of the Court was finally upheld by the House of Lords, against a claim brought by John, the son of the third Baron Ampthill by his third wife. The play was revived in 1931, and there was a television version in 1952.

Noël Coward wrote: 'Dear Brutus and Fryn. I have seldom been so moved by a play. It is perfectly written, perfectly constructed and perfectly acted. This isn't effusiveness, I really mean it. All congratulations. We left the theatre shattered.' And Gerald du Maurier wrote: 'Gladys took me to *The Pelican* this afternoon, and I came away with a red nose and a pain in my "innards". My word; what a good play! And beautifully done all round . . .' Indeed, he liked it so well that he and Gladys Cooper produced and played in it at the Playhouse later on.

With *The Pelican* safely launched, Fryn and Tottie boarded *Moby Dick* on 21 November for a six week cruise of the Italian coast, described by Fryn to her French publisher: 'Our great love was sailing. We sailed "foreign" in the Mediterranean without even an engine, and our crew were proud of us because, instead of going down with the Blue Train to join them at Cannes, we went through the Bay with them. Coming back, we carried away everything, every scrap of sail, our ratlines hung in little tags from the shrouds, our rudder was split in half and only held together by the brass sleeve at the top. This was the result of being pooped by an eleven-foot wall of green water that had apparently travelled the whole way from the Atlantic with that express purpose. There was no shore we could run for; we were half way across the Bay. I sat on the companion stairs and handed out the signals and at times served rum to the men. We played poker patience in the evening, one sitting on the floor of the saloon and the other on the seat, because that was the angle the table was at. Finally we made Plymouth.'

On 12 March 1925, Fryn's first solo play to be staged, *Anyhouse*, made its appearance. It was dedicated: 'With love to May, who makes my house a pleasant place,' and was published by Heinemann and produced at the Ambassadors Theatre, but not by Tottie for some reason. Hilda Moore played in it, and Tom Nesbitt, Cathleen Nesbitt's brother, and Margaret Scudamore, Michael Redgrave's mother, and Walter Hudd, and Carleton Hobbs. The unusual thing about the play was that the body of the argument was below stairs, and 'kitchen-sink' hadn't then come in. It was about right and wrong, and about doing the right thing for the wrong reason, and the mother – above stairs – was Fryn's idea of her own mother; a frigid, pious hypochondriac: 'No, mother's not religious, she suffers from religiosity. Loathing sex . . . she's always ill and unhappy because she thinks it a sign of a shallow nature not to be.' The critics gave the play such a lambasting it was taken off in a fortnight. It was not Tottie's collaboration that was lacking, for this was no scintillating comedy. It may be that because Fryn had been poor she thought she could speak for 'the poor', but that she could not portray a young servant-girl sacked for becoming pregnant, without talking down, however kindly. A letter from the Stage Manager reads: 'Every night at the end of the play there were always four, very often five, good hearty calls. One thing was obvious; the audience were not at all in agreement with the critics.' Other letters volunteered: 'There were moments of great beauty and power and I feel it received very bad treatment indeed from the press. You must on no account be discouraged.'

When these letters arrived, Fryn had left Adelphi Terrace and returned to Cut Mill, which was filling up with visitors, and Tottie joined her there. Athene Seyler and Nicholas Hannen came, and Marie Tempest and all the Nares. There are photograph albums full of these darlings, and the house came into its own again. 'We swam and did our beauty exercises,' Fryn remembered, 'and played human chess on the large black-and-white floor-tiles of the hall.'

However, a failure is a failure and, particularly when it is the first, it demands self-examination. As soon as Goodwood and the tennis-party were over, Fryn took her chastened person into a London nursing-home and called for a dilatation and curettage. This was not the only time she had made a bid for medical help in conceiving. It did seem to her cruelly frustrating that the doctors couldn't do more. 'She was always in and out of nursing-homes at that stage in her life,' said May. 'Whenever she could snatch the time, which wasn't easy, that's what she did. She wanted a baby so very much that her eyes grew haggard.'

It happened that a thirteen week run of *Hayfever* at the Ambassadors was coming to an end then, and Tottie was about to put on *Emperor Jones*. Paul Robeson was in it, and he and Fryn had greatly taken to each other during rehearsals. When he heard of her 'retreat', naturally he went to see her, and he sang to her softly for an hour, while the entire nursing staff gathered in the corridor outside her room and pressed their ears to the wall, entranced.

Had Fryn and Tottie, right from the beginning, left their yachts lying at their moorings and sent their guests away, while they followed patiently a routine for both, with the hormone treatment that obstetricians nowadays recommend, she might have achieved her heart's desire, despite the bad habit her body had got into. For Fryn had had a second miscarriage, and then a third, each more advanced in the pregnancy and more spontaneous. The last time had been the most inexplicable. At home in Cut Mill, she had been peacefully enjoying what she called her only vice – reading in the bath. The warmth of the water was comforting, and she hadn't had time to be anxious before the book had leapt from her grasp and her heart had seemed to leap into her throat. Swift spasms had racked her. She had felt faint, yet steady, and the same emotion that had filled her in the 'pusher' aeroplane, when she had looked down at her hand lying in its blood, had filled her anew; a feeling of desolation, of loss beyond pain.

It had not been at all like that the first time, she mused now. That

pregnancy had come too soon; inconveniently soon. Tottie had been
away in Syria, and their marriage was still their secret. Feeling out of
sorts, she had put her feet up, taken a sedative, and hoped for the best.
But the dragging sensation in the small of her back had persisted. By
the time she had begun to miscarry it had been almost a relief and she
had accepted it philosophically. The second time had been of the stuff
of nightmare. In her miserable state of mind on leaving *Gudgeon*, she
had not cared what happened to her body. The ominous thing about
the third time was that she had rejected automatically what she
wanted to have and to hold more than anything in the world. Why?

Fryn has described how, lying in the London nursing-home,
languid after the curettage, she put her two palms on her tender sides
and pondered with dismay on this physical aspect of her dilemma.
Her bones had always been rickety, she knew; which wouldn't help.
And to submit to the ordeal of an operation, even a minor one such as
this, was not easy for her. She loathed any attack upon the flesh,
except in the way of love. She was thirty-seven, and her hands moving
lightly up and down told her something else that was hurtful. She was
no longer beautiful as she had been, beautiful as Giambologna's figure
in the fountain at Petraia of 'Venus wringing out her Hair'. Her
breasts, which she mockingly called Beatie and Babs, were firm still,
but bigger and deeper; not a girl's breasts any more. Her waist felt
solid. Her neck too, instead of rising fine and tense, seemed heavy
and shorter. Only the thighs and ankles were as slim as ever, and the
arms and hand. She loved them and was proud of them, silly though it
was to be proud of something that was sheer luck. Faulkner's in Bond
Street, who made all her shoes, displayed the 'last' of her lovely foot
in their window, and if it had been an Order of Merit they were
displaying she couldn't have been more gratified. Her face, heart-
shaped, was miraculously ageless too, she was aware, but what did
that avail her when she had this treacherous body that was turning
against her? And now her play was a failure!

She had accepted that in all humility. But she also knew the fierce
creative urge that at intervals took hold of her, and would again
without pity or by-your-leave. She was not condemned to failure in
her writing, as recent work of quality already existed in manuscript to
reassure her. She would tackle that later, in her own way.

But from early years she had envisaged herself bringing up a baby
girl such as she had been, to be encouraged and confident as she was
not. In *The Milky Way* she had instinctively equipped Vivian with a

child to care for, finding it essential to the adventure of life. Well, she must trust the future, that's all! She and Tottie loved each other, and he knew how she wanted his child. He had his son, but no other woman had given him a daughter. A girl like Peta, now? If Peta had been hers? For the space of a few breaths she indulged in this fancy, before impatiently denying herself its false comfort. Peta was not hers, she was Ethel's ewe-lamb; ugly, frog-like Ethel Vaughan-Sawyer, her gynaecologist and obstetrician, in whose skill she was now trusting.

So musing, Fryn had made up her mind what she would do. She must first get rid of any remaining tensions between herself and Tottie and allow herself to relax. And he must help her. She would write all this to Tottie. And in her letter, with mesmeric sleight of hand, she laid her heart at his feet and the blame on his head. A mutual stock-taking followed. Calmly she spoke of leaving him, which precipitated such a vehement counter-protest from Tottie that she wrote him this letter:

'I told you there was something you had got hold of wrong. You seemed to think there was something in our personal relations "not good enough" – that that was what I found wanting when I took stock. There was never, once you found you cared for me and we began to be happy, a time when I have not been utterly content with our relationship, as it only affected each other.

'The only thing that has made me unhappy (not every three weeks but whenever I have been unhappy), desperately, unforgivingly unhappy, is the third person you have not only allowed, but encouraged, to keep in your current life. You haven't "failed", as you call it. The three-cornered arrangement you attempted is impossible, as far as making both women happy goes, that's all.

'If it hadn't been for that, I should have been the happiest woman in the whole world for five years past. Even as it is I have been very happy, just as I have been very unhappy. But the happiness is the everyday fare, the unhappiness spasmodic – though always waiting to jump out. All I meant was that it was bad enough either not having a child, or having the other woman; and that with both, and the other woman being pleased I didn't have a child, it was too much.

'I don't know how you knew it had grown even worse this last year, but you're quite right. I lack self-confidence and am fool enough to show it. I am a fool in matters of love. Nothing is any good to me unless you are happy, and if the impression left on your mind is of "scenes every three weeks", you can't be happy. In that case, I don't think I can, or should, go on living.

'This letter sounds hard and cold. It is because I love you much too much to try and weigh the scales in my favour.'

There were people who knew of Tottie's previous love-affair, and some of these had remained in the circle of their friends and acquaintances. Part of Fryn's problem was that, after their marriage was made known, those who had been discreet enough while they thought he was pulling the wool over the eyes of both women, had found it necessary to pass on to Fryn Harwood anything they heard concerning Tottie and her predecessor or their son. It seemed to Fryn that the other woman took a perverse delight in supplying information, and that the friends enjoyed conveying it to her. Yet, while she scorned both sources, she could not ignore what was said. Instead, she had tried to repress its effect upon her; to batten down the hatches on her pain. All she wanted was to love him in peace.

As usual, they left for the Mediterranean before the cold weather. But that winter was to be their last in *Moby Dick*. Sailing was something incomparable that they had together, for derring-do is not for boys only. 'Eventually,' Fryn wrote, 'we sold the yacht to Lord Rennell of Rod, a great scholar and a most charming man.' But, while sailing down the Gulf of St Tropez, they had caught sight of Sabi Pas, a mellow old house, and Tottie came back to Cut Mill saying: 'I've bought a house.'

'But you've got a house,' protested May, who had often accused him of having ants in his pants. 'You've got a lovely old house already!' Tottie nodded: 'Yes, well – Fryn fell in love with this one when we saw it over the sea wall. So I bought it.'

They had arrived back in time for the publication of *Tom Fool*. Heinemann published it in May 1926 and there were three new impressions that year and another in 1927. A new edition was published by Evans Brothers in 1952. Fryn dedicated it: 'To HMH and our sailing days together: But O the ship, the immortal ship! O ship aboard the ship! Ship of the body, ship of the soul, voyaging, voyaging, voyaging.'

Tottie wrote to her from the Midland Hotel in Manchester, where he had become chairman of directors of the old Gaiety Theatre:

'Dearest. Yes, it is – I feel sure – a classic of the sea. In a new way, because it deals with it, not from the externals, but as it reacts on *him*, from within. How large a field this may cover in the way of an audience I do not know, but for those to whom it *does* mean something it will be a treasure, of that I have no doubt. It is full of wisdom. Also of beauty. Not necessarily *better* than *Secret Bread* – unless to do a more difficult thing is better – but it has the same feeling of bigness, and of detachment. *How* you have used your batteries too – wet *and* dry! And so well that no one – but me – will ever know. I am very proud to have my initials really *printed* therein. All love, B.'

Who was Tom Fool? The young face pictured on the frontispiece Fryn had found by chance in a Victorian album displayed in an antique shop in Lymington, and had 'recognized' him. Tom Fould was a sturdy boy with a heart for weak and tender things and an eye for the breathless beauty of an eagle's flight. He was a bold young man, whose passion for women was lyrical and who steered his burning ship into the path of a waterspout. But Fryn poured herself into him. Tom Fool was a part of her that was not of the earth; the quintessence of pure sensation that is in sailing, in love-making, in the exultation on the crest that divides death from life.

There are hundreds of letters, from friends and strangers, offering homage. One, to the publisher, says: 'I feel called upon to commit sacrilege and say that she has written rings round Conrad in his own medium.' Another says: 'I have just read *Tom Fool*. You say in it: "Not in the scene, however wonderful, spread before a man, did beauty lie, but in the one moment during which it struck at his breast like a sword." I can only say that for me the whole of your book was the prolongation of such a moment.' So they go on: 'This is the strange wild fancy of a human soul ever alert for ecstasies.'

The Times Literary Supplement, after relating Tom's quest for high and dazzling moments of danger, summarized: 'Miss Tennyson Jesse, who writes when she has a mind to, when she has something to say and no oftener, never says the same thing twice. Her books, widely as they differ in subject, have in common a distinction of workmanship and a considered beauty of thought.'

Hugh Walpole stayed at Cut Mill in the summer of 1926. Also Fryn's American publishers, the Fabers and the Knopfs. At that time, Cousin Hebe, who had done the *petit point* embroideries, had developed a cruel cancerous growth on the side of her face, and was being cared for at her home in Chelsea by Marjorie Greig, a young widow. One day, Hebe laid her tormented head on a pillow in front of her gas oven, and that was where Marjorie found her. Fryn's response, straight after the funeral, was: 'Come at once. Close the house and stay with us.' Thus Marjorie became a quasi-member of the Harwood 'family'.

Marjorie had been sixteen when she married her first husband, a barrister of thirty-eight. He was over-sensitive, and worried so intensely during the general strike of 1926 that he committed suicide with her big silk scarf over his head. She was not yet twenty, with a living to make and nothing but a crack boarding-school education to recommend her. Her doctor introduced her to the Curwen sisters, Henrietta, married to Valentine Goldie, and Geraldine, married to Sir Adrian Dingley. Fletcher Christian of *The Bounty* was one of their forbears. They had been clever and beautiful girls, but both became eccentric and then progressively mad. Marjorie had the attitude to life that whatever might happen was natural, so that nothing seemed to surprise her. Until Henrietta died and Geraldine was committed to an asylum, Marjorie cared in turn for these lunatic ladies, who treated her as a house-daughter and grew attached to her. It was through Henrietta that she had met Hebe, another Curwen, their cousin and also Fryn's.

By the time Marjorie arrived at Cut Mill, Somerset Maugham and Noël Coward were staying there and the house was full, so she shared May's bedroom, and it became an understood thing, whenever Fryn and Tottie were off on their travels, for her to keep May company. She often came at other times too because she made everyone laugh. She was irresistibly funny in retailing the calamities that befell her. It was never possible to tell if they were 'true or fictious' – as the Methodist fishermen-models used to query sternly of the Newlyn students – for strange adventures happened to Marjorie, as to Baron Munchausen; so strange that Fryn was compelled to revoke her judgment that 'you'd never find a nice girl in a trunk'. Marjorie was so nice, and so eminently trunkable.

Eustace
Tennyson
d'Eyncourt
Jesse, and his
daughter
Wynifried
Margaret, who
was to become
first Fryniwyd,
then Fryn.
There is no
portrait of his
wife Edith
among the
family papers.

Stella

May

Fryn by Jean de Bosschère. He used her as a model when he
was illustrating a children's book written by himself,
which she translated.

Tottie – H.M.Harwood – soon after he and Fryn got married.

Fryn at about the time of her marriage.

Fryn at Cut Mill
(top) and at
Sabi Pas.

Three homes. *Top*, Cut Mill. *Bottom*, Sabi Pas *(left)* and
Pear Tree Cottage.

Tottie, by the French caricaturist G. Augsburg.

TEN

—••€)(Ʒ••—

Sabi Pas

FRYN AND STELLA were greatly exercised over their papa, for Eustace had become excessively absent-minded, and the excellent arrangement at Gordon Place was no longer practicable. He got lost on his walks, and when Stella went to the trouble of getting him seats for the theatre and he was put on his way to meet her, he quite forgot to go. 'He really is getting too woolly-headed, poor darling,' Stella told Fryn. By then, Aunt Jenny couldn't cope any longer, as he was constantly tipping his pot of tea into the bedclothes. Finally, a nursing-home had to be found for him, to which Fryn and Stella were to contribute jointly. Auntie stayed on in the little house, and Papa's room was reserved for May, should Fryn need her while at Adelphi Terrace.

At the end of 1926, Tottie and Fryn, Somers and Stella, decided to spend the winter in Egypt, travelling from Cairo up the Nile to Wadi Halfa and back on a sailing *dahabeah*, and Fryn wrote of the journey: 'The north wind, that was essential to us, rarely blew, and when it did it took us flying past places of interest. However, going and coming, we did manage to see everything. We went at the wind's pace, neither faster nor slower, and it took us four months. Stella started to write a novel as we went along. In honour of the Prophet, I had had my hair dyed with henna in Cairo, and floated up the Nile looking like a giant tangerine.' Despite Somers' lament that she had thereby sacrificed all claim to beauty, Fryn was in merry mood as they had basked under the benevolent care of Massa their dragoman, 'descended from a long line of eunuchs'. Tottie's sole anxiety, watching her stretched out on cushions in a long chair, was lest she turn before his eyes into a flat fish on a marble slab.

On their return, Fryn was invited by James Hodge, of William Hodge and Company in Edinburgh, to write the introduction for a new edition of the trial of Madeleine Smith. James had recently taken over the Notable British Trials series from his father, Harry Hodge, who was preparing to retire. Not in the least abashed at the modesty of the fee, Fryn saw it as 'money for jam'. Thrilled at the honour, she went up to Edinburgh and on to Glasgow 'to sniff the air of the venue.' This could hardly be in the manner of a detective, for the scent was cold, the crime having been committed seventy years earlier, but Fryn had a fine nose for the feeling of places.

The Trial of Madeleine Smith came out in 1927, 'edited by F. Tennyson Jesse, author of *Murder and its Motives*, to Margaret James and H. Somers James, barrister-at-law, this volume is affectionately dedicated.' After a graceful preface thanking Professor John Glaister for taking her over Madeleine Smith's house in Blythswood Square, the introduction plunges characteristically to the heart of the matter: 'On Thursday, the 9th of July 1857, the trial of Madeleine Smith for the murder of her lover, Pierre Emile L'Angelier, by the administration of arsenic, ended in the verdict of "Not Proven", and she left the High Court of Judiciary in Edinburgh, by a side door, a free woman. Only twenty-one years of age, handsome with a bright, hard, defiant beauty, a beauty unabashed by an experience that might well have ravaged it, she passed into obscurity from obscurity . . . but it is those months between April 1855 and June 1857 which present a riddle that has never lost its fascination.'

By the clarity and pungent humour of her style, Fryn established herself as one of James Hodge's favourite contributors. From that time on, too, the police were immeasurably helpful to her in the work on this and the subsequent five trials she edited. Her introduction was reprinted by Penguin in their series of Famous Trials.

Heinemann had at the same time published her novel *Moonraker*, with end-papers, frontispiece and four other black-and-white illustrations by Fryn. It was also published by Alfred A. Knopf of New York in 1927 and in translation by Holger Schildt of Stockholm in 1929, titled *Piratbriggen*. Its full inscription was: '*Moonraker*, or the Female Pirate and her Friends: this book is dedicated to Captain I. Rice, Master, and the Crew of the Yacht *Moby Dick* with the friendship of the author and in memory of two winters at sea with them.' It was re-issued in paperback as a Virago Modern Classic, in 1981, with a new introduction by Bob Leeson, who marvels at how many light years its author was in advance of her time in glorifying the theme of freedom, both for a gallant woman and for a black people.

The story of this second tale of the sea is in strong contrast to *Tom*

Fool. It is briefer and, being told through the mind of a cabin-boy, it is in a simpler idiom. It tells of piracy on the high seas, and of how a noble young Frenchman, Raoul de Kérangal, sets off for San Domingo on a merchantman to warn Toussaint l'Ouverture, the peace-loving and peace-giving black Governor-General of the Island which became Haiti. Napoleon had been persuaded by the white ex-planters in Paris to send an expeditionary force against Toussaint under his brother-in-law, General Leclerc. The merchantman is sunk by the pirate ship *Moonraker*, whose master, Captain Lovel, spares de Kérangal and falls in love with him. Against the mounting fury of the crew, he takes time off from piracy to further the Frenchman's idealistic aims. Under cover of the child's-eye-view, a love story is subtly developed, until the critical moment when the pirate-Captain proudly displays herself as a woman who realizes her cause is hopeless. Then she orders out the long-boat for the Frenchman and the survivors from San Domingo, and blows herself, the mutineers and the *Moonraker* into fiery fragments. The mouthpiece in *Moonraker* is Jacky Jacka, a sweet-faced Cornish boy, to whose lot it falls, when the adventure is nearly over, to get the survivors off the beleaguered island, and the only craft he can find to charter is a little sloop, called by the natives a *maman-prend-deuil* – or mother goes into mourning – which traditionally carried a black pig and a black dog. An old piece of the stuff of Fryn's life is woven into young Jacky's, and in the cold wet night he wakes – as she did – to feel a pointed hoof digging into one side of him and a shivering dog snuggling against the other.

Gerald Reading wrote: 'I must thank you for having written *Moonraker*. My only complaint is of its shortness, I enjoyed it all so hugely. It is a magnificent story, none the less enthralling in that, in the familiar words of the gentleman who swore an affidavit: "the funny thing about it is that it is true." And you will acquit me of being too philistine if I add: what a marvellous film!'

Fryn was already engaged on another introduction for the Notable British Trials series, that of Samuel Herbert Dougal, who had been found guilty in 1903 of the murder of his wife. Gilbert Hair, who was the Governor of Chelmsford Prison where Dougal had awaited trial and where he had been hanged and buried, took Fryn to the Moat Farm, near Saffron Walden in Essex, which was the scene of the murder, and brought her back to Adelphi Terrace only just in time for the first night of Tottie's play *The Transit of Venus*, which was produced at the Ambassadors Theatre by Raymond Massey on 26

April 1927. The next morning, May came over early from Gordon Place to read the rave notices to Fryn and Tottie in bed. Her eyes were shining with pleasure and pride that she should actually know someone who walked in this kind of glory. Tottie's eyes were shining too; but for a different reason, as he explained. What he was marvelling at was that anyone could be so simple-hearted as to revel in another's good fortune.

Nicholas Hannen and Athene Seyler were in the cast, and Allan Aynesworth and Nigel Playfair and Archibald Batty, and they all came down to Cut Mill for a week-end's celebration. The story of *Venus* opens in the British High Commissioner's house somewhere in Mesopotamia. A spoilt 'beauty', by getting herself abducted, forces a diplomatic showdown. This greatly enriches the neighbouring land-owner, a very civilized sheikh who had wanted to leave his oil unexploited, by releasing that oil to an Anglo-American Syndicate. The play was published by Ernest Benn, as were all Tottie's successes, and Lloyd Osbourne, the stepson of Robert Louis Stevenson, wrote: 'Nobody can write such dialogue as you, Tottie; it is *really* brilliant, and as witty as Wilde was supposed to be and wasn't.'

In June 1927, Fryn wrote to Tottie:

'To my dear – I hoped and hoped your head would get better, and that you'd have a good night, and a lunchless day today, and that you'd give me a thought. Are any of these true?

'The first two are the most important and after them the fourth. You see I do not build for the future but only for the present. That you should not have a headache and should have a good night *now*, is much more important than your possible – or probable – figure in the future. And that you should think of me *now* is all I ask.

'Enjoy yourself, my heart. See whom you like. If your self is faithful to me, I mind nothing on earth. My confidence, my deep-rooted placid yet intense (can there be that mixture?) content in, and belief in, our love, grows more strongly. Am I right? It makes me so much less anxious and feverish than I used to be, but one can't force these things or make them come sooner than they will. They're a question of growth, suitable climate, and manure. (The manure of your love!!! Do you think *that* symbol has been used before?)

'Answer this letter. You easily can on your way to Manchester. Tell me if you're glad, if you understand, and if you sometimes keep my letters?'

It was at this time that she began to call him 'My fatty', so the concern expressed for his figure is natural.

Marriage had not caused Fryn to lose sight of Nan, who lived in a series of boarding-houses after her uncle's death. That year she went to one at Southsea, kept by an elderly woman who looked like a grenadier. Fryn was about to go ahead to the South of France, to get Sabi Pas ready for that winter, when an agitated letter from her mother, saying that Nan had gone blind and was not allowed out, urged her to go down and look into it. So Fryn called on the grenadier, and was told that Miss Roberts could not see her. Thoroughly alarmed, she went to her old friend George, the doctor at Chichester, saying she believed Nan was being sequestrated. Then she went to the police at Portsmouth. They'd had trouble at that address before and said that, if she brought an ambulance, and her doctor from Chichester attended, they would give her three plain-clothes men. Next morning an ambulance drew up and George got out and Fryn went and knocked at the door: 'I have come to fetch Miss Roberts,' she said. She walked in and found Nan in bed, her fine white hair flying. She was deaf as well as blind, but Fryn put her arms round her, and dressed her, and the plain-clothes men followed behind the doctor and carried her on a stretcher to the ambulance. Fryn followed after, with the grenadier just behind, big gnarled fists shooting out on each side of Fryn's face as she abused her: 'You dirty . . .' blustered the grenadier: 'You dirty little theatrical manageress!' And with that benediction in their ears, they left her house.

Then began the patient search for somewhere permanent near London. Eventually, Fryn got Nan into the Anglican Convent at Chiswick; a haven of refuge for such as she. Instead of smelling sour, as she had at Southsea, she smelt clean and fresh. And Edith was a well-known figure there, so the choice went well with her. 'Badly as my mother had behaved to her, she loved her more than she did anybody else.' Fryn wrote. 'I think Nan had cherished something in the nature of a rave for her when she was a young woman. My mother was never pretty, but she was graceful and confident of her attraction. She had herself photographed beside Nan in her bed and, though Nan could not see the result, I do believe she would have felt a sense of pleasure in being told she was being photographed beside my mother. I only know I came across a copy of it, when Nan and my mother were both dead.'

Eustace's, however, was the first death. He had scarcely left Aunt Jenny's to go into the nursing-home when he died. Much later, Fryn and Stella were overheard, in indignant tones but with one voice, discussing their dear papa's next move. They had discovered that they had been paying for years to have his ashes 'lodged' on some dusty shelf within the crematorium precincts. This was too much to bear. How long had he been made to submit to lodgings, and in just such a drab depository? Now at last he and his random thoughts should be allowed to blow where they would. Unanimously they had sent instructions for his ashes to be given to the four winds of heaven.

Fryn and Kitty Roseo had been staying at the Hotel Beau Rivage at St Raphael while they kept a watching brief on the renovations to Sabi Pas. From there, Tottie had received this letter from her:

> 'Here it is perfect summer heat, and so still. I am hot in a shantung suit and straw hat. This is the part of the world to live in! The house is really getting on. It looks ghastly at present of course; glad you can't see it, you would gloom! But it will be almost perfection, I think.
> 'I should have started writing you all my thoughts in the train coming here – but I can't get over the chill of our parting, and that evening. Even parting you were kind and tender, but I don't want kindness, I want mutual love. Without it, whatever our houses are like, I must give up. One dreads the publicity and the awful rending of tissues, but the something within oneself is more important; to keep the integrity of that. I love you too much to keep on, if that was really a sign that things are changing. I hope and hope that it was just tiredness that made the lack of spark.'

Tottie collected his enormous motor-car and, with Mr Hunt the chauffeur, picked up May from Gordon Place, and set out for Dover and the Channel crossing. They stopped at Lille and at Lyons, where, to May's shocked indignation, a breakfast-tray for two was brought to her room. But Tottie only laughed. Gallantly he showed her round the towns *en route*, and took her out to dinner. It was a happy and exciting journey, as May remembered it – a sort of honeymoon *manqué* – and they duly met Fryn and Kitty, who had devised a *rendez-vous* in Kitty's car *'sur le pont d'Avignon'*, to exchange ladies and drive in stately convoy to Sabi Pas. Already vague shadows obscured the bright vision which had lured them across the Gulf and over the sea wall, and Tottie's heart must have quailed with foreboding at the increasing frequency of Fryn's unhappy spells. But from autumn 1927 to autumn 1932 the entire Harwood household spent their winters at Sabi Pas, Beauvallon, and their summers at Cut Mill, entertaining lavishly at each. Though part of Tottie's idea in dividing the year into halves had been to save taxes and thus economize, it did not quite turn out that way. At one point in his economy programme he discovered that he had no less than eighty pairs of sheets. He protested, astonished at May's extravagance, only to be assured that these were in constant circulation between guest and laundry and there was not one too many.

'At Sabi Pas I had a beautiful little sailing canoe,' wrote Fryn, 'bought from a boat-builder on the Seine. She was practically unsinkable, had a roll of kapok round her, outside the gunwale, and a lovely sail with a fish stamped on it. I am a strong and good paddler, and I used often to paddle all the way to St Tropez if the wind were tiresome. We were living on the Côte des Maures, in an old straggling house set at the edge of the sea. We fell in love with it as we sailed across the blue waters. We landed in the small boat and walked through the garden gate and explained to the beautiful old gentleman who owned it that we were from the ketch that had just come to anchor. He had sea-blue eyes and a creamy-white beard and had once served in an armed brigantine. We discussed sail excitedly and in half an hour the house was ours.'

Somers James was an early visitor. As guest-present, he bought sets of hand-embroidered *crêpe-de-chine* undies at St Tropez for the five girls then in residence: Fryn, Stella, May, Guylet and Josephine Blumenfeld. Josephine was holidaying in the village when Fryn met her and asked her for a week-end. Their first encounter had been on the beach, where Fryn's renown for omniscience had preceded her, to Josephine's trepidation. But, settling herself on a rug beside her kitten, Fryn had started to twist the fringe between her fingers, murmuring to the intent animal 'Mama make a mousie!' and Josephine had exploded into relieved laughter. After her week-end stay, she packed to go home, and Fryn kissed her goodbye and said: 'Darling, why must you go?' – 'I don't know,' said Josephine sadly. 'What?' shrilled Fryn. 'Then don't go. Unpack at once.' And so Josephine did, and stayed three months. One day Fryn, burbling with pleasure at Josephine's talk, said: 'You ought to be married, you're wasted,' and Josephine said: 'Yes. I'd like to.' So Fryn lay in her bath and thought; then leapt out crying: 'I know the very thing: Alan Bott! He's as mad as you are,' And when Josephine did leave, his name was tucked into her handbag. The next thing Fryn heard was that they'd married. He was then editor of *The Tatler*, and became chairman of the Book Society and of Pan Books.

Josephine's father was chairman of the Express Group, and she herself wrote the drollest of short stories. She also wrote an article called 'Sabi Pas', which Fryn included in her book of that name published several years later:

'It's name is Sabi Pas,' wrote Josephine, 'Provençal for "I do not know", and really a better name has never been put to use. You don't know – that's just it. Literally speaking, it is a house. It has a front door, windows, bedrooms and places to eat and sit in, but that's not the point . . . the front door never will open when shut, or vice versa; there are always six people in each bath; and the bedrooms, as far as privacy is concerned, are a farce. Why knock? How can it help? You will see no more by going into any of the bedrooms than you have already seen downstairs or met flying along the passages. The head man, the owner, the host, doesn't understand the feelings people have about clothes, although sometimes when real people come to lunch he fixes on a pair of white corduroy shorts and perhaps an open-necked sort of sack which laces up the front. But by the time the meal is half-way through, one or other of these garments has fallen off and been kicked under the table. There is something about his body which doesn't seem to feel the need of a covering. It is so obviously there, covered or uncovered. You see him, listen to what he has to say, and wild ideas of how right he is, how futile civilization, modes, manners and clothes are, rush to your head. You don't even bother to dress much for dinner or comb your hair. With a sense of complete freedom you cry: "Be like him, the thing you saw downstairs!" But it is just at this point you realize how wrong you've been, just where you start to "Sabi Pas". For the door opens softly, a high-pitched laughing voice drifts across the room, and down the steps trips the Lady of the House. She doesn't walk, she picks; each slender foot waving its delicate stem above it in mid-air before touching the ground. She comes towards you slowly picking her way, and talking all the time about a hundred different things at once. You stand up, shake hands, and gaze aghast at what you see. Patou, Raville, Molyneux and Chanel fade away from your thoughts as tawdry second-class dress-designers. There is a little cry from those she lives with, and innocently, daintily, with round flat saucer-eyes she turns appealingly and pleads: "But darlings, I don't know what you mean. It's only a very ordinary, frightfully old frock, the only one I could find!" And feebly you take your cocktail and swig it down, hoping to drown your dress, your hair, and the stockings you haven't got on, and whisper: "Sabi Pas!".'

*　　*　　*

The Trial of Samuel Herbert Dougal, with Fryn's introduction, was published in 1928, dedicated to Harry Hodge, 'the onlie true begetter' of the Notable British Trials series. It tells how, in the year 1898, Miss Camille Cecile Holland, a lady of fifty-six years of age, was living in a boarding-house in Maida Vale, when she was wooed, for the first time since girlhood, by Samuel Herbert Dougal, a man 'of strong animal passions and skilful address, incapable of fidelity or of ruth'. He had earned a long-service and a good-conduct medal with full pension for twenty-one years in the Royal Engineers, during which time he had been twice married and twiced widowed. Both wives had died suffering great pain and vomiting, but life without a woman to molest was impossible for Dougal. He had since had innumerable relationships with women, young and old, and had spent one year in a lunatic asylum. He was still big and virile at fifty, when he met Camille Holland, and she was a pretty little woman, somewhat faded though with full pouting lips. By powdering her face and dyeing her hair red-gold she hoped to remain 'attractive to the gentlemen', and she did indeed, according to her landlady, drop fifteen years 'between waking and when "got-up" for the day.' She had once been courted by a young naval officer, and she treasured his simple ring set with a cornelian. She played the piano, wrote verses which she set to music, and painted small water-colours. Dougal recognized his 'meat' at once; she was the born 'murderee'. She had inherited seven thousand pounds and, though she had always been religious and chaste, she allowed him to beguile her into setting up home as his 'wife' at the secluded Moat Farm, on 27 April 1899. In the middle of May he drove her off in his trap for a shopping expedition. She was dressed in a sailor hat and with a fall of white lace at her throat. She was never seen alive again. Four years later her body was found, with two bullet wounds in the head, in the drainage ditch of Moat Farm, which had since been filled in and planted with trees. Dougal had in the meantime transferred her property to himself. He had advertised for a sequence of young servant girls, who became pregnant by him to the scandal of the countryside. It was tittle-tattle that set inquiries in motion, then the digging began, and when Dougal was eventually apprehended, Camille Holland's cornelian ring was found upon his person.

Without ever mentioning the words 'women's rights', Fryn's introduction is a fulmination against the lack of them. The mind of the murderer held a fascination for her, with its fatal combination of cleverness and idiocy. It was this that had led Dougal to the gallows on 8 July 1903. Chelmsford Prison is built like a fan, and Dougal was buried in the precincts. On and around his gravestone there flourished an evergreen shrub with the bitter-scented leaves of rue. Edmund Lester Pearson wrote to H.G. Wells from the Harvard Club in New York: 'I was in London a year ago, and Mrs Belloc-Lowndes asked of me did I wish to meet any writers. I told her yes, two: Miss Tennyson Jesse and Miss Dorothy Sayers. As it was August, both were naturally out of town. If you should ever happen to write to Miss Jesse, I wish you would say that I hope she will edit some more of the Notable British Trials. Her introduction to the Trial of S.H. Dougal is the most fascinating of the whole series. I have read it over three of four times, and I think it is in the very first rank of them all.'

Charley Evans, C.S. of Heinemann's, was a regular guest at Sabi Pas. John Masefield has said of him: 'He was interested in people, in the theatre, in the cinema, and in every branch of literature. I used to wonder if he ever went to bed.' Well, he was so exhausted once at Sabi Pas that he had to spend his whole visit in bed, which was sad indeed for one who enjoyed sparkling talk as he did. Luckily for Fryn, C.S. had begun publishing at precisely the same time as she had begun writing, and he had a taste for large books. Like William Heinemann whom he succeeded, he had a flair for discovering the right author at the right time, and he was faithful to his chosen.

Sometimes Lloyd Osbourne and his tall and slinky wife Ethel came over from their own house at Cap d'Antibes. There is a snapshot of Ethel and Fryn, Fryn knee-high to Ethel, kissing hullo or goodbye with the utmost dexterity. Each is wearing a vast cartwheel hat, which required to be circumvented at an acute angle if their faces were to meet in the kiss.

Sometimes Rebecca West and her husband Henry Andrews drove over from the house they rented on the Coast, but Rebecca has confessed that she didn't care for Sabi Pas, finding it oppressive. Fryn may have been the root cause of that feeling of oppression, for she was in a bad state at that time. Nobody knew what was wrong. She couldn't sleep, she couldn't eat and she couldn't work. She got odd ideas into her head too:

'Fryn could say the most impossible things sometimes,' Rebecca remembered. 'Once she said to me something cryptic about a magic strain she had in her that kept her from getting old. That was perfectly true in itself; she foxed us all with her everlasting youthfulness. As to her sister Stella, one occasionally wondered if there might even be something wrong with her, that she should look so immoderately young. But of course there wasn't, and there was nothing immature about Fryn most of the time, and nothing predatory except that parrot voice which she called "my little pipe". She and Tottie had an agent at one time, who had embezzled a lot of money from them and others. So good of the Harwoods not to prosecute him! They were nice people. Wilfrid Greene, Master of the Rolls, and Nancy Greene too, were devoted to them both and often stayed with them at Cut Mill, and that's an interesting connection. I was never at Cut Mill. Gordon Place was altogether charming. But Sabi Pas was neither a happy place nor a beautiful one.'*

For whatever reason, nothing her doctor gave Fryn there seemed to do her any good; rather the reverse. Sometimes this morbid state was short-lived, sometimes it went on for weeks and it was purgatory for everybody. Tottie went about like a bear with a sore head, and May shelved any attempt to explain it with the laconic: 'Half the time at Sabi Pas Fryn was mad.'† People began taking sides, saying: 'Poor darling Fryn, so lovable and so lovely still; it's tragic!' They thought she had somehow got hold of 'that drug' again. Others said: 'Poor darling Tottie, what he has to put up with! How *can* she?' They thought she was playing him up like a spoiled child – to punish him for the hand perhaps, or for her childlessness? Unaccountably, too, she would take dislikes and look upon some innocent victim with suspicion. It became a question of hoping her condition was not becoming obvious to strangers.

Lt Col Robert Francis Gore-Browne and his wife Margaret, called Gorey and Gorette by the Harwoods, came often through the years, and something that happened while they were there gave Gorette a bad fright. It was the first time she had seen Fryn off-balance and apparently under the influence of drink or drugs. Robert and Tottie were good friends, as well as collaborators after 1930, and though Robert had affection and sympathy for both, seeming to understand that Fryn couldn't help herself, Margaret was condemnatory of what she found unforgivable in Fryn, and a mutual antagonism sprang up between them. She, too, was a childless woman, and she saw the fact

* Dame Rebecca West in conversation with JC.
† May King in conversation with JC.

as no reason to play such sad havoc with a wonderful marriage. Fryn's behaviour struck Margaret as reckless self-indulgence.

Outside the medical profession, at any rate, "mad" means different things to different people, and half the time at Sabi Pas Fryn was not mad by any standards. Imperceptibly the oppression would lift and there she was again, her sunniness unimpaired, radiant at the hub of everything. She was back at her desk, working; or in a deckchair by the round pool, laughing and talking with the old verve. Spirits leapt to meet hers, the misery of the last days or weeks was all but forgotten, and nobody wanted to think there might ever be a next time. Survival was all that mattered.

Survival, for Fryn, meant work; work meant a secretary; and Guylet, who had been billeted at St Maxime, had gone back home when work had stopped. So Fryn began to send out signals around the Coast, and these were picked up by Noreen, a wild Irish girl, the wife of the architect Derek von Berg, who had built the additions to Sabi Pas. They lived at St Raphael, and Noreen said she had the very thing: Moira Tighe – or Tiger – who had been at school with her. She would make the perfect secretary for Fryn. Fryn didn't quite believe her, valuing Noreen more for good fun than good judgment, so she prudently arranged for Stella to ask Tiger to tea at Albert Hall Mansions. They met, they took to each other, and Tiger came to Sabi Pas at once. She was twenty-five and had always longed to travel. She remained with Fryn, on and off, for the next eighteen years.

What Fryn required in a secretary, besides a feeling for words, was not great speed but empathy. Tiger had that quality by nature and was also well-bred, well-read and well-trained. Fryn was fond of saying of her that her beautiful blue eyes were so large they looked almost hysterical, and her beautiful behind was so vigorous she broke every chair she sat on, until one of steel tubing with a leather seat was found, which long outlasted her need of it. By the same token she played a fine game of golf, which meant that Tottie need never lack a worthy partner.

Of herself, Tiger said simply: 'I was born in Galway, and educated at a French convent in Wales where I spent a lot of my time in tears. The education was adequate, stress was placed on deportment, and every activity frowned on by the nuns was classified as *"manque de delicatesse"*. My father was twenty years older than my mother, a pretty and iron-willed *petite blonde*. Mother was fond of us in a detached way, but enjoyed golf more. Somehow or other, we had three servants – cook, housemaid-into-nurse and gardener. There were five of us, and our first nurse used to dose us – and dope us – with Mother Siegel's Syrup, which I believe contained laudanum, so that mother never could make out why we were generally so docile and then screamed our heads off with withdrawal symptoms on nurse's day off. Father was a delightful eccentric and a good architect, responsible for some charming churches in the West of Ireland. He was permanently in debt, as he either forgot to send out bills or was blackmailed by priests to reduce his fees: "Ah, Mr Tighe! Surely you would be giving this work for the glory of God?" He would try to protest that he had five children to feed and educate, but this was brushed aside. He was a keen archaeologist too, and used to take us to old castles, where we clung perilously to the crumbling stairs while he forgot all about us. He didn't bother to read out to us any nonsense like Beatrix Potter; he chose what he liked himself. All ten volumes of the Arabian Nights in the Richard Burton edition he read to us, and we were charmed by the sound of it and neither surprised nor corrupted when the Princess and the Cobbler "fell to toying with each other," and when she thrust her lip "like a titbit into his mouth" and got her deserts, we all agreed with the Princess there was "no harm in that". We had one of the earliest cars in Ireland – a de Dion Bouton – though father was completely unmechanical and wherever it broke down we had to walk home crying.'* It appears that Tiger's emotions were readily tapped at that stage. Undoubtedly Fryn would have adored the delightful eccentric, had she ever met him. Instead she acquired a healthy respect for the *petite blonde*, having an open mind regarding other people's mothers.

There was a disturbing incident for Tiger's emotions not long after she moved in to Sabi Pas. One night, as she was on the edge of sleep, Fryn crept into bed beside her. She felt the small, weightless body pressing up against her, and the mothlike hands, that were yet so strong, clutching spasmodically, and for the first instant she stiffened angrily against a lesbian assault, before realizing that this was not an expression of any desire, however misplaced, but of grief. Concerned, she waited till the tearing sobs subsided and Fryn could voice her sorrow in broken snatches: how she and Tottie, secretly married, had spent a lovely night on *Gudgeon*, and of how he had then cruelly driven her from their only sanctuary, for the sake of his son and the

* Moira Tighe in conversation with JC.

mother of his son, and she had had her second miscarriage. Gasping with tears, Fryn had brought out these bitter accusations against Tottie, and Tiger was puzzled. To her it all seemed long ago and far away, and she could not forget, as Fryn had obviously forgotten, how happy the two had been together only yesterday. She listened as patiently as she could, wanting her bed to herself, and then she gently led the woebegone little figure back to her room, with words of pity and comfort in her soft Irish voice, for the grief was real.

At intervals, Tottie would go off to Paris or London or both, for, notwithstanding the interruptions caused by guests, or those centred on Fryn's health, a tremendous amount of work saw the light. He had adapted a Paris production, *L'Ecole des Cocottes*, renaming it *Excelsior*. It was produced on 5 September 1928 at the Playhouse in London; one of his many successful adaptations from the French.

Fryn's second collection of short stories was published the same year by Heinemann and by Alfred A. Knopf of New York. It was called *Many Latitudes*, and was dedicated to Kitty Roseo, 'as a small token of affection and admiration from your cousin FTJ.' Of the seven stories, only 'Baker's Fury' had been published before. It had appeared in *Georgian Stories* by Putnam, New York, in 1925. 'The Two Helens' is the long-short story – or novella as it is listed in America – with which the book opens. It tells the life story of a ship, from its beginnings as the *Prince Charlie*, a summer excursion steamer belonging to the Western Highland Railway Company, to its hijacking and overnight metamorphosis into the *Helen of Troy*, a rogue ship plying for cargo from Newcastle to Iquique, and along the Chilean coast. Changing her appearance, bluffing the port authorities, risking liberty at every port, 'it was with every rope-yarn and every wire thrumming that she sang her way like a giant harp across the seas.' David Martyr, the young writer son of a wealthy ship-broker, sailed all unknowing as mate. Years later, while living in a cottage on the Helford River in Cornwall, he watches the *Helen of Troy*, holed in a collision and beached on a strip of coast between Lamorna Cove and Land's End, breaking up on the rocks.

Fryn had watched that ship die, by another name. If she had known one end of a horse from another, she might have written a story like *Black Beauty* instead of 'The Two Helens'. But she had chosen ships as her love object, and she was on the cliffs when this one was beached: 'Where she lay, between two jagged headlands, the fields sloped down to the boulders, and from the cliff's crest she looked as though she had wedged her nose in a sea of daffodils that made a Field of the Cloth of Gold around her bows. Crowds, trampling the flowers to death, came to see her floating thus magically.' It was that sight that had prompted Fryn later to follow the ship's history.

Though she had none of the usual illnesses like measles or mumps, so many mysterious things happened to Fryn's person that sudden death would have been no surprise to Stella, who told May: 'If Fryn does die, you and I will set up home together.'* They were merry in each other's company, though Stella couldn't do a thing for herself and took the whole morning just to get up and make up and make her appearance by mid-day. Since leaving the stage early in the twenties, she had apparently been lying fallow, in the manner of all good Tennysons. But in the autumn of 1929, she was commissioned to write a series of travel articles for the *Daily Express*. She wrote of Peru, the Falkland Islands and Brazil with refreshing individuality, and of crossing the Alps, Apennines, Rockies and much of the Sudan in her baby Austin. And then her book, *Eve in Egypt*, was published by Geoffrey Bles on 22 October 1929, under the name of Jane Starr. Out of the journey to Wadi Halfa, she had made an attractive travel-book romance. It was dedicated: 'To FTJ and HMH, the parents of EVE, in memory of a £10 bet', because Tottie had betted her ten pounds she couldn't do it. She did it well, and the book has a delicate flavour. Fryn said: 'We are all mixed up in it,' and their ingredients are indeed switched and switched again, but each confection succeeds independently and, here as in life, the two sisters of the foursome are exquisitely feminine and funny with it. At one point, Serena the married one, stares with melting eyes at what had been the Ras-el-tin hospital in Alexandria, from which Tottie had come home from the war to Fryn. Elsewhere she is described as indolent and placid and a mother, while the love interest belongs to Eve. The question asked about idle Eve: 'But what does she *do*?' remained an open question all Stella's life. But she had a seeing eye, and what she told of Egypt was both fresh and factual under a pleasingly frivolous crust. The book was not a great success, though it was amusing and light-hearted. The

* May King in conversation with JC

notices varied from: 'a charming piece of work, spoiled by Eve, whose maddening infantility we get thrust upon us at every line,' to 'this singularly vivacious and mirthful book.'

The same day that her book was published, Stella married Eric Andrew Simson, of Marykirk, Kincardineshire. One of several brothers, he was a powerful athlete and had been head-boy at Wellington and captain of cricket, rugger and fives. Perhaps the fact that she had imagined a romance for Eve had put Stella in the mood for one of her own? She was forty-two when she married and Eric was nine years younger. When she came to register her wedding at Kensington on 22 October 1929, she whispered to him: 'Don't you think thirty-two would look better?' and he beamed at her and said: 'Yes, thirty-two is a nice age.' She looked much, much less. For the wedding, Tottie had booked a suite at the Savoy, and Fryn lent Sabi Pas for the honeymoon.

Eric wrote under the name of Laurence Kirk. He had a graceful prose style and had then written several novels and had contributed short stories regularly to *The Sketch*. Later he collaborated with Tottie in a play, and his best known novel, *Halfway to Paradise*, was exhibited at the Festival of Britain. His work shows a good comedy sense and he was very good company and inexhaustibly kind and gentle. He was very good-looking too, and had been a pilot in the Royal Flying Corps in the first world war.

It seemed that until her marriage Stella had not grown up emotionally. She had suffered a series of set-backs: when she was repudiated by her mother; when her adored Squire died; and when her success on the stage was snatched from her. Fryn has explained the last: 'Stella's stammer had been no trouble to her when training or when acting; her skill at *ad libbing* in any emergency was spontaneously comic and would often be incorporated thereafter into the lines; but unfortunately during the air-raids she began to stammer on the stage. She went to every specialist in the art of speech, but eventually she had to give up acting. There was a sort of break in her life, and she did not enter whole-heartedly into anything she did. She travelled about the world and had plenty of admiration, but nothing seemed to touch her personally. She was very young in outlook, and she still looked very young when she came to marry, but she was nothing of the sort.'

Stella's dark hair was meticulously cared for, her skin beautifully made up, her shoulders bare whenever feasible, her childlike face rising from a choker necklace set with sapphires. Stella, in fact, was often accused of being over-dressed, and so was Eric, while Fryn and Tottie tended to underdress, especially Tottie. Fryn was a quick dresser, never even glancing at herself, unlike Stella, and seldom wearing any ornament other than the diamond solitaire ring Tottie had given her. Red was Fryn's colour. It is said that anaemia impels its sufferers to wear red, so she should have been very anaemic and at times she was. Certain it is that most of her clothes were red or had red in them, and she had quantities of gorgeous clothes. She detested blue for herself and professed to scorn it on others. 'The sort of woman who wears pale-blue' made her lip curl with disdain, and 'if blue's bred in the bone it comes out on the flesh,' she would say, absurdly. But Stella, with her dark blue eyes, knew she looked well in blue and often wore it.

Towards the end of 1929, Tottie had been working on the three-Act play, *A Girl's Best Friend*, and he produced it at the Ambassadors Theatre on 22 October, Stella's wedding day. Marie Lohr was the star, and *The Times* described it as 'of little substance but of infectious gaiety and sparkling feminine animation.' Marie Lohr loved it.

In November, *The Lacquer Lady* was published by Heinemann. It was reprinted twice in that year, twice in 1930, and further editions appeared in 1933, 1936, 1938 and 1945. It was dedicated to Sir Harcourt Butler, GCSI, GCIE, with affection and gratitude, and the Pan-scorpion mark was in its place on the cover, ensuring that any sweetness Fryn might dispense would be tempered by her sting. The end-papers were decorated with a fine pen-drawing in vermilion red of the Golden Palace of Mandalay. The preface acknowledges the help of 'those living brains, so generous with their memories and their knowledge' in providing the true story of the causes which led to the Annexation of Upper Burma – how it was 'Fanny' and her broken love affair, not the pretext of the Bombay-Burma Corporation, that drove the Indian Government into action at last.

Evans Brothers published a new edition of *The Lacquer Lady* in 1951, and the book appeared in paperback in 1979 as a Virago Modern Classic, with a new introduction by myself. It has been reprinted by The Dial Press, New York, and by Lester & Orpen Dennys, Toronto, in 1981.

With the same skill in imagery by which she had used the waves and troughs of the ocean to conjure with the passing of time while Tom

Fool was drowning, so in *The Lacquer Lady* Fryn used the weaving of the Royal *tameins* to reveal the devious pattern of the palace intrigues and the tinsel thread defining Fanny's own heartbreak. As the tale of massacres and treachery unfolds, a great red stain spreads across the silken surface, the shuttles move faster and faster, till the barbaric groundwork is complete even to poor jilted Fanny's vengeance. With the last thread in its fine appointed place, 'the whole fabric, compact of so many lives and deaths, pleasures and miseries, had been trailed in the dust like a captured banner.'

It is all as Fryn had absorbed it, in the Burmese winters of 1922 and 1923. 'I am a slow writer,' she has explained, 'and it took me three years. I finished it in a great burst at ten o'clock at night, not having gone down to dinner, and Tottie came quietly into the room with a glass of wine and some sandwiches. It is the book by which I should live.'

The Daily Telegraph wrote: 'Miss Tennyson Jesse is to be congratulated on achieving an artistic triumph.' The book was acclaimed everywhere, Gerald Gould in the *Observer* quoting great chunks of it. And it was the Book Society's choice for January 1930. Among the hundreds of letters that reached Fryn was this from W. J. Locke: 'I have read *The Lacquer Lady* in two long fascinated spells. This is a marvellous achievement. It has been a wonderful year in that it has produced two great novels, yours and *The Good Companions*, and of the two yours is the greater . . . It has passages of extraordinary, abiding beauty. Your last paragraph is unforgettable.'

It occurred to Tottie that Vivien Leigh and Myrna Loy would be superb as Fanny and Supaya Lat, respectively. But, before putting the proposition to Alexander Korda, he wrote to Vivien Leigh, inviting her to consider the part of Fanny. She replied: 'It would have been lovely to do *The Lacquer Lady*, which as I told you I absolutely love. And of course you are right, it should be filmed,' but she went on to explain that she was engaged to do *Caesar and Cleopatra* and a string of further films for A.K., and was therefore 'not much use for the furtherance of the plan, dear Tottie. I *am* so sorry,'

Tottie was busy throughout 1930 with two important pieces of work. The first of these was *The Man in Possession*, which was produced at the Ambassadors Theatre on 22 January, with Raymond Massey and Isobel Jeans in the cast, and played for thirty-eight weeks initially. The title in Paris was *La Route des Indes*, and it ran for over a year there with Michel Simon and Alice Cocea. It was repeated many times both in London and Paris and the film rights were sold to Metro-Goldwyn-Mayer, who renamed the screen version *Personal Property*. The play toured the United Kingdom right through 1930, and Scandinavian, German, Hungarian, Italian, French and Dutch rights were sold that year. It was produced in the United States at the Shubert Theatre, and a musical version was made in German in 1937 and repeated in 1947. In 1939 there was an adaptation into an operetta in France. A straight German version was produced in 1951 and 1952 in Vienna. Television rights were taken up in 1953 in the USA, and Rex Harrison and Lili Palmer acted the star parts, royalties being claimed by MGM. A tour was arranged in Belgium, France and Switzerland in 1955 with Michel Simon, and Peter Cotes has written: '*The Man in Possession* is perhaps the most constantly performed of all his plays by repertory companies.' Its success in London and New York undoubtedly led to Tottie's going as script-writer to Hollywood.

Six months later, *Cynara*, adapted from the novel *An Imperfect Lover* by Robert Gore-Browne, was produced at the Playhouse Theatre on 26 June 1930, with Sir Gerald du Maurier as 'the man', a barrister. The three women were splendidly contrasted: Gladys Cooper played the 'happy' wife, Ann Todd her 'naughty' sister, and Celia Johnson a too-loving little shop-girl. The lyric in Act I, 'Goodbye, you daffodils' was written specially for it by Noël Coward. The play brought H.M. Harwood's name before the widest public of his career, as Robert Gore-Browne has written: 'After its West End run, it toured the British Isles with Owen Nares, before transferring for six months to New York, to end in Hollywood as a vehicle for Ronald Colman.' In 1955 it was televised in New York, and there was an ITV broadcast in 1959 by Associated Rediffusion.

May had always detested her forenames, Ada May. As a child, Church and Sunday School used to be treats for her; she knew all the hymns and Psalms and sang them lustily. But she had been harrowed with embarrassment when the kind man who taught Sunday School had read out each week 'The May Queen' when he came to her turn on the roster. He had meant to draw her out, but she knew she was lamentably plain and fit only for obscurity. Her parents had found two pleasing names for each of her sisters, Winifred Lucy and Madeline Maud, and why – thought May – should she have had to suffer two such horrid ones? If only she had not been so bashful when she first came to Gordon Place, Fryn would have provided her with the very thing. But, by the time Fryn knew, the hated name of May had stuck. 'Yes, indeed. What a pity it's too late to begin again,' Fryn had condoled. 'Full of thorns and unlucky to have in the house! Why ever didn't you tell me before, darling?'*

In 1930 May's father died, and she had travelled with Madeline to the house on the outskirts of Burton-on-Trent where their parents had lived. They were not a demonstrative family, but May had left Fryn, and Madeline had torn herself free from the hospital, in order to be with their mother. The three had sat down to a meal at the kitchen table, and Elizabeth the mother served; her sharp eyes concentrated upon the task, while her sharp tongue began to tell of the dying of her husband in the work-house and his return to the bed upstairs. She ladled out three helpings of hot-pot, picking up the jacket potato for each in her fingers. She was given to eczema, and the backs of her hands were scarred with it. Madeline had leapt up, protesting: 'Mother, how can you be so disgusting?' and that was the last word they spoke to each other in the three days they spent together. Essential information passed through May, who could not break the deadlock. George the father, in his droll way, could have found a text to thaw their frozen lips, but he was up above, mute as they. Intensely conscious of this, each knew it was terrible that their silence banished him, but each knew she was entirely in the right. Stern eye warred with buttoned mouth as they stood side-by-side at the graveside later, as May has recorded: 'when we buried father in silence'.

Neither May nor Madeline attended the funeral of their mother, not long after. Their brother Cyril had written to tell May, but the post hadn't reached her at Sabi Pas, where a letter from Stella was being read out at the breakfast table on the verandah, accompanied by gusts of laughter. Into the limpid air the postscript escaped with the rest: 'Does May know her mother is dead?' and there was a howl of incredulous mirth at the incongruity of Stella's lines, which met May as she bore the coffee-tray out into the sunshine. Their feelings about their mothers had been among the things that Fryn and May had shared, but in May's ears echoed quite different words her father had once spoken to Aunt Jennie: 'She's a tartar is my Betty, but dependable.'

---

* May King in conversation with JC, and so, too, the details which follow about May's parents' deaths.

ELEVEN

——•◦€)(3•◦——

Astray in Hollywood

BY 1931, Fryn's publishers had had nothing from her since *The Lacquer Lady* in 1929, and C.S. had pointed out that, though natural enough, that was not politic. He treated her like a queen, so she strove to live up to his expectations if she could. Long ago, while keeping the roof of 46 Gordon Place precariously over the heads of herself and her girl-friends, she had invented a character she called Solange Fontaine; a pale, slim young woman, half French, elegant and intelligent, with a delicate instinct for semeiosis or the inspired guess. It is a gift she has, like the bloodhound's sense of smell. In the presence of evil a chill apprehension flows over her, which she calls her 'feeling', and which guides her unerringly to the detection of crime. The earliest Solange stories had appeared in the *Metropolitan Magazine* in New York, and in 1918 to 1919 seven of these were published in *The Premier Magazine*. Fryn therefore selected five more on this theme under the title of *The Solange Stories*, and they were published by Heinemann and also by the Macmillan Company in the USA, dedicated 'for the Beloved W.J. Locke – *Frater, ave atque vale*!'

A frolicsome foreword defines the rules of detective story writing, in which surprise is the only essential, whereas the function of the crime story is above all to give the nerves a *frisson*. Through the stories that follow, Solange's intuitive gift leads to the discovery of a wife-murderer in 'The Pedlar', enabling her to save the next naive victim. For Solange also works in the legal anthropological department of the police laboratory, where her father Professor Fontaine conducts scientific investigations into crime. 'The Canary' has appeared in anthologies, on BBC radio, and on television, in which Fay Compton took the part of the medium who gives a séance, while the canary dies in its cage by the same evil influence which so powerfully affects Solange. 'The Black Veil' is staged near Sabi Pas, amidst the pine-clad hills of the Côte des Maures. It tells of the recurrent dream of a young prisoner awaiting trial for the murder of a prostitute. He dreams that he stands under the guillotine, covered by a long black veil, and Solange discovers in the course of her investigations that, in France in the nineteenth century, parricides were executed in this grotesque garb, and that the youth all unknowing has killed his own mother.

One of the letters which reached Fryn in response to this collection was from A.E.W. Mason, who wrote: 'I read your book with great pleasure in my little yacht during the summer, and I liked the stories very much; especially "The Canary", where the charlatan holding a séance is alarmed by finding something real creeping in.'

The Solange Stories, with their very feminine style of detective, still crop up in magazines, anthologies and on American television. A second collection, to be called *The Original Solange Stories* – those previously published only in magazine form – was unearthed in 1981 by Ferret Fantasy Ltd, London, and is being prepared by them for publication as a book for enthusiasts of the detective genre known as the Queen's Quorum.

Back in 1931, however, the first collection served merely to fill a gap. For at that time Fryn and Tottie had problems; the worst of these being that her creative work was at a standstill. He was back in London, at the Ambassadors Theatre and working on a film script, when she wrote to him from Sabi Pas:

> 'I'm so sorry for all your worries, my sweet, but so thankful you share them with me. Don't worry about me; we'll get out of this flat spin somehow. And then, when we've simplified life by getting rid of our possessions, we'll be all right again.
> 'Dearest, don't you realize that, if at last we're free to be ourselves – if the burden of thirteen years is lifted from me – I could be happy with you in a Bloomsbury boarding-house. Poverty doesn't worry me at all. As long as you want me to have anything there is, I don't care if there isn't anything. This is very female.
> 'I think I shall soon be able to work again. I'm *much* better. Do take care of yourself. Come back and love me. That is all I mind, except your work and my work. I have no child to share you with – you are everything – that has to be my distinction now, and I think a real one? Bless you, my heart.'

and a little later, from Sabi Pas again:

> 'My dearest – First, would you like to sell Cut Mill, and this house, and buy the river house, so that we could travel every winter, and you could

really do the sort of work you like in the summers? I know you like practical work; so do I. I get more thrill out of painting furniture or putting a Notable British Trial in order than out of most things. Also, your writing does require rubbing up against people. I should like London very well, with nothing but the river in front of my eyes. The only thing I should dread would be that it would be impossible to avoid being too social. But it is *your* life *I* want you to live and, as long as I can work, it is *your* life *I* want to live. Think it well over.

'You may not believe it, but it wasn't only fear of my own uncertain position and a dread of losing you that made me put up with so much unhappiness. I think you were wrong. I don't think you weighed up values. And it remains that it was I who have been sacrificed. But I still should hate to blackmail you emotionally into doing what you felt wasn't right for *you*; even though you've not been quite honest with an essentially dishonest person, but have let her think the thing that is not.

'Oh my heart, I'm so excited at the thought of seeing you.'

Tottie's first film scenario came to nothing, but it did indicate the direction towards which he was turning. Then, without warning, he had to dash over to Marseilles to support Fryn and May, who had driven there for a funeral. Inexplicably and shockingly, young Peta Vaughan-Sawyer, while on her way to stay with them at Sabi Pas in the last week of August 1931, had died of an epiglottic spasm. It hit Fryn hard, wrung with pity as she was for the mother.

That year, she too was indicating a new, and ominous, direction in her work. An essay of hers called 'Death and Deportment' appeared in an anthology called *Essays of the Year* published in November by the Argonaut Press, and it foreshadowed a new low in her state of mind. Not that the essay was lugubrious in its attitude; rather it was mocking, and after quoting Walter Raleigh's thoughts before his execution: 'But from this earth, this grave, this dust, My God shall raise me up, I trust,' it concluded, 'to anyone who can believe those lines, the trappings of death seem a small affair.' Yet, while playing with the idea of death, a mood of morbid despondency overwhelmed her, and one melancholy night Fryn took an overdose of sleeping pills and was found the next day in a coma. All the hideous pother of stomach-pumps and prostration followed, and she was accompanied by a private nurse to a nursing-home in the neighbourhood while Tottie pondered what to do next. Nobody at Sabi Pas at the time remembers precisely when this occurred; a general amnesia has overlaid it. 'That was only the first,' they say. 'There were so many others.' This time, Fryn was taken by ambulance from the nursing-home to Cut Mill to be under her own doctor, and Tottie tried to urge her to see a consultant. But this Fryn resisted strongly. With her eloquence, even when *hors de combat*, she could easily parry any hint of her need for a psychiatrist, then and later. And so depression settled over once-peaceful Cut Mill, which was contaminated with the misery of it all.

To Tottie then it seemed that the whole confounded exercise, involving the Ambassadors Theatre, Cut Mill and Sabi Pas – his great tax-saving economy programme – had been nothing but a farce. The success of Fryn's books, his plays, had been rendered worthless. The scale on which they were squandering their joint resources, in time, money and health, let alone mutual love and trust, was appalling. Fryn was becoming a formidable burden to carry, and though he knew better than anyone that she was infinitely worth her weight, for the present he was drained.

Nevertheless, in the beginning of 1932, Tottie had two plays produced in London on successive nights. 'No playwright of the "middle",' according to the *Observer*, 'could ask for better than that.' *So Far and No Father* was produced at the Ambassadors Theatre on 16 February and had some very good lines for Marie Tempest in the principal role. *King, Queen, Knave*, written in collaboration with Robert Gore-Browne, was produced at the Playhouse Theatre on 17 February, with Gladys Cooper and Leon Quartermayne. But as soon as these successes were behind him, Tottie threw in his hand. Because of the stultifying entertainment tax, he ended his contract at the Ambassadors. As he wrote in explanation: 'On three plays covering twenty-seven months, the profits were £2,500 to the producer, £15,000 to the Exchequer.'

There was mourning at his departure, and one grateful actress, Marda Vanne, wrote to him: 'Dear, dear Mr Harwood – Oh *NO*! Directly and indirectly, all my successes – such as they are – have been connected with you and the Ambassadors Theatre.' Peter Cotes has since said of him: 'He was that rare mortal, a blend of successful business man and talented creative artist. It was during his reign as lessee that the Ambassadors enjoyed its most golden period.' But he threw it all up. He relinquished the flat in Adelphi Terrace. He put Sabi Pas up for sale. He arranged to let Cut Mill. He accepted a proposal that he should go to Hollywood to write scenarios for Metro-Goldwyn-Mayer, and invited Archie Batty to accompany him as his Managing Agent. Robert Gore-Browne had preceded him there, under contract to Fox Studios.

*   *   *

When Fryn had left Sabi Pas for Cut Mill, she was secretly afraid that she had cancer of the womb. She also feared that Tottie's purpose in deciding to go to Hollywood was to escape from her. But she masked these fears from him, having a talent for approaching every new situation vis-à-vis their relationship with a clean slate.

In September 1932 there came a great storm, that devastated St Maxime and Casino, and Tottie wrote to her from Sabi Pas:

'Darling – We returned to an incredible desolation. Wet and grey. As we turned into the head of the Gulf, I knew that I didn't any longer "belong". The whole place is like a scene when the limelight has been turned off – just cardboard. If places have souls, this one's, for me, has gone out of it. The man comes on Tuesday. My only wish now is to sell quickly and have done with it. I shall try to fix it. Then, I have several suggestions to make, but I shan't do that till I hear from you. Nor, just now, will I talk about *us*. Let us leave that for a few weeks. We've been in deep water and must come up to breathe first. That's all I want to say just now.

'But one thing I do know. It is that your presence in a house is a strange thing. It may make or mar, but it cannot be a matter of indifference, to the house or those in it. It is a ferment like yeast, so you have to be doubly sure that it's working the right way! But there isn't a house without it.'

Sabi Pas was sold that September to Monsieur Combaste, the proprietor of Vins de Postillon, who pulled down the simple old house, the round pool and the sun parlour to build a sumptuous villa and a real tiled swimming-pool. Fryn wrote in her book *Sabi Pas* that where it once stood 'there is now a building of concrete and glass, horse-shoe shaped to catch the sun, but in the days when we lived there it was a yellow-washed house with a roof of fluted tiles. Pine trees, ilex and mimosa grew there. A garden like an apron stage thrust out towards the clear water.' But they had had to leave it, and nature had reinforced the necessity, washing away the ground on both sides of the house, and washing the goldfish out of their pool, so that everything that had been Sabi Pas was wiped out.

Tottie had arranged to take one of the towers of Princes Hotel at Hove, and there Fryn was transplanted by ambulance, and there they all stayed, Fryn, May and Tiger, for the remainder of the winter, Tottie joining them when he could. Actors and actresses arrived from London continually and they talked and ate with them every day. Cancer still menaced Fryn, and on the days when she had it she had to have a wheel-chair. Their daily walks along the promenade made quite a cavalcade, with the chair-man at the controls, May on one side, Tiger on the other. On the days when she didn't have it, the wheel-chair was dismissed and they went foraging in the dress-shops in extravagant spirits. One day Fryn bought each one of them a model suit with hat to match.

But under the high spirits and under the low spirits, Fryn was jousting with Tottie for place, and she wrote to him in London:

> 'Sweetheart – your letter makes me very sad. That you, who always enjoyed life so, should feel that either nothing matters, or that things are suicidal! I remember your once saying to me: "I should like to have put on my tombstone: 'If there is another life, I hope it's half as good as this one, but I doubt it'."
>
> 'I worry terribly lest it's partly my fault you don't feel like that now. Yet we have had such happy times, and have won through to something of value when all around us has gone phut, that I can't believe it's my fault, or even the fault of my illness. It's the fault of life. You see, though you're the most unselfish man I've ever known, you have also an enormous strength and violence of egoism. You cannot imagine the world going on without you, while I can imagine it only too well. And so the gradual slackening of youth and the powers of youth hurt you even more than they do most people.
>
> But you are wrong in thinking anything has happened to your brain. *I* should know if it had. But if you seriously feel you can't go on, I don't mind a bit as long as we do it together, knowing what we're doing. I've always felt that every human being has a perfect right to say "Finish!" when he pleases. And I've never, though I've lived so acutely, been violently attached to what is called life. But you must never do anything without me.
>
> 'Dearest of my heart, come back to me soon.'

By this time, neither was unhappy, though she was still indignant with him for daring to contemplate Hollywood without her, and played him up in every way that came to hand. Yet it was all rather fun; she was sleeping and eating as she had not done for years, and Tottie's face lost its savage look and was seen to wear a grin. He did go alone, though. Just before his departure, having been to see his old friend Frank Towle, manager of the Dorchester where he was staying, he wrote to her:

> 'Darling – Frank will do anything he can for you, either about staying in London or getting you fixed up on ships. He told me to tell you this. Goodbye my very dear. I love you.'

So she had won. When he sent for her and Tiger to join him, Fryn's cancer symptoms had ceased, and she had written and told him about it. His reply on 8 February 1933 showed all the concern she could have hoped for:

'Darling – my poor, poor darling – Your letter arrived and I have cabled you asking you to wire possible date of *safe* departure (by which I mean that no further treatment for *anything* is considered necessary). I also want you very much to see Ethel, who is good on this particular thing, and to hear that she is confident that nothing is to be feared, and that there is nothing to be *watched*. As far as that goes, I am now in touch, through University people here, with the best advice, but in these cases it is of the highest importance that the thing should be seen by those who have already seen it earlier. It is *change* in the condition that makes the diagnosis.

'I suppose you don't realize that I had to read right through your letter not knowing what *had* been found. I won't tell you what I went through. As for your not telling me – I don't know what to say. I do appreciate your motive, and your thought for me, and of course I should not have started if I had known, until I was certain what was the matter. And I ought to have been given the chance of deciding. What should I have felt like if there *had* been an operation?

'And then I try to put myself in your place, and hope (and think) that I should have done as you did. And yet I feel that that isn't right – that a thing like that is something that we ought to share. I know of course that you will think that, as I had wilted already under the rain of physical ills, it wouldn't be any good telling me of this. But I can't bear to think of your going through all that anxiety alone.

'As for lies; if you had made up your mind I wasn't to be told, what else was there for it? It all hangs on that. I've always known that you would tell anything necessary, once you'd decided that a secret had to be kept. It's the decision, not the way of carrying it out, that matters. But I don't now feel quite sure about anything.

'Of course you must come out as soon as ever you can. And I must know about when, because of getting a house for you. I want to know how you feel about having Archie and Molly to run it, because although it would make it ever so much easier for me, I don't want you to feel you have always people about.

'Longing to see you, and – if you feel like it – might have some work for you!

'I think it is too terrible the things that happen to you. I don't know what fate is thinking of. Please add to your cable how you are *everywhere*.

'Your letter found me facing a really heavy day on this first job, with people panting for it at the studio. I still work hard. I read 4 plays and 3

movies, including *Painted Veil*, in one day this week, and wrote reports thereon. More in your line than mine!
'Oh darling! I don't mind your lying to me, but I do *hate* not being given a chance to take my share.'

May did not weep when Fryn left for Hollywood with Tiger; she had grown to welcome periodic release from her little friend. As always, she threw herself into the business of spring-cleaning, and in Tottie's gift she booked front-row theatre stalls once or twice a week for herself and Marjorie. She also kept a diary which she knew would make Fryn and Tottie laugh, for she was a rare clown when it pleased her. But her first task had been the nostalgic one of helping Auntie move from Gordon Place to a basement flat in Warwick Gardens, Kensington, and of moving in with her as lodger.

Fryn and Tiger sailed on the *Aquitania* on 9 March 1933, Fryn having had a reassuring session with Ethel Vaughan-Sawyer to remove what she called 'a thriving family of billiard-balls'. All her friends had been warning her about the American Banks' Moratorium, but Tottie had cabled: 'Splendid firmness in a rocking world', and that was good enough for Fryn. When, minutes before sailing, another cable came from him: 'Stop Fryn at all costs', she had remained unmoved. She was very well and being her most amusing self. They were put at the Captain's table and were an instant success with him and with Lord Clive, their table companion. In New York they booked in at the Hotel Pierre on Fifth Avenue, to a suite of what Tiger found 'inconceivable grandeur'.

A series of memoranda, for circulation to Stella, May and all at home, trickled from Fryn's pen in the ensuing months:

'17 March: Hotel Pierre. I have had two letters and two telegrams from Tottie, who seems slightly madder and sweeter than ever. They have all been living on tick, so I suppose I shall live on tick too. I didn't mean to smuggle, but I suppose it is in me an ineradicable vice, for I did my usual trick of handing over all my keys at the Customs and got through with a bottle of brandy, a bottle of gin, and all my injections. The nicest friend we made on board was Lord Clive – Mervyn to me after two days – a tower of strength, as poor Tiger was very sick. I was dreadfully anxious about the Californian earthquake, but got a telegram from Tottie: "Welcome Napoleon Love," which reassured me I'd made a right decision in disregarding his cable to stop me sailing.

'19 March: We lunched with darling Archie yesterday, and today are lunching with my new agent at a speakeasy. I go quite sick and ill when I think of meeting Tottie again, as though something will prevent it.

'23 March: A seething mass of boy-friends pushed us on to the train. We missed them frightfully. A white-haired negro optimistically made up two double-beds in our compartment. You never saw anything like the Middle West, there's so much of it! Miles of country with one hen-coop – except that human beings lived in it – and nothing else. Across this desolation runs a magnificent high-road with a white line painted pathetically down the middle of it.'

Tottie, grinning broadly and accompanied by two cars, met them at Pasadena Station, and they arrived at the house to find a log-fire, a Scotch parlour-maid and her husband the butler, a Czech cook, an airedale and a bulldog. Outside were lawns, a swimming-pool, and a tennis-court so white it had to have red tennis-balls. And Fryn wrote:

'25 March: Beverley Hills. Now we are safely here, met by little Fatty looking marvellous. His secretary – Jewish-Austrian-French-American – polishes him off in half a day, is also good at golf, drives her own car, and orders all meals before leaving at lunch-time. Tiger says gloomily that all there is for her to do is turn backward somersaults off the springboard, which will not get her very far. At the beauty parlour where Tiger and I went to have the dust of the Middle West removed, the girls led one from cubicle to cubicle, arms round one's waist, and called one "honey" in the intervals of smoking and eating a carrot salad. When I explained that I was suffering from a bad inferiority complex, mine kindly said: "Well, I'm not sure you aren't happier without brains. You don't suffer so much," and I was so touched and pleased I tipped her a dollar. We have dined with Lynn Fontanne, Alfred Lunt and Noël Coward, and on to *Design for Living*; superb acting and Noël angelic as usual. Then the Goreys dined with us, Gorette looking like an innocent schoolgirl with white collars-and-cuffs on a navy frock. Vita Sackville West and Harold Nicolson lunched with us yesterday, and last night we went to dinner with Clemence Dane, a pet as always, with an Edwardian figure and masses of hair in a bun. Diana Wynyard was there, looking perfectly sweet. Tottie goes off every morning to the studios, just like a London clerk.
P.S. Poor Tottie does hate the work so.'

There is a postscript too from Tiger, saying: 'Fryn had slight migraine after the train journey, but is now very well indeed and very happy to be with Tottie again. The great difficulty is trying to settle down to work in this unsettling atmosphere.'

Fryn's next letter took up the thread:

'10 April: I haven't begun work yet. Everything is so kaleidoscopic and I shall be a ruined woman. Our frightfully nice Scottish maid observed to me this morning that she thought it was too exhausting for me to butter my own toast and she would do so in future. How far away from everything this place seems; cut off from time and space it has no roots of any kind.

P.S. It makes me sad too about Gordon Place. Get Auntie a bottle of port to cheer her up in the basement flat!
P.P.S. Ethel is a genius. Matilda as regular as clockwork!

'25 April: Beverley Hills. Darlings – two people murdered in the next street a few nights ago, but here we still are. Everyone has firearms here and even burglars have cars, which makes us so sorry for our poor little English burglars, who have to walk to work carrying a suspicious-looking bag of jemmies. Tiger and I have been over the Los Angeles prison on the tenth floor of the Hall of Justice. No exercise-yard, no gymnasium, a stale smell like the lion-house at the Zoo. The men and women lie about reading and playing cards all day long. Everybody is proud of this prison, as they treat the prisoners kindly and smile.'

They met actors, playwrights and critics; gossip-columnists and designers. Everyone came to dinner with them, and they went every-where. To tea at the MacCormacks; charming manners, log-fires, home-made bread and scones, strong tea and two priests. To a party at G.B. Stern's; exquisite supper and potent cocktails. To lunch at Beverley Brown Derby; photographers snapping the beautiful wait-resses in ultra-short starched skirts. To Long Beach: Fryn radiantly well and bathing in the ocean with Laurence Olivier – 'A beautiful diver, but too lanky to be physically attractive!' so Fryn confided to her Fatty. Harmless pleasure was the order of the day, and she wrote home:

'12 May: The Hearst newspapers have been conducting a great agitation to save the life of Ruth Judd, who murdered her two girl-friends and cut them up and put them in trunks. Sob-sisters write articles calling her "this frail little tuberculous woman", and a headline ran: "Sanity Quiz ordered for Moody Tigress." By her photographs she is a beautiful creature; though her hands are large enough to strangle an ox. If she had been coloured, she would have hanged long ago, but the Defence doctors say she is suffering from "condemned-cell neurosis", meaning she doesn't want to be hanged any more than you or I do. Everybody has forgotten the unfortunate murderees, although I expect they suffered from trunk-neurosis at the time.

'I have a good idea for a short story about Siamese twins: "In Death They were Divided". Not a money-maker, I think! Tottie is suffering agonies with *Queen Christina*, and Garbo is arriving at any moment and will probably undo all he has done. It is a quite mad industry, in which nobody can read or even listen.'

Tottie had lunch with Greta Garbo. They bathed together after-wards, and Greta said she couldn't bear to wear anything on her top half, with which Tottie warmly concurred. Tiger noted in her diary that she had high cheek-bones, grey eyes, and wore grey flannel slacks. 'She talked intelligently and he liked her. She is a good swimmer, has a simple manner without affectation, and Tottie is now the envy of Hollywood.'

By the middle of June Fryn was not so well, with a return of migraines. But she had done some work on the novel she called *Julia*, and she planned to get right down to it after her wisdom-tooth had been removed, as she wrote home:

'22 June: Your poor little friend has been having a difficult time. The only comfort is that the impacted wisdom was at the root of more trouble than we knew. I had abscess after abscess after its removal at the Cottage Hospital at Santa Barbara, which took two hours under ether. Naturally I had an awful migraine, but these have cleared up since in a manner that staggers me. If only I were at home I could be working at the top of my form, but this is a very relaxing place, and it isn't one's own house, and Tottie seems to have taken a "scunner" against Cut Mill, and I am going to be trailed around the world for the rest of my life.

'I expect you feel pretty bad, Stella darling, at giving up your lovely flat, in spite of the relief as far as money was concerned. We Gudgeons have an attachment to our homes, and we marry people who haven't, but who like careering about the world. That is all very well as long as one can afford the two, but if one can only afford the one – then I am all for home and work!

'We've been to the Four Square Temple to hear the Angel of Broadway, Sister Rheba Crawford, deputizing for Aimée McPherson who is ill in Italy. The hymns are all sung to well-known tunes: "In the bosom of Jesus" was sung to "Champagne Charlie".

'Well darlings, I wish we were all at Cut Mill. I wish all sorts of simple

things that apparently can never be, I don't know why. I am so thankful,
darling Gudge, that you are so much better.'

Stella had been to Paris for deep-ray treatment to her throat, and
their cousin Kitty Roseo had invited her to stay at St Cloud while she
followed the course. Naturally, no mention of cancer was made in
these open letters, but did Stella already know she might have it? And
did Fryn? Did either yet entertain the dread idea? And was this why
Fryn suffered the counterfeit pangs in her own flesh? She had cabled
anxiously: 'Take May. I'll pay all'. She couldn't bear Stella to go back
and forth alone every day for her treatments. So May went too, and
she and Stella had had a happy time in spite of the ordeal, walking the
parks and quays and galleries of Paris. And May at least had had no
inkling beyond a new cure for Stella's stammer.

On a night in August 1933, a murder was reported in the Los
Angeles newspapers, described as 'The Pent-roof killing'. The pent-
house was over a florist's shop in Pasadena, and one Harold Wolcott
was arrested for the shooting of his blonde lover Helen Bendowski.
The trial was to take place in the Pasadena court-house, and Fryn
managed to get the front-row seat reserved for the *Alabama Star*,
close to the jury of ten women and two men. They fanned themselves
in the grilling heat with large palm-leaf fans, and rocked to and fro in
their rocking-chairs. Russell Gleason, son of the film stars James and
Lucile, drove Fryn from Hollywood in his sports car, and every day
she observed with fascination the differences in the way the law
worked out. 'It was a curious trial, to one accustomed to the austeri-
ties of the Central Criminal Court in London,' she commented.

Fryn was forty-five now and had lost that beauty of youth which
was all she had ever laid claim to; but the golden glow hung about her
still, as if she carried a source of warmth like a lamp within her. In the
early days at Beverly Hills, while she was triumphantly well, she had
held her own effortlessly at the quick-fire repartee of Dorothy Parker
or Alexander Woollcott. And Tottie's charm and wit had made
everyone, men and women alike, his devoted slaves. Naturally they
were asked to every party going, and as their circle increased so did
their round; attractive, destructive. Although Fryn did write the grim
short story, her further efforts were frustrated.

Tottie's work, meanwhile, was running down. He was still hating
the damnable way everything was duplicated, with scripts shared out
to several writers. According to his contract with Metro-Goldwyn-

Mayer, he was to have so much on approval and further contracts at increased rates. Money was not the problem; it was satisfaction that was lacking, and he again threw in his hand.

Towards the inevitable end, they all paid a visit with the Gore-Brownes to Joy Boy Rogers and his pansy chorus at the Hollywood Barn. Some of the men were like beautiful girls, and one would have been a peach in any sex, though the best sight was the expression on Gorey's face when they came and waggled their bellies at him, in sheer organdie frocks, falsies, cache-sexes and a scattering of diamanté. But it was too sick to be funny, or clever, or beautiful, and Fryn said so in ringing tones and had a migraine for days after. In fact, she had begun to feel wretchedly ill, and a trepanning operation on the skull was seriously proposed by her doctor. One night, shortly before leaving, they were treated to an earthquake by way of parting shot. To a noise like cannons going off, Fryn leapt out of bed and ran in to protect Tottie, with the sleepily confused notion of 'Let us die together!'

On 27 October 1933, enormous crowds saw them off at Los Angeles station with enormous bunches of flowers, and on 1 November they sailed home again without a home to go to.

In some ways it was a wasted year for both of them. Fryn was in worse shape at the end of it than at the beginning, and Tottie never quite regained the eminence he had reached as a notable as well as a successful dramatist. E. Phillips Oppenheim wrote in his memoirs: 'Tottie Harwood everyone loves. I should describe him as a thoroughly sound dramatist and cannot understand why he has not met with even more appreciation. His *Man in Possession* was almost a perfect piece of work, one of the best constructed modern plays I have ever had the good fortune to see.' But then he added: 'I believe he was once led astray by Hollywood.'*

Yet in the long term their Hollywood interlude was not a dead loss, since they both came to look back upon it with increasing pleasure, and could never bring themselves to regret it. Friendship was what they gained. As well as the Lunts, and so many other actors and actresses; as well as Carl and Sonya Hovey, from Fryn's first voyage in search of a surgeon; they got to know and to love the Mount

* *The Pool of Memory* E. Phillips Oppenheim, Hodder & Stoughton, 1941.

Wilson astronomer, Professor Edwin Hubble and his wife Grace, the playwrights Sam Behrman of *Brief Moment* and John Balderston of *Berkeley Square* with his wife Marion, and Alexander Woollcott the journalist, actor, broadcaster, critic and wit; 'wasp or honey-bee at will' as Fryn has called him. These last eight were to combine with Fryn and Tottie in a transatlantic correspondence between like minds, which later formed the basis of two books designed to help the war effort against Germany.

The immediate aftermath, however, was disastrous. Fryn's health had been visibly declining, causing speculation from the curious owing to her erratic moods and behaviour, and what happened to her between the farewell ceremony at Los Angeles station and the embarkation on 1 November will always remain obscure. Tiger's diary dismisses it with: 'Four tiring days on the train. I felt sick and Tottie had a septic tooth.' On board the *Aquitania* the pair behaved to each other scrupulously politely but distantly, not talking unless they had to. On arrival in England, Tottie provided Fryn with funds which he insisted were hers, and told her to make her own plans. He refused to discuss anything, and left for Paris alone.

In September 1933, some weeks before their return to England, an essay by Fryn, called 'Joseph Conrad 1857 – 1924', had appeared in an anthology, *The Post Victorians*. It was published by Ivor Nicolson & Watson of London, who had it in hand before Fryn left for Hollywood. Such old friends as Alan Bott and R.D. Blumenfeld, Hugh Walpole, Rebecca West and Harold Child were among the other contributors, and no doubt Fryn was invited to join their number because of her old friendship for Conrad, who had so admired *The White Riband*. His feeling for the sea and ships struck a chord of sympathy in her. The taking of risks had been his lot at sea, and 'that grimmer danger of the lean larder was his also,' as Fryn recognized. Never did she cease to feel for those who had to live on 'the edge of circumstance'. She honoured him as a man and as an artist, but most of all must she have felt kinship with Conrad as a fellow-sufferer, at this stagnant juncture in her writing life, when the spirit had left her, as it had so often left him, 'under the strain of a creative effort in which mind and will and conscience are engaged to the full hour after hour, day after day, away from the world, and to the exclusion of all that makes life really lovable and gentle.'* In these desperate terms he had been driven to ask himself 'whether I am bewitched . . . After such crises of despair I doze for hours still half conscious that there is that story I am unable to write . . . I feel my brain . . . My story is there in a fluid. I can't get hold of it, no more than you can grasp a handful of water.'†

How many times had Fryn's recurrent illness taken a similar form? His gout had its counterpart in her migraines; and, judging from his howls of protest in letters to friends and publishers, Conrad endured that scourge too. Medical evidence suggests that, though the pain of migraine feels as though it is in the brain itself, it is caused by dilation of the blood vessels and in fact is outside the brain, in the scalp, muscles, veins and arteries, and that sensitive and talented people are the most susceptible to it, authors and philosophers being especially prone. It is also recognized as being hereditary, and pent-up emotions are a prime cause. No wonder that Fryn, with another huge novel evolving in great travail, should have felt at one with Joseph Conrad!

On 21 December 1933, *The Old Folks at Home*, a play in three acts by H.M. Harwood, was produced by the author and W. Graham-Brown at the Queen's Theatre, dedicated to Marie Tempest who played the principal role. She had written to him: 'Do I understand you have a play for me? Indeed I hope so. I read nothing but "typical Marie Tempest plays", and my heart sinks lower and lower. Will you save me from this Slough of Despond?'

On 21 January 1934, she was writing to him again, at Villa Mauresque, Cap Ferrat, where he was staying with Somerset Maugham: 'Just a line to tell you how splendidly the play is going. They stand up and shout at nearly every performance, which is unheard of in a London theatre. It's all tremendously thrilling. But, in case you get above yourself, I enclose some letters which will steady you.' She added a big hug for himself and love to dear Willie and enclosed a rich mixture of opinion: 'I consider the play not only *unworthy* of your wonderful acting, but one which struck me as more entitled to have been enacted in the courts of *hell* than in this dear land of ours. Three adulterous women! It is a *grotesque* play, and so ludicrously immoral that, thank God, one can spit it out on leaving.' And this: 'It is only the peer of a Bernhardt or a Duse who could have

---

* 'Joseph Conrad 1857–1924' FTJ, in *The Post Victorians*.
† *Joseph Conrad*: A Critical Biography, Jocelyn Baines, quoting an excerpt from a letter to Garnett from Conrad of 29.3.1898.

driven home so effectively the honest message of that excellent play, the production of which was to me perfect. If by your very human presentation of a wholesome lesson you succeed in helping lots of boys and girls, you will have gleaned a rich harvest.'

The press notices were uniformly excellent, the *Sunday Times* writing: 'I must declare Mr Harwood's play to outshine everything this brilliant writer has done before, Miss Tempest to eclipse the French Réjane and the American Ada Rehan, and everybody in the cast to contribute to the greatest first night since Genesis.'

At the end of the run, Marie Tempest wrote to him again: 'I can't tell you how I have loved playing your beautiful play. Go on, dear, and write more and more. There is no one today like you.' That was in the summer of 1934, and Fryn too wrote to him then, from the Royal Palace Hotel, Kensington:

'My love – It was sweet of you to come and see me, but it makes me still more firm in my belief that I am unable to cope with the aftermath of your absence.

'Don't cheat yourself by telling me to go out and mix with people. The reason they loved to meet me and stay in our house was that we had happiness and so diffused it. I don't wish to diffuse unhappiness.

'At the beginning of our last year at Sabi Pas, the man whom I wrote "A Garden Enclosed" about, wrote to me from a nursing-home where he was dying. I wrote back and said I couldn't follow all his dissections of being "in love" or "not in love"; that I lived on a love that had been my common daily bread for years. I never dreamt it could fail. But it has, and it's not your fault, it's my own blind stupidity. But don't tell yourself and me lies. You know that I didn't sleep-walk in the USA, that I never lost my "me". You know perfectly well how I tackled that whole subject at Hove, because I had something to fight for.

'Of course, I never travelled in places like Upper Burma, or in the yacht, without medinals. I took one about twice a month. And I wrote *Tom Fool* and *The Lacquer Lady*!

'Now I shall have a shot at this book, but I really don't see much good after that. What am I working for? To go back to Cut Mill – without you? To take an obscure cottage somewhere, and try to build up a "home" again – for May and me? What inducement is there for me to do such a thing? No more going about the world, between books? No more you? No, thank you.

'And, by the way, tell Archie I think it would be a good idea in the Spring to advertise Cut Mill for sale, with photo in the back page of the *Times*.'

And Fryn had written to Stella as well:

'Darling – I got your letter, and evidently Tottie didn't write you what he promised.

'This is what happened – I am dictating this to Tiger, who was with us – When we got on the train at Los Angeles he saw that I had a migraine, which naturally I had been concealing all day. He, poor thing, had had a tooth out. He gave me an injection and, in an effort to stay asleep and not disturb him, I then took two "blues".

'I have written to you about the earthquake at Santa Monica, and the noise it made: well, the train made the same noise, and it woke me up in the night shouting: "Earthquake!" and calling "Tottie! Tottie!" to know if he was saved. I had no idea I was in a train; in time and space I was back in the Santa Monica earthquake.

'I got out of the top bunk, and he – I don't blame him in the least for this, he was in great pain – put me back. I then, with my odious officiousness, began to worry about Tiger's safety, and again got out of my berth and started looking for her. Tottie caught me and brought me back, infuriated, and I was so annoyed that anybody should mind being saved so much I said: "All right then – go to hell!"

'In the morning I got up and dressed, quietly so as not to disturb Tottie, and went to the breakfast car. I couldn't understand why the waiters didn't mention the earthquake, till about half way through breakfast a shutter sort of slid through my mind; and I knew there had never been any earthquake – that it had only been the noise – that we had been in the train the whole time.

'When I went back, Tottie said he was going to move into Tiger's berth, and she was to come into mine. Although I implored him to listen, he wouldn't speak to me the whole of the way to New York, or in New York, or on board the *Aquitania*, except in public. He kept on repeating: "You can't have it both ways. You must have known you were on the train, and that a train couldn't run through an earthquake." He repeated this in London. My answer was that I had the best reason for knowing that such a state of mind is possible, because it had happened to me. And I begged him to go to Ernest Jones, Maurice Craig, or anyone he liked, without me if he preferred. He spoke kindly to me before he went away, but he still wouldn't go and see a doctor. This was what did me in.

'I asked him the other day – when he admitted he had been wrong, and had been reading papers to do with the brain in France – to tell you what had happened. I was afraid you would naturally think it a recurrence of the dopey affair at Sabi Pas. I was under no dope whatsoever. And I think and hope a perfectly good patient to Dr Liston, who is writing a footnote to this letter. I have always said, most humbly and gratefully, how good you all were to me during those years at Sabi Pas. And if I had been in a state to realize what a strain it was on you all, of course I should have left there. I did leave directly I realized it.

'I blame Tottie for nothing except the fact that he left England without going to a doctor and finding out about this particular condition of the brain. Even when he said he would write to you, he said: "And how frightened do you think I was, with a brain that can do that?" To which I said: "And how frightened do you think *I* was?"

'This is the thing that has stood between us two. I have never for a moment doubted your love. It is true that I could not refuse to listen to someone I loved, for weeks and weeks, but people are differently made. I cannot bear that you should not know what it was that did me in.

'I should have stayed in London anyway to write my book. But it was the fact that he had gone away without going to see a brain specialist, and kept on repeating: "I know all about it; you can't have it both ways," that made life so impossible.'

There are two footnotes to this letter to Stella. One from Tiger: 'This, as far as I know, is exactly what happened,' and one from Dr Liston: 'When I heard the facts some months ago, it appeared to be the obvious explanation of Hurlingham.' For, left to her own devices, Fryn had put up at an hotel till Marjorie had found her a furnished flat by the river; Valentine and Henrietta Goldie's flat on the edge of Hurlingham. Tottie was at Cap Ferrat, May was living with her as usual, and Tiger was coming in daily; and one morning Fryn's bed-room door was still shut when Tiger arrived. May had thought it best to leave her sleeping, but at 10.30 Tiger over-ruled her and peeped in. Fryn was unconscious. She had arranged her hair and made up her face and clasped on her chest was a photograph of Tottie. She had swallowed all the pills in the drawer of her bedside-table, and on the table was a goodbye letter to him:

'Dearest – It isn't that I don't love you, but I felt your hatred of me was setting me back. I know you can't help it, but I wanted to get well as soon as possible for your sake, so that I could get away.'

Dr Liston had come then and she was rushed to a nursing-home with a private nurse, Mary Morris, who remained with her when she returned to the flat. Most of her life Fryn had suffered from insomnia, and she had been in the habit of taking sleeping-pills since before she was out of her teens. She mentions them in her diary at Newlyn, and she mentions migraine injections there. The 'blues' were medinals, which she took when she thought she would need a great many of the milder 'pinkies', or soneryls, to be effective.

On her return from the nursing-home, Fryn was in a black mood, antipathetic to everyone except her nurse. May went to stay with

Marjorie, suffering a complete loss of confidence, her place usurped, and Tiger left to take a new job with G.B. Stern. Tottie was more worried than angry now. Not for the first time, he found that the only way he could reconcile himself to the cruel changes that happened to Fryn was not to be there to see them. It was years before he was able to watch and wait right through these transformations with open eyes, with open arms, for her return. Her migraines, and the melancholy that sometimes overcast her bright spirit, he could bear with, but this was something different. In order that the tenderness between them might survive, he needed distance. But he had appointed someone less vulnerable than he to chart Fryn's progress towards recovery. Archie Batty, being the gentlest of men as well as the truest of friends to both, carried out this ticklish charge uncomplainingly, sustained by his peerless humour. In the guise of Puck, he shuttled between the estranged pair, and presently Fryn was able to write to Tottie:

'My darling – I want to tell you that you are free of me at last. I love you as dearly as ever, but no one can go right down to death deliberately, knowingly and thankfully as I did, and be pulled back, without something happening to them. That something has happened to me.

'I see the faults of our marriage were initially yours and later mine, in my blind dependence on you. You didn't want this and had always said so. I can only plead in extenuation that I wanted to be protected. I had been the protector to so many people for so long, and it *is* a woman's natural feeling towards her husband. But it was wrong *for us*! I ought to have been strong, as I was at Hove. Today, much as I long for a sight of your beloved face and the sound of your voice, it is suddenly happiness enough for me to know you exist on the earth and are well. I won't say I shall be able to dwell on these heights, but let us drop this strange hatred, which is so wrong for us and which has fallen from me like a cloak. Forgive me, and let me occasionally write that I'm trying to get well – that I love you.

'I have been dead and come back, and it does something odd to one. I will willingly take money from you for our poor May, who is on the edge of an awful breakdown. That I find it hard to forgive myself, but I had too little margin of safety, and it went.

'It seems terrible to be wasting the last years of our life, which ought to be together. It is a curious sensation, but my resentments are all gone. You gave me the only happiness I have ever had, if you gave me the rest. Dearest, you are right; love is not enough. And I do know how impatient you have naturally become of human relationships. But always, if we join up again or not, the only love I have and all my thoughts are yours.'

There is an undated line from Tottie, which seems to be his answer: 'I love you. I only want to meet again as soon as you are well.'

TWELVE

—••€)(३••—

Taking to Crime

ACCOMPANIED BY HER NURSE, Mary Morris, Fryn had managed to attend a murder trial at the Old Bailey. Reginald Ivor Hinks, an electrical engineer and part-time thief, young and personable but for the hair that stood up stiff and straight from his forehead like a scrubbing brush, was accused and found guilty of murdering his gentle, senile father-in-law. The old man had settled his life's savings on his daughter and her new husband, with whom he lived. He had been found dead, with head and shoulders in the gas oven, after the greedy Reginald felt he had established himself in the eyes of the world as a devoted son-in-law. But he had a tendency to lay on the devotion unnaturally thick. 'He was the only prisoner whom I have ever seen who wore a black tie and a black mourning-band round his arm as signs of sorrow for the person whom he was accused of killing,' observed Fryn.*

She had already been working tenaciously at her novel, and had found the courage to plunge headlong into the terrible climax. She had written gratefully and lovingly to May: 'I have longed for you more than I can say,' and adding: 'yet there is a point of unhappiness through which one cannot live, but I promise you I will, till the book is done.' She had also found whatever it took to turn the tables on Tottie: she had forgiven him. Although they still hadn't a home to go to, there was no difficulty in finding a roof; Frank Towle saw to that. According to May's diary, they enjoyed twelve addresses in the year following. Furnished flats in London alternated with the Dorchester or The Old Drum at Sandwich. This was a fine specimen of sixteenth century black-and-white, and it belonged then to Frank Towle's daughter Mollie Carthew, who let or lent it to Fryn and Tottie several times: for Stella and Eric were staying nearby at Walmer, while searching for a house to buy down there.

* *Comments on Cain*, FTJ, Heinemann, 1948.

James Hodge had again invited Fryn to write an introduction for his series, and this she now did, finding it a welcome form of relaxation from reading the galley-proofs of the novel, an exercise she detested. It was the Trial of Sidney Harry Fox, and she went with May to Margate to see the layout of the hall and staircase of the Metropole Hotel, and the bedroom where Fox had burnt his mother. The Trial was published in 1934, and a reprint in Penguin's Famous Trials appeared in 1950. It is dedicated to Sir Vincent Baddeley, KCB, 'unofficial proof-reader and kindest of friends.' In her introduction, Fryn wrote: 'Matricide is uncommon, but even apart from this obvious truth, there was something so peculiar, not only about the character of the son, but about that of the mother, that the case remains to a certain extent mysterious to this day.' Sidney Harry Fox was charged with murdering Rosaline Fox on 23 October 1929. His trial, at Sussex Assizes in Lewes County Hall, began on 12 March 1930.

She was a heavy, white-haired old woman, with a big genial face, loose lips and trembling hands. He was the youngest of her four sons, and she adored him above all. His expression was cherubic, so that he had come to be nicknamed Cupid. He was also an invert, and to indulge his extravagant tastes he had developed a talent for forgery, posing successfully as a gentleman. For years he had swindled and blackmailed, and his partially paralysed mother had accompanied him on a round of hotels, leaving without paying all the way. This regime of luxury and anxiety had gone on until by October 1929 the two had only each other and a wad of pawn tickets. From the first of May, when Rosaline Fox had made a Will in his favour, he had kept her life insured, and he had just secured short extensions of two policies totalling £3,000, payable should his mother die before midnight on 23 October. There was no time to be lost.

At 11.45 that night, Fox rushed into the hall of the Hotel Metropole, calling: 'Fire!' By the time several guests had helped to drag Mrs Fox's unclothed body out of the thick smoke that blanketed her room, artificial respiration was of no avail. Fox walked up to her and his eyes filled with tears. '*Homo sapiens*,' wrote Fryn, 'is a strange animal. His grief may not have been entirely assumed. Probably, in his reluctance to make use of her, he saved her up for his last effort; if at any moment a perverted rich man had come his way, Rosaline Fox was the human being with whom he would have shared his spoils.'

Three medical experts argued long over whether she died of strangulation, or of heart failure, or of suffocation. Without doubt the fire was feloniously lit. Finally Sir Bernard Spilsbury drew the unshakeable conclusion, from a recent red bruise at the back of the larynx, that death was due to manual strangulation. By that time, both insurance companies had smelled a rat. When the trial was over and Fox was found guilty, a woman spectator cried out: 'If his own mother were here, she would forgive him.'

Artists with a proved talent in one genre often set their hearts on triumphing in another, though it may be a Will-o'-the-Wisp. Alfred Tennyson and Joseph Conrad each allowed themselves to be weaned from poetry and prose, while they eagerly tried their hands as play-wrights with far less success. It is said that Gainsborough, strolling round Reynolds' studio, remarked sourly: 'The beggar's so various!' So might a rival have said of Tennyson; or of Fryn, in her extra-ordinary diversity. The two novels and the numerous short stories she wrote about the sea differed each from the other as much as from the two books on Burma, or from the love stories, the plays and the poetry. So that it has been said that this 'beggar' was too various for her own good as author. Time and again, Fryn had her *succès d'estime*, book-of-the-month, or all-time classic, but she went on to other things, leaving the idolators to go hungry. 'That is why I have never been a best-seller,' she apologized. Yet, not content with these accomplishments, she hankered to become a criminologist. The first time she had been praised for her grasp of legal matters was when Lord Reading, then Attorney General, had offered to coach her, saying that a mind such as hers would have no difficulty in mastering law finals. Sensitive insight and the power of clear analysis were natural assets. Dealing with true crime, as she did in the introductions and the essays she took to writing on famous cases, called for no creative energy. It was a way of limbering up between the absorbing demands of fiction. But the crime novel then in the pipe-line was a very different matter.

Linked with her interest in the criminal mind, Fryn had always been interested in prisons. She had been to the Tombs, Sing Sing, San Quentin and Botany Bay, as well as Birmingham, Dartmoor and countless others around England; to Broadmoor too and of course to Wormwood Scrubs and Holloway. Mary Size was Deputy Governor there to Dr Morgan during the time when Mrs Thompson was awaiting execution, and she became Fryn's friend and invaluable adviser in the course of the many visits and letters they exchanged at the final stages of her novel. 'As to my method of writing,' Fryn told her Paris agent, 'for that book I wrote Day Piece to Julia and Night Piece to Julia, the beginning and end chapters, first. And in that frame I placed the life of an over-emotional, under-educated, suburban London girl, who had no more idea of murder than the unfortunate Mrs Thompson had.'

The Notable British Trials introduction to the Thompson and Bywaters murder trial had already been written by Filson Young while Fryn was in Burma, but the story and the woman haunted her mind, and only by re-creating them in fiction form could she rid herself of the uncanny knowledge of the affair that seemed to possess her. Thus it came about that Julia Almond grew from the same stem as Edith Thompson, and Herbert Starling married her and bored her in Percy Thompson's place. Leo Carr became her young lover, doomed to receive her stirring letters, to strike the murderous blow, and die for it like Frederick Bywaters. Fryn immersed herself so deeply in their lives she almost suffocated. While the book was in the making, she had thought of it just as *Julia*, and had no title that pleased her, until one day she heard May describing a game she had played as a schoolgirl.

May was not alone in her generation in practising the game, but the names given to it varied from place to place, and Flora Thompson's *Lark Rise* says: 'Sometimes in the summer the "Pin-a-Sight" was all the rage. Two small sheets of glass, a piece of brown paper and plenty of flowers were required, to form a kind of floral sandwich; a little square window was cut.' The girls expected to be rewarded with a pin to be stuck into the front of the pinafore. And in *The Peaceable Kingdom* by Ardyth Kennelly, a small boy builds a 'Pinny-Peep-show' from a shoe-box full of scraps of silk and tinsel, with a peep-hole: 'and everybody who looks in has got to pay a pin, even my father and mother.' It was one of those fashions that sweep a school, and it cost nothing. With a variety of coloured fragments, the boys and girls May played with at Burton-on-Trent constructed little private worlds; a winter scene, a garden, or a desert. A peep cost a pin and there you were, lost in illusion. 'It was a wonderland,' May was saying. 'You could fancy almost anything in there as you glued your eye to the hole. We called the game A Pin to See the Peepshow.'

'*A Pin to See the Peepshow*,' Fryn broke in: 'May, darling. That's my title! It's what I've been waiting for!' Once embedded in her book, it fitted into Julia's schooldays as smoothly as if it had been part of *Day Piece to Julia* from the beginning. 'She was so enraptured at the solution,' May recalled, 'that she took me straight up to town and bought me the loveliest and most costly flowered-silk dress I had ever seen.'

A Pin to See the Peepshow was published by Heinemann and by Doubleday Doran of New York in 1934 and was reprinted the same year. From the novel, Fryn and Tottie collaborated in 1948 in a play version of the same name, which has a separate history. There was a Penguin edition of the book in 1952. Then in May 1973, Heinemann issued a reprint, to coincide with the BBC television production of the play, which was dramatized by Elaine Morgan. St Martin's Press of New York brought out a paperback a year later when the play was televised in America, and the Hearst Corporation serialized it in 1976. Virago published yet another paperback edition in 1979 in their Virago Modern Classics series, with a new introduction, again by Elaine Morgan.

Fryn dedicated the novel 'To Bobby', a mongrel dog she had adopted, which is also Julia's dog in the book, and she went to Shakespeare's *Measure for Measure* for the foreword:

> 'But man, proud man!
> Dressed in a little brief authority;
> Most ignorant of that he's most assured,
> His glassy essence — like an angry ape,
> Plays such fantastic tricks before high Heaven,
> As make the angels weep . . .'

The letters she received all tell the same story. Harry Hodge's was one of the first: 'Your *Pin to See the Peepshow* is wonderfully good; I enjoyed it thoroughly. Every now and again I had to lay it down and quieten myself with a little Bach on the piano. At night I had a sort of nightmare, dreaming about Julia. I wonder if Mrs Thompson is able to read the book in her heavenly home? What a waste of life! Your reviews have been good.'

'Joe' Jackson, for long her adviser on any difficult point of law or Court procedure, wrote: 'I read the whole of the manuscript with such breathless interest that my critical faculties may have been impaired, but as far as I could see you have made no mistakes at all. I found the whole of it most intensely interesting and think the book should have a very great success.' Fryn had first met Sir Richard Leofric Jackson when he was in the Office of the Director of Public Prosecutions. He became Assistant Commissioner at New Scotland Yard, in charge of the CID and the Special Branch. A most enthralling talker, he was a favourite lunch guest of Fryn's, for he was a big man and a gourmet, and she delighted to prime him with good victuals while they exchanged hair-raising legends of the Courts and the underworld. His name alone was an Open Sesame! while she was working on a case.

Ethel Mannin's review said: 'It may stand beside Dreiser's *An American Tragedy* for dramatic power and as a social document. It is a book to move one to tears and anger.' And Herbert W. Wilson, a barrister friend of her uncle Somers James, leads straight on to Fryn's next project: 'When I got in last night, I could not put your wonderful book down. It seems to me head and shoulders above your rivals in fiction. Arnold Bennett never did anything as good, and as for the much over-boomed Lawrence, his works are not in the same street. But how tragic it is and how terrible! I have never read any study of the last days and hours of a doomed soul which compares with yours in power and psychological insight. I am sure you will give us another masterpiece on the Rattenbury case in the Trials series.'

That letter was written on 13 June 1935, when the trial of Rattenbury and Stoner was barely over, so that hardly had her *Pin* been launched when Fryn set to work on a case in many respects its carbon copy; or so it appeared at first glance. Mrs Rattenbury was, like Mrs Thompson, a woman of mature years, accused jointly with her young lover of the murder of an older husband, and the parallel did not appeal, till closer study revealed such a stark contrast in the characters of the women that Fryn was won over. Instead of the fantasies of romantic love with which Mrs Thompson-into-Julia had seasoned her meagre existence, Mrs Rattenbury had indulged her generous nature. She had had three husbands, two little sons she loved and cared for, and a weakness for writing love-lyrics and drinking cocktails. And instead of struggling to save her own dear skin regardless of her lover's, Alma Rattenbury ardently confessed to the murder she knew nothing about.

At the trial, this confession was shown to be nonsense and she was found Not Guilty, but the moral judgment of society had changed little in the dozen years between, and she was hounded by press and public alike. Her life was handed back to her, her lover's was forfeit, and 'in her fear and grief for Stoner, in her misery for her children,' as Fryn described it, 'she bought a knife and went and sat beside the little stream where she had been happy,' and there she 'thrust the knife six times into her breast. The blade penetrated her heart thrice.'

The *Trial of Alma Victoria Rattenbury and George Percy Stoner* was published in December 1935, and a new edition appeared in 1950. It was translated into Danish for the Crime Club of Copenhagen in 1973. It was dedicated: 'To the dear memory of H. Somers James, Barrister-at-Law, who would have judged no human being without mercy – and all with humour.' The same correspondent, Herbert W. Wilson, wrote: 'I find it wonderfully good, the finest and most absorbing of the whole series,' and he adds: 'Your dedication to poor Somers is most touching. I condole with you on such a terrible loss, and what it must mean to Miss James I scarcely dare to think.' Somers had collapsed after a day's shooting, and though Margaret had rushed him to hospital he had died of a coronary thrombosis. Among Fryn's letters was this from Desmond MacCarthy: 'I have spent a day reading the trial of Rattenbury and Stoner, and your preface struck me as a fine piece of work, as remarkable for legal analysis of evidence as for understanding and moral judgment. It is just and moving and enlightening. It contains a lesson men need to take to heart, and so well conveyed that I cannot but believe that it has gone home, and that you have done a piece of work of real importance to your fellow human beings.'

In the summer of that year 1935, Fryn's little volume, listed among her *belles lettres* and entitled *Sabi Pas or, I Don't Know*, had appeared, 'dedicated to all the animals and most of the guests at Sabi Pas.' On the flyleaf was written:

For that which befalleth the sons of men befalleth beasts; even one thing befalleth them; as the one dieth, so dieth the other; yea, they have all one breath; so that a man hath no pre-eminence above a beast; for all is vanity. All go unto one place; all are of the dust, and all turn to dust again. Who knoweth the spirit of man that goeth upward, and the spirit of the beast that goeth downwards to the earth.

ECCLESIASTES, REVISED VERSION

I said in my heart concerning the sons of men, that God would prove them, and show them to be like beasts.
Therefore the death of man, and of beasts is one, and the condition of

them both is equal; as man dieth, so they also die; all things breathe alike, and man hath nothing more than beast; all things are subject to vanity. And all things go to one place; of earth they were made, and into earth they return together.

Who knoweth if the spirit of the children of Adam ascend upward, and if the spirit of the beasts descend downward.

DOUAY VERSION

The book illustrates how animals have 'a spiritual communion, a flamy intensification of the friendship that can exist as truly between beasts as between men,' and in it Fryn contends that Sabi Pas, or 'I don't know' is more than a name, it is a phrase; more than a phrase – it is a philosophy.

After Josephine Blumenfeld's descriptive article, which Fryn included in the early pages, there is nothing more about its human inmates. It is a beguilingly reticent book, in which the animals – all strays except the goldfish – are allowed to take the stage throughout. The heroine is Mistinguette, that strange wild kitten, so gay and dauntless, who would go mad in the drawing-room after dinner and leap from one piece of furniture to another uttering little cries. The 'hero' had been picked up by the police and would be destroyed if a home could not be found; a large dog of a deep tan shading to black, slender delicate legs, and beautiful appealing eyes, Valentin proved to be mis-cast and had to be re-named Valentine. Valentine and Mistinguette enriched the population at about the same time, and it is around the lives and fortunes of their descendants that the tale revolves. The gift of several goldfish in a glass jar was let loose in the fountain in the garden and named after King Mindoon, Supaya-lat, Thibaw, and others of the Court of the Golden Palace at Mandalay, and there was a small brownish one called Fanny. The true heroes arrived later: Michlum, a mongrel dog, gave the appearance, like a waiter, of being in evening-dress in the day-time, which added an indescribable vulgarity to his appearance. He constituted himself tutor to Pataud, Valentine's vast puppy. But whereas Michlum was a charmer, Pataud was a grand dog, the greatest watch-dog imaginable, and both were to die by the hand of man. 'Man alone creates works of art. In building, birds, beasts and insects have skill and knowledge – witness the artificial mounds of the Magapodes, the dam of the beaver and the high red castles of the ant. But awareness of beauty and the conscious creation of it are the flowering of the troubled soul of man. Yet a man killed our animals, who were so beautiful. "Who knoweth the spirit of man that goeth upward, and the spirit of the beast that goeth downwards to the earth".' Who indeed?

According to Fryn, she wrote her books in an atmosphere of companionable high spirits, coming straight from her workroom, be the matter never so grim, to laugh and talk and enjoy her leisure. Leaving behind her the jottings from which she had dictated, she relaxed as if she had no care in the world other than to amuse. That is how she saw herself and how she often was. Tottie, on the other hand, never dictated. Scowling morosely, inward-looking, he handed over his tiny note-book, filled to the edges with the faint scratches he had written against the palm of his hand, and waited in the doldrums to have the typescript of his friskiest dialogue in front of him, before his face could light up once more. 'He writes his comedies in a foul temper, while I toss off horrors with my sweetest smile,' Fryn boasted with some truth.

In 1935, Tottie was occuped with two plays. He was dramatizing the novel, *La Foire aux Vices* by Germaine Ramos, and he was for once enjoying the writing of a play, *These Mortals*, always his favourite though few mortal eyes have read or seen it. He wrote to Paris from Cap d'Ail: 'The main theme of *La Foire aux Vices* is that prostitution of the mind is infinitely worse than that of the body, and that if one has to choose between the latter and the cheap, lying, blackmail rife in certain political, financial and journalistic circles, then it is better to choose the more honest way. This play is getting on extremely slowly, but you will see from this resumé that what I want to concentrate on is integrity of mind.' He had transported his family to the South of France, from where he commuted to Paris, and he first took the Château Barlow at Eze in the Alpes Maritimes from August, but it was gloomy and Fryn found the walled town oppressive. 'We got out of it as soon as we could,' she wrote, 'to the banal joys of a white marble villa.'

Tiger was still with G.B. Stern, accompanying her and Willie Somerset Maugham and Gerald Haxton on a lecture tour of the States, and Noreen had brought Mack to Tottie, who needed a secretary with faultless French for *La Foire aux Vices*, just as she had produced Tiger for Fryn in 1930, saying: 'I've got the perfect secretary for you, darling!', and she was right both times. Mack was Marjorie McCall from the Cape, who had a teenage daughter, Bridget, at finishing-school. It was a strange routine they followed then, for Fryn was again suffering an eclipse, her mind clouded by the incalculable flaw that marred its wholesomeness. Every single day she would be driven in to Monte Carlo, to Dr Michaelov's surgery hung and covered in yellow satin; for a migraine injection, so she said. And Mack would while away the time having a flutter in the Casino, while May went incessantly to the library to change Fryn's bed-books; always an unhappy sign. And when Eric and Stella came to stay, Fryn was constantly getting him to drive down the precipitous hill to Monte Carlo to fetch the doctor to give her yet another injection, till Stella burst out: 'If anything happens to Eric on these awful night drives, I'll never speak to Fryn again.'

The house they had moved into was the Villa Primavera at Cap d'Ail, said to be where Mata Hari received her instructions from the Germans, with a front hall looking like the foyer of a cinema, all marble floors and columns, and with mosaics depicting scenes of slaughter and sacrifice. Fryn didn't like it any better than Eze, having not wanted to go to France anyway. But when Tottie chose a house he took it willy-nilly; he was, for all his powerful charm, the very model of headstrong wilfulness, though Fryn's will was the stronger, grinding slowly and exceeding small.

These Mortals was performed by the Repertory Players for one night, 8 December 1935, at the Aldwych Theatre, with a splendid cast headed by Basil Radford as Zeus. Isabel Jeans played Helen and Glen Byam Shaw played Paris. Heinemann published it in 1937, under the title *These Mortals*, *A Scrapbook of History*, by H.M. Harwood, from Notes by Homer and R.F. Gore-Browne. There is a preface which is not only funny at the fifth reading and the tenth reading, but positively valuable to all authors, producers, actors, generals and women. Robert Gore-Browne wrote of the play: 'It is a rationalization of the Trojan War, which was judged unsuitable to the general taste of the day. Its close contains the tolerant, smiling philosophy of the man and explains his partiality to it.' A letter to Tottie from Irene Brown the actress deplores his decision not to proceed with its production: '*How* I enjoyed it,' she wrote. 'What a pity if you discard it as an unpropitious time for doing it,' and the letter ends: 'you are so wise, so witty and so kind, and you know about everything and all of us.' *These Mortals* has been performed once more, produced by Peter Cotes at the People's Palace in 1950. The National Theatre considered it in 1973 and found it very enjoyable, but was deterred by the vast cast.

*   *   *

In his autobiography, John Cowper Powys observes that 'every time a living being gathers itself grimly together, and draws on its inmost vitality to be happy in spite of all, it is doing what our sturdy ancestors called "praying".' So it was with Fryn then and, leaving the marble palace without regret, once again astonishingly recovered, she and her entourage returned to Sandwich. They moved, complete with Mack and Noreen, into Manwood Court, a very grand house, Elizabethan and beautiful, before taking The Old Drum again. It was opposite Stella's and Eric's new house Ninepins, and Tottie and Eric, the latter as Laurence Kirk, collaborated on a play, *The Innocent Party*, which was produced in 1936 at the St James's, London, and also at Edinburgh.

Fryn had begun work on another novel, *Act of God*, the concept for which she had been absorbing in Eze and Cap d'Ail, but she turned her attention first to the light-hearted play, *Quarantine*, which she had written in 1922, between the two Burmese winters, and that too was produced in 1936, at the Comedy in London, with Edna Best and Owen Nares.

In the same year, Tottie wrote *Married Life Behind the Scenes*, in collaboration with Harold Dearden. Dr Harold Dearden was not only handsome, he was amusing company and he stammered, which somehow added to his qualities as a raconteur, for he handled it with such skill. In many respects his life ran parallel with Tottie's. He too came of a Lancashire cotton family. Born at Bolton, son of a cotton manufacturer, he too qualified as a doctor, served in the first world war as a Captain, and later turned his whole attention to writing. He too was an athlete with a great zest for life and an ironic sense of humour.

With Fryn he was equally in tune then, for he shared her love of animals and of humanity and a rare perception into sick and criminal minds. The wife of his youth had been a morphia addict and died from an infected needle, self-inflicted, and he had made a study of drug-takers and their psychology, of passionate interest to Fryn. A copy of his autobiography, *The Wind of Circumstance*, has a flyleaf inscription: 'To Fryn with love, this lowdown on her friend,' and in it he describes his young wife's addiction. Fryn confided in him.

Early in 1937, Tiger came on a visit to The Old Drum, and it was mutually understood that, when Mack departed for the Cape with her 'finished' product, Tiger should come back to Fryn; G.B. Stern having proved quite as demanding and without the lovable qualities.

Naturally Tiger saw Stella again, and she saw her as 'a deep one', much more than met the eye. 'She was a professional ingénue, you see, exquisitely made up for the part,' she recalled. 'But there was strength behind the mask, and it always sounded odd to me that she and Fryn should carry on their otherwise enlightened exchanges in baby-talk!'* Gudgeon to Gudgeon, they had a special brand of it, even simpler than the old double-inversion of the Myrtage: such as 'pandy' for hand, 'womby' for womb, and 'no moany, darling' to Tottie, or to Stella's old spaniel. They never grew out of it.

That summer, Tottie took a house at Lelant in Cornwall, and Primrose-née-Tregurtha came with her young daughter Betty Strick from Newlyn to act as cook and housemaid. Eagerly Primrose and Fryn talked of Tregaggins and swopped memories, Primrose reminding Fryn how 'you would all put on your gear after supper and go to the quarries in search of ghosts, and I remember when you all went to sell strawberries, dressed up as gipsies, and you pretending to be an imbecile and looking just like one! But they bought your strawberries off you all the same.'*

At Lelant, Fryn worked her quiet best with Mack, who used to drive the car, and people used to come and stay as of yore. Damit came, and Gilbert and Lucy Hair. Lucy was a convert to Catholicism as was Gilbert. She was also very pretty and a great flirt. She amused Tottie and doted upon him, displaying two enormous photographs, besides Gilbert's, on her dressing-table as on an altar – Pope John's and Tottie's. 'What a man!' she recollected admiringly, 'and what a brain! Fryn too, of course, but she was such a nutcase. I met her sister Stella there at Lelant, an enchanting person. She was everything Fryn should have been, but wasn't; the human and lovable version. But dear Fryn was generous beyond belief. When I became ill, she sent me down to Lelant again, hired a nurse which she knew I couldn't afford, and paid for everything. But she was too, too unpredictable!'†

When *Act of God* was with the publishers, Fryn and Tottie went up to London, and Tottie announced on their return; 'I've bought a house!' or words to that effect. Forthwith he set off for the Riviera with Fryn to stay with Gertie Miller, Countess of Dudley, and thereafter as guests on a yacht lying at Dubrovnik. A letter from Archie Batty to Stella gives some elucidation; Cut Mill had finally been relegated to the past:

* Moira Tighe in conversation with JC.
† Lucy Hair in conversation with JC.

'My dear Stella – I mean my *darling* Stella. In contradiction to the unflagging personal attention which the Harwoods are wont to give to their affairs, you may have heard that they are in the Adriatic at a time when they are selling one house and moving into another. By some inexplicable coincidence, that personal attention seems to have been lacking also at the time of the purchase of Cut Mill. For the Deeds, which are very numerous, stand in the names of F. Tennyson Jesse, F.T. Harwood, Fryniwyd Jesse, Mrs. H.M. Harwood and F. Tennyson Esq. Now, by my Power of Attorney – signed against the window of the Blue Train while the guard was blowing his whistle – I have to dispose of these Deeds to the purchaser of Cut Mill. But, owing to the diversity of nomenclature, I have first to go into open Court, and take oath to an Affidavit that all these are one and the same person, and that I can produce witnesses. Would you on oath be prepared to swear that Fryn was ever known as F. Tennyson Esq? Archie B.'

Cut Mill was bought by Percy Harry Thompson, better known to the music hall profession as Percy Honri of concertina fame. What it cost him was not given out, but the word went round that its previous owner had spent some £50,000 upon it.

Act of God was published in 1937 by Heinemann and by the Greystone Press, New York, bearing the inscription on the flyleaf: ' "Act of God is something which no reasonable man could expect." Lord Young'. A Tauchnitz edition appeared in 1938, and these early editions were all dedicated: 'For Peta Vaughan-Sawyer. August 31 1908 – August 30 1931.

> *She was so young and lovely when she went*
> *It seemed that youth and beauty too were spent:*
> *Yet, though she did but pause upon her way,*
> *Her beauty lives with us for all our day.'*

It is a novel about the miracle of Fraxinet, which was vouchsafed to man in the year of Our Lord 1929. Haut Fraxinet, a pure bare mountain, towered higher above the town than the town towered above the port, and there beside a spring the Mother of God appeared to two shepherd children. Miraculous cures began to take place, and eventually the Bishop at the assize town of Draginoules issued a Mandate authorizing Haut Fraxinet as a place for pilgrimages. A hideous basilica was built where the frail harebells had swayed.

But it is a dangerous thing to let a miracle loose upon the world, particularly one perpetrated by a vain and idle woman whose vanity led her to confess to her little fraud to a gathering of Oxford Groupers. *Act of God* tells of the indigenous fishermen of Port Fraxinet and the bronzed parasites who had made it their playground, and of Haut Fraxinet perched 'under the clear bell of Heaven'. It tells of the lives engulfed in spiritual confusion, and of the protagonists who had to deal with the distressing effects of the miracle: the learned and sensitive Curé; his agnostic friend, an English writer, who had spent many years sailing the Mediterranean; the worldly-wise Anglican Chaplain at the Port; and Monseigneur the Bishop at his Palace in Draginoules.

It was the Curé, 'a man who lived in the thought of God as a fish lives in the sea,' who proved most vulnerable to the cruel hoax. The writer's story, his beliefs and thoughts, are based firmly on Tottie's, and when the Tauchnitz edition appeared, one copy specially bound in yellow leather for him was inscribed: 'From Fryn, who knows more of act of man than act of God and who loves Tottie – to him.'

Hugh Walpole's was the first reaction. He wrote: 'What a beautiful, sincere, moving book. Surely your best! I am not with you in your conclusions. There is too much wonder in this little world for physical death to rob man of a longer continuance. And one love experience at least in my life has proved to me that some sort of immortality lies at the root, quietly and irremovably, of poor human nature. But that doesn't matter; the book is lovely. And the technique, wisdom, knowledge – wonderful.'

The *Freethinker* wrote: 'One occasionally comes across powerful and penetrating criticisms of current religious assumptions. A case in point is *Act of God*. Few who have read this scathing satire on Lourdes and Fatima are likely to forget it.' Professor Edwin Hubble, whose giant telescope had so enthralled Fryn, was her authority on the handling of the expanding universe, as it was experienced by a small yacht in a great storm in the Mediterranean. Hence the new dedication: 'To Grace and Edwin Hubble, with love and thanks,' when the book was published by The Thinker's Library in 1940.

The house that Tottie had bought was in St John's Wood, in the north west of London. It was number eleven in a short cul-de-sac, Melina Place, and it was called Pear Tree Cottage for the proper reason. Fryn spent the last months of 1937 running up to London from Lelant to oversee the preparations for her final move; for without doubt this home-making must be for ever. All these years past she had not seen any of the chattels she had collected with such joy. They had been dumped here and there when Sabi Pas and the flat in Adelphi Terrace had been summarily vacated. Hollywood and its aftermath lay between. Succeeding tenants had made nonsense of the Cut Mill inventories. Precious pieces had been lost for ever, Nefertiti's beautiful head among them. But gradually a mountain of 'junk' converged upon the house in Melina Place.

Pear Tree Cottage was a back-to-back, so that from the narrow pavement running alongside its outer wall it looked only the width of one triple-windowed room, but when the arched wrought-iron gate linking that wall to the garage was breached, a series of windows and doors stretched away on the left-hand side, facing upon the garden enclosed and ending in a covered loggia among trees. Six rooms stood flat upon the ground, four rested upon them, and two capped the low pyramid, so that at each end of each floor was an expanse of flat roof with a low coping. The house was generously proportioned for all its compact design, and the face of the outside walls had been painted rose-pink. Fryn had mixed the shade herself and planned the lay-out of the garden, the fountain, and the green-painted flower-boxes, to adorn the flat roofs in season alternately with daffodils and trailing pink geraniums.

Their wisdom of choice in settling on this spot only became apparent after the event, when unsuspected charms emerged. For a start, and for all, there was the blessing of possessing no guest-room; and there was the blessing of living in one place instead of in two or three. Tottie's clubs, the Bath and the Garrick, were near enough; his friends Robert and Margaret Gore-Browne were nearer still, in Hamilton Terrace; while his play-pen was just round the corner at Lords. Then, Rosie Headfort née Boote, Marchioness of Headfort, long dear to Fryn and a regular front-row companion at first nights, lived no distance away in Elsworthy Road; while in St John's Wood village was Cochrane Street, the site of the manger-studio of delightful memory for Fryn, where Clare Collas had put her up while *The Milky Way* came into being. A stone's throw towards Maida Vale, she and May had first met in Winnie's flat and had there plighted their troth. Thus this bond was shared by May who, terrified of the new in all its forms, drew comfort from the familiar pavements. She found too a vicarious pleasure in living unsmirched in what might almost be called a red-light district, for this corner of St John's Wood was

supposed to have sheltered many a 'soiled dove'. It became her pride
that she had lived in three famous houses, or houses of famous
women: the house in which D.H. Lawrence had placed Lady
Chatterley at Eastwood, which was that of May's final nurse-maid
post before joining Winnie in London; the Villa Primavera at Cap
d'Ail, where Mata Hari had received her orders; and Pear Tree
Cottage, in which Mrs Fitzherbert was said to have received her royal
protector.

Incidentally, it was a perennial puzzle to Fryn how those billowing
skirts could have been manoeuvred up and down the prettily carved
and spirally curved staircase, but this was a myth she was willing to
accept. She had written to Edmund Lester Pearson, in praise of his
treatment of *The Trial of Lizzie Borden*, in his introduction to that
case for the first American version of a Notable Trials series. Lizzie
Borden had served a breakfast of mutton stew, and she had then
murdered her mother and father with an axe, and these two circumstances appealed equally to the macabre in Fryn. She had added: 'We
have found a lovely little house, in a cul-de-sac and beautifully quiet.
It used to belong to Mrs Fitzherbert and it has the original panelling
and an exquisite staircase.' To her publisher she described the new
abode: 'From the outside it looks like a cottage in the South of France,
as it is painted bright pink with veridian green casements, and has a
walled garden with a goldfish pool and a fountain which plays in the
middle of it. This part of St John's Wood was a pear orchard when the
Prince Regent built the cottages there to be hunting-boxes, while he
hunted in Regent's Park as Prince Florizel.'

According to legend again, before Fryn took possession of it the
house had been occupied by Mrs Theodore Wessel, née Jessie
Smither. She was formerly Lady Churston, married to Richard
Francis Roger Yarde-Buller, 3rd Baron Churston, and was later to
become the Duchess of Leinster. She had numerous lovely daughters
by her first marriage, the Yarde-Buller girls. There was Denise, and
Lydia, and Primrose, each of whom made fairy-tale marriages, and
there was Joan, who once married Aly Khan and became the mother
of the young Aga. The legend went that Aly Khan had sometimes
occupied the narrow rear apartment of the garage at Pear Tree
Cottage while paying his court, and the chilly cell came to be known
in the Harwood family as 'Aly Khan's bedroom', though it held
nothing more intimate than the garden chairs.

Fryn and Tottie had been prepared to take up residence in time for

Christmas, with fanfares, a great big Aga – the cooking variety – and two living-in maids. For the nonce it was May who foiled this plan. Normally in perfect health, though prone to blush, she got erysipelas or St Anthony's Fire, and was so ill she had to have day and night nurses. And Tottie, already staying at the Bath Club, got influenza and had to remain there. So Fryn made her entry unsung, and uncontaminated. But, swift upon the recovery of the invalids, there began 'the Year of the Parties'. It was almost Cut Mill over again, with forty guests to be served with champagne, Guinness and oysters in the long drawing-room. These evenings were attended by old friends as well as by new neighbours; by judges and prison-governors as well as by fans. And as the days grew warm, forty guests would be served in the garden with champagne, whole salmon and strawberries, and these lunches were for the delectation of Hollywood friends, and for all those who had shared their chances at the Ambassadors.

The family came: Stella and Eric of course; Aunt Margaret, now known to Fryn as Crossauntie; Maggie, and yes, even Mama. Edith brought all her ammunition to bear, when she arrived for lunch. She was driven by her chauffeur, escorted in on the arm of her nurse-friend, and her fragile hands were weighed down with rings. She discarded the delicacies carefully chosen to tempt her, and talked in her high whine about the Church and herself, and May found her a tiresome creature. It would have shocked Fryn immeasurably if she had ever imagined that they had traits in common. 'There was nothing of my mother's family in me,' was her boast. But when Edith came to Pear Tree Cottage she was an honoured guest, till the time came to summon the chauffeur from the loggia beyond the kitchen where his meal had been served.

Maggie had lately left her black-and-white house in Kent for a farm at Mayfield in Sussex. At Pear Tree Cottage, she sat and rubbed Fryn up the wrong way with consummate lack of finesse. Despite her devotion to Tottie, she had never scrupled to step heavily on Fryn's little feet. At the fish course she demanded: 'What *is* this, Fryn?' 'Langouste, Maggie dear,' said Fryn. 'Mongoose? Really, Fryn!' complained Maggie. But Fryn just smiled, disdaining any denial. She had a theory that deaf people did not want to hear; that while blind people took pains to see, deaf people were content to leave all effort to others.

As party followed party through the length of that glowing summer, Fryn reckoned that the Harwoods were back in circulation again. It was their twentieth together, and they and their house were featured in a series of Two-Career Marriages for the *Evening Standard*. 'I don't see that a wife's career need affect a husband's,' Tottie commented, 'unless she's a saxophone player and practises an awful lot.' – 'What matters is – just being good at marriage. Either you are or you aren't,' offered Fryn.

It was Munich that brought the party mood to an end. Fryn couldn't but sympathize with her little hairdresser's puzzlement after Chamberlain's speech: 'Peace in our time, Ma'am? Whose time does he mean? I'm seventeen and he's seventy.' But, for the time being there was a respite, and Fryn decided to use it while she could, in a way that was second nature to her. In March 1939 she went to Paris, and thence to the Trianon Palace in Versailles, with the authority of a *Daily Mail* reporter covering a multiple murder trial.

The trial of Eugen Weidmann was taking place at the court-house at Versailles, and Fryn had a seat on the floor of the court for the three weeks that it lasted. She went to see the villa, La Voulzie, where Weidmann had lived and killed in December 1937, and to the Forest of Fontainebleau where he had buried one of his six victims. And she invited Madeleine Masson – a family friend of Mack McCall in South Africa and now living in Paris – to help her with the case. Through her she met the novelist Colette, who was attending for *Paris Soir*.

The brilliant Swiss cartoonist, Géa Augsbourg, was sitting in court, dashing off drawings of the accused and their judges and defenders, and of Fryn and Madeleine. Fryn begged to see them, and he gave her his original cartoon of Weidmann in the dock, and his artist's proof of Paris en fête in lascivious enjoyment of this last public guillotining; a gross and graceless scene, depicted in a fine and graceful line. Later he made a drawing of Tottie, who joined them at the Trianon Palace. Fryn had never been vain about her looks but, as her sight called for increasingly strong lenses at work, she had grown shy of the camera or artist's tools. No Augsbourg drawing of her vulnerable face survives, but Madeleine's looks out unafraid from the pages of her autobiography: *I Never Kissed Paris Goodbye*.*

There was such excitement about the Weidmann trial that 'all Paris' was struggling to get in. The crowd ate oranges and never stopped talking. Dignified it was not, yet Fryn realized that the Prosecution was more than equitable to the accused – just *because* he was a

* *I Never Kissed Paris Goodbye*, Madeleine Masson, Hamish Hamilton, 1978.

German and every Frenchman knew that Germany was on the eve of attacking France once more. Her record of this trial was to form the high point of Fryn's next collection of true crime cases, but it's publication was inordinately delayed by the war, and four other books were to intervene before her *Comments on Cain* eventually came to the surface.

Part Four

—••⁌)⁌ ⁍••—

Winter

THIRTEEN

——•⊷ ⟨ ⟩ ⊷•——

A Tough Pair

FRYN HAD ALWAYS enjoyed writing letters, regarding it as one of her natural functions. At the German occupation of the Rhineland, she was quick to express her unease in this way to the press and to her friends. Upon Hitler's gobbling up of the Sudetenland from Czecho-slovakia, followed by the Prime Minister Neville Chamberlain's obstinate trust in the Munich agreement, she had rung the tocsin in a series of letters to America, originally addressed to Grace and Edwin Hubble, who had become enthralled. Before the march into Prague, Grace had been passing on these letters to their mutual friends Sonya and Carl Hovey and to the playwright Sam Behrman. By the time Stalin concluded the pact with Hitler to divide Poland, Sonya – as a screen writer for Metro-Goldwyn-Mayer – wrote clamouring for more such unblinkered reports, and Carl was so impressed by the style and content that the editor in him was aroused: 'Both of us were back to the old *Metropolitan Magazine* days emotionally, Fryn dar-ling, when a remarkable manuscript came to hand.' He offered to circulate instant copies of everything she cared to write, and that was the course afterwards followed. As Fryn told Sam Behrman, they would write their letters, 'I to the Hubbles and Hoveys and Tottie to you, with copies of each others.'

It happened to be a letter from Tottie of 29 August 1939 that set the pattern for the two-way correspondence that ensued. The tone was confident and frankly bellicose, as this excerpt shows:

'Here we are, waiting for the bell. The fact is that for 150 years the Germans have been a cancer in the world, and it is time they were removed. The people they are up against are not international bankers, anxious still to look on Germany as a potential customer; they are the descendants of those who cut off King Charles's head, and who have been out of business now for 300 years. When the bell rings we want to be our own time-keeper and referee.

Our chief asset in my opinion is Hitler. Why it should be considered a sign of greatness to have turned an industrious people, with a record of scientific and technical achievements, into a mob of lunatics, I do not know. He happened to find himself up against those who were afraid of a bully, and who could apparently not recognize epilepsy when they saw it. If – which Heaven forbid! – there is to be a treaty of any kind, it should be signed on Mr Hitler's coffin, and should be such that his memory will stink as much as his body. Yours T.'

Distrustful of the current policy of appeasement, anglophile Americans were immensely cheered by this rallying-cry. The Hubble-Hovey correspondence spread to the playwright John Balderston and Marion his wife, who wrote: 'Your letters, lent us by the Hubbles, seem to have come from another world.' Then Sam Behrman began to pass his copy on to Alexander Woollcott, and these were the eight who took it upon themselves to write the answers.

Since the first week of January 1939, Fryn had been entertaining five or six Jewish refugees from Austria to lunch every week, wanting to show how welcome were these victims, and she wrote:

'No further harrying of Jews must be allowed. We are now waiting for our dear old friend the frightfulness to begin, but you would laugh if you saw our precautions. We have three buckets of sand and two of water – to the deep confusion of our animals – and we hang an eiderdown over the window to save us from splinters.

A very kind and beautiful friend has lent us her radio for the duration. And I, the least mechanical-minded of human beings, spend my time sitting on the floor, twiddling three buttons whose relation to each other is interdependent yet dependent like the Trinity, and when I do anything wrong, a round green light with a red centre pulsates in a rather rude way and sudden roars and screams come out at me in every language of the earth. Cathleen Nesbitt, the actress, was here to tea with me, having been lunching with a newspaper editor who believes apparently that the secret weapon is to be a gas which will make everyone deaf and dumb. Alarmed at this – for what should I do if I were deaf and dumb? – I appealed to Tottie, who merely remarked that he could think of no better way to ensure peace in the world. And, talking of deaf and dumb, the ARP inform us that it is important during an aerial bombardment to sit with a cork in your mouth, as the blast may snap your jaws to, and then not only may your tongue be cut off, but your ear-drums are blown in! I intend to practise talking round a cork.'

To these early letters, Sam Behrman reacted:

> 'I can't tell you how people like myself feel here: the most painful sensation it is possible to have – impotent rage. We feel that this fight is our fight as much as yours; that you are bearing the brunt of it and yet we are even cavilling about sending you supplies. Your letters made a sensation. Alfred Lunt wants to read excerpts at every performance before the curtain.'

Sam had also passed the word to Haggerty of the *New York Times* and to George Backer of the *New York Evening Post*. Soon, other groups of interested people were attending regular readings, and were among those who later formed the kernel of a great variety of relief organizations and action groups of many and far-reaching kinds.

After lamenting the loss of the *Royal Oak*, and Poland's fate, Fryn poured scorn on Hitler's speech from the Beer Cellar. Needless to say, her letters were not solemn; she mocked, or rejoiced, or scolded in turn. Then cosily she reported a private murder:

> 'A charming incident occurred after the death sentence, when the two condemned men turned to leave the dock. One of the police officers, with a scandalized face, pointed sternly to the floor, and meekly the two rapers and murderers stooped to pick up their gas-masks. I presume that, even in England, with our respect for authority, they will not have to take them to the scaffold.'

Tottie's services had been refused by the War Office; 'too old' was what they said. So he had walked round to the neighbouring hospital, St John's and St Elizabeth's which had been fitted up as a Casualty Clearing Station, and had signed on for duty during air-raid warnings. Typical was his comment upon Finland's stand against Russia:

> 'The war seems to be developing along the lines of Midshipman Easy's triangular duel, when one of the parties was finally shot in the backside by someone with whom he had no quarrel at all: if Sweden helps Finland, does Germany attack Sweden, and does that constitute a Russo-German alliance?'

and Sam wrote: 'Your simply wonderful letters must certainly be made into a most eloquent, humorous and enlivening "War Book".'

Towards the end of May 1940, Fryn and Tiger were enrolled to act as interpreters at the railway stations, to meet and give tea and aid to train-loads of refugees, many of whom had been machine-gunned up and down the roads to the coast, and all of whom were exhausted from foot-slogging and lack of sleep. Once a carriage-full of young Belgian soldiers was disgorged, with enough spirit left to sing '*auprès de ma blonde.*'

Fair news or foul, the letters continued to make their way across the Atlantic, and always the undercurrent was indomitable. Throughout the events of that year – Poland, Finland, Denmark and Norway, Holland and Belgium, King Leopold's surrender, the *dégringolade* of France – their refrain was the only one that mattered: 'We are certain to win.' Upon the French surrender, Tottie wound up:

> 'And now dear Sam, we enter on a new, though probably not a final phase and, speaking for myself alone, I look forward to it without dismay. I have had explained to me with a wealth of detail exactly how an invasion of England is possible. I do not find them convincing.'

With this conclusion, Fryn passionately concurred:

> 'Great Britain is now the hope of the world and I do not think we shall fail. I cannot beat the big drum; my talent is too small, my inclination too faint and my taste too fastidious. But my capacity for sorrow, scorn and anger remains to make me a burning bush, even if we are left unsupported by other countries who say that our ideals are their ideals, and even it we are over-run by those nations whose ideals are in direct contradiction to our own. And so farewell, my dears, while we wait to know what else is going to happen.'

London Front, *Letters Written to America (August* 1939 *— July* 1940*)* by F. Tennyson Jesse and H.M. Harwood, with Answers from Marion Balderston, S.N. Behrman, Carl and Sonya Hovey, Grace Hubble and Alexander Woollcott, was published in 1940 by Constable, and by the Macmillan Company of Canada, and by Doubleday Doran of New York. It is dedicated: 'To our American Correspondents, to May and Tiger, and to One Another.' The Constable jacket depicts the dim shapes of innumerable barrage balloons floating over roof-tops in a lilac dusk.

Pamela Hansford Johnson, writing in *John o' London's Weekly*, found it 'an extraordinary feat. A feast of good reporting. No one who has lived through this terrible and miraculous year could fail to find it of vital interest.' From America, the *New Yorker* expressed the opinion that 'their letters have vigour, clarity, humour and elegance. They are a tough pair, these gentle writers. *London Front* is not all fire-eating and politics. The Harwoods, being hopelessly civilized, write of Cathedrals as well as bombings, pet cats as well as Dunkerque.'

Among the letters received is one from author and publisher Michael Sadleir, Director of Constable: 'I have read *London Front* almost at a sitting. It is an enthralling experience and will crystallize the feelings of thousands of your countrymen. The contrast between the man-written and woman-written letters continuously fascinated me. The *difference*, the amazing difference, between the male and female expressiveness gave the lie to all the modern chat about there being only a physical difference between men and women.' And, to Tottie: 'I trust the letters are being continued, and that we can have a second instalment this autumn at latest. Yours is an exceptional gift of pungent lucidity and my letter is a plea.'

It was a plea often repeated on both sides of the Atlantic. Fortunately, as Fryn mentions in her foreword to the second series: 'Letter-writing to those whom one knows and loves and who stimulate one intellectually is one of the best means of avoiding claustrophobia,' and one of her first sentences on picking up the tale in July 1940 was: 'Tottie is now Vice-Chairman of the Fine Spinners Association and has to go back and forth every week' to Manchester. Fryn and he had consequently been scouring the Cheshire countryside, in case they were impelled to live up there should the railway-lines be bombed. They went on to stay with friends in the beauty and peace of the Lake District, where their hostess, 'the most normal of human beings, with an admirably balanced mind', murmured as they picked peas and beans in the jewel-bright sunshine: 'We have no intention of living under a German occupancy. We should put the children out first and then ourselves.'

The occupation of the Channel Islands by Germany put Fryn in mind of her childhood days in St Peter Port's ancient streets:

'The glass-houses full of tomatoes, all the lovely lackadaisical old-fashioned island steaming with gossip like a tea-kettle, unaltered since the days of Edward VII, passed from freedom to tyranny with hardly a remark made in the London press, so much greater was the tragedy of France.'

By August, the Battle of Britain was going strong:

'The fate of the world is being settled in the air over England. Tremendous air battles, bombs, sirens are incessant and everyone is sick for want of sleep. This little house shakes like a loose tooth, but no worse than when Tottie walks across an upper floor,'

wrote Fryn. They were both raging that America was selling oil to Japan: 'Oil is the most powerful instrument of policy in the world today, and should never be in private hands,' protested Tottie. Then in the middle of August, he took over as Chairman of the Fine Cotton Spinners. He was still spending three days a week up in Manchester, confident that he never came across alarm or despondency among his 18,000 work people; still insisting that America was infinitely more use to us as an arsenal than as a combatant. He was asking for something else from them:

'The question is, how much is America sorry about Hitler? We are sorry ten million pounds a week. Of course if America doesn't really believe it is her war too, there's no reason why she should pay for it. It is for America to say whether she turns away, sorrowful, having great possessions.'

Friends marooned in London came to spend a night or two at Pear Tree Cottage. Angela Baddeley slept on Tottie's divan one night and Emlyn Williams the next. Wilfrid and Nancy Greene came for lunch and fetched Fryn and Tottie for a peaceful weekend in the most English of all countrysides, that part of Surrey stretching away from Leith Hill to the sea. Wilfrid had been appointed Master of the Rolls in 1937:

'A sweetie-pie, so clever and so simple, like Edwin Hubble', wrote Fryn. Indignantly she added: 'And now has come this frightful thrust, aimed at England's heart; but they don't know what terrific blows England's heart can take and still go on beating.' Lunching in the garden of Pear Tree Cottage in the divine September weather, despite the incendiary bomb that had landed the week before, Tottie rejoiced: 'I shall always remember this summer for the raspberries and the lettuces', which Fryn capped with: 'You'll be damned lucky if you remember this summer at all.' And when Lord Greene said that he thought Hitler couldn't any longer afford not to have an invasion, she countered that neither could he afford to have one; and when

Wavell took Benghazi she said longingly, Tottie's hands in hers: 'Darling, you know I love you, but how I *wish* I was Lady Wavell!'

In October, the railway journeys having become too unreliable, they all four moved into a house fifteen miles from Manchester, and Fryn told Grace:

'We have got the most enchanting puppy, who has made the whole house feel alive. A house always feels dead without children or animals. He is a miniature French poodle puppy, and we got him cheap because he was born without a tail. He is silver grey, with soft silky curls. He has a glistening blackberry of a nose and two glistening black eyes which make a perfect three-point landing in his face. He is a loving little creature and we have called him "Brother".'

The big house in the garden next door to Pear Tree Cottage had been hit by a Molotov Cocktail and gutted, but it didn't prevent Fryn from harbouring the notion that she would go up and spend a night or two, popping in and out of shelters in London's West End, 'so that I can write about it better.' The letters themselves were therapeutic for her, often transmuting bad news into good cheer:

'One good thing the Germans have done is to open up St Paul's Cathedral; at last it may be in a setting worthy of it, green lawns and fountains playing. Amongst the blackened walls, it stands beautiful and triumphant, and so do the spires of the Wren churches that, lit by pale moonlight, spring like white lilies.'

Invasion date had come and gone when Fryn took train for London with Tiger. There were three air-raids during the journey and the train crawled. When they reached the entry to Melina Place they found it roped off, a bomb having landed plonk in the mainroad beside it. Another raid had begun when they set out, hungry and tired, after dumping their luggage. London's new troglodytes were calmly lugging rolls of bedding here and there, making their preparations for the night. The will of the people had taken over the underground railways and Fryn wrote:

'The sirens wailed like infernal dogs baying the moon, mingled with the strophe and antistrophe of bombs and guns, the whistles of wardens, the tap-rap of running feet. The bright moon was riding high. It seems absurd one can't put out the moon on such occasions. The bombers came back and back like swarms of jungle bees. At every brutish blast rang the now soundless chimes of Westminster and Paul's. We saw a notice saying "Air Raid Shelter" and in we went.'

It led down some steps into what proved to be the basement of *Punch*. Old bundles of the publication formed platforms for bedding and there, crowded together with young and old, they spent a night of almost continuous bombardment:

'till at last the All Clear sounded, triumphant as the crowing of a celestial rooster. We all streamed up and out into the early morning light after twelve hours of darkness and danger, crumpled and shabby and tired-looking, a job lot of human beings, crunching over the broken glass that lay thick in the streets. And as we walked through the ruined Temple, bombed that night, Tiger and I could have wept for what once was one of the beauties of London, were it not that everyone in the streets was smiling at us and at each other.'

Back at Pear Tree Cottage, after a bath in Eva Reading's apartment at the Dorchester and a breakfast there of bacon and eggs, Fryn wondered what her feelings would be like if this cottage were destroyed? It contained the library of a life-time and lovely old bits of furniture which had taken years to pick up. Would she feel that sense of being new-born that one used to have in one's youth when one went to confession and received absolution? Or would the little bit of one's heart that was not engaged in this struggle be broken? Eight years in hotels and other people's houses had hurt so much that probably one would just shrug.

Up in Manchester, Tottie was anxious to test a vitamin scheme on his work people in various mills. He believed that vitamin feeding in the form of synthetics and concentrates could guarantee the people of this country against starvation even if no foodstuffs were to arrive for six months, and he wrote: 'The next generation would be free from a number of old-fashioned diseases, particularly if everyone also ate less.'

He advocated communal feeding instead of subsidies to deal with inflation also:

'Large-scale inflation never rested on an uncontrolled demand for caviare and diamonds. If every member of the community is assured of shelter, food and reasonable clothing, as they are in the services, you can safely leave the prices of other things to sky-rocket as they will. Sooner or later, the Government will have to assume responsibility for a standard of life for everyone. This is the time to do it. A standard of life sufficient for health is as much a public need as air and water.'

John Balderston had become a member of the White Committee, a pressure group working for increasing aid to Britain since the collapse of France, and a cable had arrived from him: 'Shipping you shortly as gift for Cotton Spinners vitamin tablets sufficient thousand men two months. No import permit needed.' The permit had been waived when Marion Balderston's War Relief Organization volunteered to undertake the shipping as medical relief stores, so cutting red tape as well as cost. The experiments were under way even while the manu-script of the second series of letters, covering the second year of war, was being got ready for press.

But there was one more long letter from Fryn, concentrating in itself everything that needed to be said to America and culminating in:

'It is what we are fighting against and not what we are fighting for that matters most. But if Americans want to know what we are fighting for, they only have to read history, both ancient and modern. If it comes to that, they have only got to read their own history. We are fighting for what the Americans fought for in the War of Independence, but we are fighting for it not only for ourselves but for the whole world. I am not good at propaganda. I hate the drumming up of the emotions to move people by their tear-ducts when they cannot be moved by their brains. If your brains are stirred by anger, pity, hatred – well and good. Anger is one of the finest of the emotions when it is directed by the intellect. A sick rage against cruelty and injustice, a hard cold determination that as far as it lies in our power the elevation of cruelty and injustice to the status of a creed must cease, is good enough for us, as it was good enough for the Poles and Greeks, the Czechs and the Jugoslavs. No slogans are needed. America is suffering from what we were suffering from – we too were too late starting. It's name is lack of imagination.'

This was her clarion call; still without dismay, but shriller.

The second series of *Letters Written to America (July* 1940 *—June* 1941*)* was published by Constable and by the Macmillan Company of Canada. It's title, *While London Burns*, was 'stolen' from Alexander Woollcott's own *While Rome Burns*, and the jacket shows the sil-houette of St Paul's, black against a conflagration. Unfortunately, owing to difficulties of production, it was a whole year after com-pletion that the book appeared, in June 1942.

The next day, a post-card arrived from one Sydney Horler: 'Dear

Madam – On the principle that a cat may look at a King – or a Queen – let me say that I think your last letter in *While London Burns* deserves to live for a hundred years.' Alan Dent's review in *John o' London's Weekly* praised 'the high political awareness, logic, humanity, honesty and Englishness in its most commonsensical sense, and the prevailing selflessness and clarity.' One critic thought fit to point out that the writers were not as interesting to the world as they were to each other, which Fryn gracefully acknowledged to be true.

Again there were appeals for a follow-up volume, but both collaborators had more pressing work in hand: Tottie's involvement in the cotton industry was increasing, as war materials using cotton-based ingredients were processed at the mills; while, to his indignation, Fryn had undertaken to write about the adventures of a burning oil-tanker *San Demetrio*, and her eagerness to do justice to her favourite service, the Merchant Navy, had made her spare herself nothing. In a letter to her at the beginning of 1942, Tottie had written crossly:

'I woke about 8. White frost and very cold. I thought of you struggling up for your bloody train – on one pat of butter – and loathed the whole idea of this job. I don't believe half of all this travelling is necessary. What they want is the writing and imagination. *Any* one can give the facts, which in any case no one is going to read about. You ought to be at home with a good fire, doing your own stuff. There! Anyhow, make it clear to them that there must be no more going to sea during the winter. You will gather that I am in rather a bad temper. I am. I hate your being away on what seems to me to be a bit of wild-goosery.'

During her absence to interview members of the tanker's crew, he had spent some days with his sister Alice in the Lake District, whence he wrote to Fryn:

'I'm just off to Hawkshead, to one of those beautiful shows where you poke beasts and where dogs and children run races. I could have easily stayed in bed all day, for I feel remarkably tired. But it is a glorious day and I look forward to seeing Hawkshead after many years. This is where my mother is buried – 50 years ago.
'I was glad to hear you had had such a long sleep. If only we could find a 24-hour narcotic, all would be well. It is beautifully still outside. I wish you were here.'

Though Fryn had no cause to love it, Lake Windermere appears to have been a sanctuary for them all from the stresses of the Manchester front, as May and Madeline too used to take their war-time holidays there.

The house near Manchester which Tottie had rented furnished from September 1940 was called Parteen. It was on the outskirts of Prestbury, and Prestbury lies sweetly in the Cheshire countryside, of all that county's villages surely the most beautiful, and full of stories heroic or macabre that should have made Fryn rejoice. Its name means The Priests' Town, and the remains of a Saxon cross in the churchyard commemorates the coming of the first community of missionary priests. The broad main-street is lined with trees and with white-painted inns, shops and dwelling-houses each more charming than the last. The River Bollin tears along under a humped bridge where the road narrows and bends sharply at the Bridge Inn, where Fryn often took people to lunch.

Half a mile along a switch-backed lane, and festooned over the hill across the road from Parteen, was the golf-course where Tottie and Tiger played whenever they could snatch an opportunity. The garden was ample, with a sweep of lawn stretching to a green valley and with an array of fruiting trees. And, though Fryn called it 'a little hired villa', the house was ample too. There was a clause in the lease enabling the owner to return when his service with the RAF expired, and vice versa in favour of the tenant. Everything about the place was eminently suitable and Fryn hated it. The north country was not her element and north country people were not her chosen people; she found their manners and their speech quite without finesse. On the other hand, it transpired that they did like to make a fuss of celebrities in their midst, particularly such generous spenders.

Generous spenders they were, and could afford to be. As head of Richard Harwood and Son of the Brownlow Fold Mills in Bolton, Harold Marsh Harwood had earned a reputation as a first-class man of business, having a remarkable rapport with work people and an effortless grasp of the financial side. When the various cotton interests had combined to form the Association of Fine Spinners & Doublers, and he was invited to become their Chairman, the industry was progressively turning its output towards the war effort, making barrage balloons and collapsible life-rafts and luminous ropes for the British Navy. It was no small responsibility for a man over the usual age of retirement, but Tottie took it in his stride.

They were handsomely treated from the start, by the County and by the tradesmen. Mr Marley, the 'big' grocer, would offer May unheard-of luxuries: a basket of cherries here, a bundle of asparagus there. And from the home-made cake-shop called The Bollin Café, right through the trials of rationing, the cakes were delectable. Shamefully, May had another friend in the fishmonger, who even took something off the hospital-basket to tempt the tiny appetite of Fryn.

Early in July 1941, Fryn got a wire from her friend Virginia Vernon, MBE, Légion d'Honneur, and some-time journalist. Virginia was energetically involved in the running of Basil Dean's ENSA Company, the Entertainments National Service Association, one of whose fringe tasks was accommodating artistes on tour. The telegram asked if eight people could be put up at Prestbury that night: Basil Dean and Gracie Fields with her musical director, manager and so on. Gracie was on her way to her home-town Rochdale for the first in a series of a hundred concerts, and wanted peace and quiet. Though Fryn had been lying in her bath when the message came, 'Mama-fix-it' arranged it all in half an hour. Instead of all going to the big Manchester hotels, Basil Dean – Founder and Director of the organization – stayed at Parteen; Gracie and her maid Mary next door; and the rest of the Company and their chauffeur were deployed nearby. The proprietress of The Bollin Café sent up a chocolate cake, decorated with Union Jacks, for Gracie, photographed sitting between Fryn and Tottie on their rose-covered verandah.

On 9 December 1941, a year or so after the household had moved north, Edith had died at the age of seventy-five. The funds under her marriage settlement of 1886, augmented by a proportion of the Henry James Will Trust, became equally divisible between her two surviving children, after payment of death duties. When probate of the will was granted, a letter from Eric to Tottie read: 'I am writing to you about your wife's inheritance, because I am told she is not very brainy about such things.' Fryn and Tottie were sitting up in bed together at Parteen, and a moment later Tottie's eyebrows arched in surprise. 'She's an heiress,' he chuckled. 'Twenty thousand pounds each, she and Stella have got!'

Stella had been living as a service wife in RAF quarters in Worcester, while Eric was serving in an administrative capacity as a wing commander. He was still only in his forties. A London posting coming up for him in March 1942 prompted Stella to suggest their visiting Fryn in Prestbury first.

As soon as they arrived, Fryn thought she saw the shadow of death in Stella's face; she was coughing a wispy soprano cough. 'What are you doing about it, darling Gudge?' she asked. But Stella pooh-poohed the little cough and said it was nothing. Unconvinced, Fryn sent for her trusted Macclesfield doctor, who diagnosed cancer of the lungs and privately warned Tottie, who had reached the same conjecture. Between them and the dumbfounded Eric it was decided to mislay the X-rays, so as to leave Stella a breathing-space while plans were made for the time she had left. The prognosis was that she had scarcely three months.

Fryn had been showing ominous symptoms of morbid preoccupation with the past, but in this crisis she became quiet and decisive. While Stella seemed to be blithely unconscious of the nature of her illness she was left so, and Fryn proposed that she should move into Pear Tree Cottage, with Eric and Aunt Margaret, and May should go ahead to prepare it. A second check at St John's and St Elizabeth's Hospital left no doubts as to Stella's condition, and when May called there daily for tea, and found the patient as full of fun as ever, she was achingly reminded of how often they had comforted each other in days past, when it was Fryn's life that was thought to be hanging by a thread. Dumbly, she saw the threesome into their fragrant house and went back to Prestbury disconsolate.

At Melina Place, Stella at first spent many an afternoon in the garden, dozing or chatting with the others, spinning absurd plans for an impossible future. After a month or so, visibly growing haggard, she could only manage an occasional hour outside, the gentle May sunshine falling on the day-bed retrieved from 'Aly Khan's bedroom'. Soon she was lying all day on the curved-backed sofa in the drawing-room. It was an ideal place to live or die in, this long room looking out upon the fountain and the creepered wall behind it. At the far end, it opened into a small square chamber where her bed lay, with its adjoining *cabinet de toilette* customarily used for arranging flowers.

Often Fryn took the train to London with Tiger and stayed at the Dorchester, whence she came by taxi each day to be with Stella. Fryn's spirit never seemed to flag, even when Aunt Margaret grumbled that she was wearing Stella out. She thought only of how to tend the light in her darling's brilliant eyes. Their murmuring voices would grow serious, then cease while Stella rested, then chime out again in delighted unison as Stella stammered some nonsense or other in baby-talk, irrepressibly gay in her weakness. And when she came to make her exit as the three months were up, no hint of distress beyond the paroxysms of coughing had shadowed her face.

Stella died on 17 June 1942 and, when Fryn went back to Prestbury with Tiger, everyone was relieved at how well she had taken it. Stella's death had preceded the final settlement of Edith's will, and her share would pass to Eric, who stayed on with Aunt Margaret at Pear Tree Cottage.

Before the calamity which had befallen Stella, Fryn had begun writing poetry again, including several war poems which were published in the *Observer*. She had also been preparing a book about Burma for the Ministry of Information, and her knowledge had been enriched by sitting at the feet of Godfrey Harvey, J.O.P. Bland and other oriental experts. It was obvious to her when France fell that Japan would strike at Burma through French Indo-China, and that Burma would become front-page news, and she went to see the Prime Minister, U Saw, in London. By degrees her Burma project had expanded, though the work had naturally suffered during Stella's illness and from a listlessness into which she had fallen on learning of the death of Penrose Tennyson in July 1942.

The two elder sons of her cousin Charles Tennyson had joined up and had gone through their Officer training at the same time. Penrose, born in 1912 and married to the young actress Nova Pilbeam in 1939, had already shown great promise as a film director, working with Michael Balcon and Alfred Hitchcock; when *Convoy*, his big naval film with Ealing Studios, had opened in 1941, he had made his mark. Julian, born in 1915 and married in 1937 to Yvonne le Cornu, had written the entrancing *Suffolk Scene* and much poetry, had fathered twins, and had just managed to land a salaried job on the staff of the *Geographical Magazine*. Both then got their commissions, Julian in the Oxford and Bucks Light Infantry in charge of the mortar platoon, and Penrose with an anti-submarine trawler, from which he was speedily filched by the Admiralty to write film scripts and run their instruction film unit. Returning from Scapa Flow, where he had been shooting films for the unit, the Fleet Air Arm plane crashed into a mountainside and he was killed instantly.

Outwardly, this accident rocked Fryn as Stella's death had not, dissolving the armour she had donned to protect herself and Stella. Somehow she had found the strength to pursue her work in hand for the Government, but by the time her book about the tanker was launched she was skinless.

The Saga of San Demetrio was prepared for the Ministry of War Transport by the Ministry of Information, and was published in 1942 by His Majesty's Stationery Office and by Alfred A. Knopf of New York. It was reprinted by HMSO in 1943 as The Book of the Film, when this had been made for Ealing Studios. The book set out to tell how an oil-tanker had been among the thirty-eight ships convoyed by the *Jervis Bay*, an armed merchant liner which had engaged the enemy enabling most of her convoy to escape. Shelled and set on fire by an enemy pocket battleship, the MV *San Demetrio* had to be abandoned. Later, a handful of her crew, adrift in a lifeboat, found the blazing tanker again, boarded her, put out the fires, got the engines going, and brought her home across the Atlantic. The salvage case that ensued was as remarkable as the feat of heroism and seamanship. The sixteen survivors, exposed and exhausted, on a diet of potatoes and onions, had made the derelict hulk shipshape. Still in danger of explosion for days and nights, she had reached the Clyde and was moored by the tired but proud survivors, to discharge her cargo with her own plant.

In the event, Tottie was wrong in thinking that nobody would want to read the little book. 'I get practically nothing for writing it,' Fryn told the people at Ealing Studios. 'The trouble is I love doing it and love meeting the seamen, and it would break my heart if anybody else was doing it. Seamen need a lot of entertaining and a lot of alcoholic refreshment to get them to talk. Then they are your friends for life. The skipper of *San Demetrio* got it into his head I was called Skiffington, John. Now, when he lands and comes to see me, there is a roar of: "Hulloa, Skiffington. Got a kiss for me?".'

The credits for the screen play *San Demetrio London* read: 'Robert Hamer and Charles Frend from the official account by F. Tennyson Jesse.' Fryn was with Robert Hamer, on a sister ship off Cardiff, while he was taking shots for the film of her saga, and a letter from him in March 1943 says: 'Thank you for the nice things you say about the film script, but please don't minimize your own great share in what has been for us a most happy collaboration. I hear the rocking platform on which most of our sets will be built provides a movement so realistic that everybody is seasick.'

Ironically, of all Fryn's novels and stories, this spare tale was the first to be filmed. From childhood, the idea of eternity had appalled her; the stress her mother had laid upon Everlasting Life having too often kept her awake at night. *The Milky Way* and *San Demetrio* excluded, she showed a strong predilection for ending the lives of the characters she created in death. Her novels carry their doom remorselessly within them, catching the breath from the very first pages. Had Tom Fool been allowed to forfeit his soul's glory in braving the waterspout to quench his burning ship, it would have been another story.

A mood of aggressive fractiousness was making Fryn more than ever impatient of religious or spiritual props. Work alone had helped her. So that when Cicely Luck wrote lovingly to her 'what life must be for you now without the endearing sweetness of Stella', and of the spiritual help the Oxford Group had given her, she had replied to her cousin: 'Naturally I am horrified about Buckmanism, as I am always horrified about anything without any intelligence content. How anyone who has read comparative religions can imagine that there has been one authoritative revelation passes my comprehension. I say this with more feeling at the moment, as I have been delving into Buddhism, which makes Christianity look quite a *parvenu*. This doesn't prevent my recognizing that Christ was the greatest of the sons of man, just as Buddha was the best man for the Far East. But Buckmanism is to me just funny. I still think it is better, prouder, and more worth while to do good for man's sake, and not for anything that may happen afterwards. As to personal immortality, it is obvious that it is man's intense egoistic credence which has invented it in every religion. Yet I am glad you have found something that is some good to you. This war is a bore. It has gone on too long.'

The well-being which had come to be accepted as the norm, since coming to Pear Tree Cottage, was slipping away from her. Tiger had volunteered for the WRNS, then under Lady Louis Mountbatten, and at this juncture her papers came through. Away she went, and a chain of temporary secretaries took her place. 'I've had so many secretaries that I have to keep one simply to write to all the others!' was Fryn's plaint. But Mack McCall was not among these. She had allayed boredom by whiling away her child's schooldays in Fryn's company, and when she had left Lelant it was to go home with

Bridget to the Cape. There, mother and daughter had been enrolled for war work, and there Bridget had met Captain Harry Frederick Oppenheimer, on leave in Cape Town. He was the son of Mack's great friend, the second wife of Sir Ernest Oppenheimer of Johannesburg, and he and Bridget married in March 1943. Mack, however, did not lose touch with Fryn, leave after leave returning for visits as surely as a homing pigeon.

Deprived of familiar support and continuity, Fryn took to writing articles. She had been writing for the *Manchester Guardian* for twenty years and they had published anything she offered, for she had an eye that could pierce the humdrum to what of beauty, or terror, or comedy lay behind. Among a series on wartime topics, she sent them a ludicrously funny column about the rationalization of the milk round, called 'Lord Woolton's Waterloo', which appeared in 1943.

Then on 22 March 1943 she wrote these lines, addressed to Tottie in pencil on Savoy Hotel notepaper, and on the back of the envelope was scribbled: 'And I'll never write better!:*

THUS LOVE ITSELF REMAINETH

Delicacy of love approacheth
Heart to heart,
Lightly love approacheth
That can break a heart.

Ecstasy of love astoundeth
Flesh to flesh,
Sweetness of love astoundeth
Heart to heart.

Bitterness of love reproacheth
Taunt to taunt
Despair of love reproacheth
Heart hating heart.

Anguish of love remaineth
Soul to soul,
Thus love itself remaineth
Till life depart. FTJ to HMH

* *The Compass and Other Poems*, William Hodge & Company, 1951.

On that visit to London, she had been to see Ethel Vaughan-Sawyer again. For it seemed that, in a corner of her consciousness, there was a mournful urge to eclipse Stella's cancer and Stella's death, and no amount of reassurance from Ethel could convince her for long to the contrary. She had entered a nursing-home and, left in the dark, Tottie had followed her, anxious for her physical and mental state. He saw both Ethel and Dr Jock Mackenzie, their St John's Wood GP, but wisely kept what they told him to himself: there was no sign of malignancy, but a total hysterectomy was advisable nevertheless. A sad little comedy followed, in which, nursing the perenniel sorrow of her childlessness, Fryn demanded the operation in secret, albeit a womb was at that time deemed to belong to the husband. It outraged her sense of fitness that one who had failed to fecundate it should alone have the right to sign it away. So Tottie, who understood, had to solve this for her unseen – not difficult in his doctor's role – and then urgently to get back to work, which he did with a heavy heart. In the fullness of time, he was replying to a letter from her:

> 'Darling – I don't know *what* to say! Why shouldn't I be told? Really I am wretched about this; far worse than if you'd told me. And what is all this about *my* not being well? I am *quite* well, though less so when *you* are not well. Like the moon, in fact, whose light comes from reflection. Now I think of it, I know how true that is. My thoughts are with you my darling darling and all my love.'

May went off to help Fryn move to the Dorchester then, and Tiger or Virginia Vernon promised to telephone him nightly. For Tiger had left the WRNS, bored with saluting the Quarterdeck in England's Lane NW3. She had counted upon getting an overseas posting and, when nothing of the kind looked like happening, Virginia had officially appealed to her friend Lady Louis to release her urgently to ENSA. So Tiger was now an ENSA Welfare Officer, about to depart for Ceylon, Burma and Singapore, and a little later Tottie was writing to Fryn:

> 'Of course with no Tiger and no work it must be depressing for you. Do try to see people, even if you don't feel like it. It will help. If London affords no company that you care to see, you might as well be in Prestbury! Am missing you *quite* a lot. Isn't that news? When so much of life falls away, it does leave the real landmarks standing out, meaning "us". And now don't say "just like the pyramids"! The sooner you

return to a decent bed, vitamins, oysters, turtle soup and champagne, the better! Much as I want you back, I don't want to press you unduly, but we must and will nurse some happiness in what is otherwise a distracted and miserable world.

I love you so much that I cannot not believe it possible to make amends for the past.'

FOURTEEN

——•◦€)(3•◦——

In Sickness and in Health

FRYN CAME HOME to Tottie that autumn and got back to work, but she was strangely diminished. It was as though a pall hung over her. It isolated her from him and from all those living and moving around her. The domestic staff at Parteen then was composed of Crystal, a dear little kind stumpy 'dwarf', who was a superb cook, and Esther, who came from the village to clean, while May took care of everything else. Another two cherished secretaries had come and gone before *The Story of Burma*, already in danger of losing its place in history due to the speed of events in the Burmese campaign, was despatched to the publishers selected by the Ministry of Information, in this case Macmillan.

It was then that 'Lest We Forget', an article written for the *Manchester Guardian* series, about a young heroine of the Resistance called Hélène Vagliano, whose family Fryn had known in France and who had been tortured to death, became a bone of contention between her and her New York agent and friend Alan Collins, the President of Curtis Brown Limited. To her request that he should place this article in America he had replied: 'Little anecdotes like this are virtually impossible to sell our side,' and Fryn had exploded in fury. For months the wrangling waxed and waned, till he wrote begging to be released, 'since your displeasure is really too fantastic,' and she was suddenly without an outlet in America.

During this exchange, the excellent relations of a lifetime with Heinemann were also jeopardised. Charley Evans' grave state of health meant that he was now seldom on hand to support and advise. 'While he was himself he was the most loyal of friends,' she wrote. But, deflected by the war, she had failed to give them a new novel; they had failed to keep certain of her existing novels in print. She had then baulked at signing their new contract for her next three books, which proposed a reduction in royalties while costs continued high.

Although they had assured her London agent, A.M. Heath, that the percentage would revert when conditions became normal, she thought that that assurance should be written into the contract.

But it was over the question of the eventual reprinting of all her work in a uniform edition, and specifically over the urgent reprinting of *The Lacquer Lady*, that Fryn reached stalemate with Heinemann, and on this C.S. had insisted on his legal right to six months' grace, while she had insisted that speed was of the essence in the light of Burma's current news value. His grounds were that, when a publisher has done well for an author, it is unfair to switch elsewhere to someone who happens to be able to put it out at that moment with the implicit bribe of getting future work.

The paper quota position was complicated. Every publisher got a fixed percentage of what he had used in the twelve months ending August 1939, and in addition could apply for a special allocation to the Paper Controller; half of this on grounds of educational use for the forces, and the remainder on the merits of the case which an individual publisher could put up. Hence, the Macmillan publication of *The Story of Burma*, requisitioned by the Ministry of Information and recommended on educational grounds, would carry a double priority, whereas a Heinemann reprint of *The Lacquer Lady*, though of comparable historical value, would have none.

On 29 November 1944, Fryn's beloved C.S. died, before the dead-lock had been broken. Professionally as well as personally, the effect upon Fryn of his absence was damaging, in that her work would never again be treated so gloriously, and that it came at the crucial stage in her writing life when a collected edition was the only way to bring her name back before the public.

There was another unlucky side-effect. Her large Burmese painting, from which the delicious illustration 'An Outdoor Court Scene' had been taken for *The Story of Burma*, had got lost 'twixt cup and lip. Having found it too big for her panelled rooms at Pear Tree Cottage, she had asked C.S. to hang it in his barn-room at Bilden's in Ewhurst, and there the Macmillan photographer had gone in order to make the block. By the time Fryn realized the painting was missing, however, C.S.'s wife had also died, the two estates had been wound up, their surviving children were serving, and no one then at Heinemann knew anything of its whereabouts. An acrimonious correspondence had ensued, which was a pity.

Fryn was in no state to look after her interests just then; she was

heading for a serious illness. Overwrought to a degree, her thoughts
tended to get scrambled. She wrote: 'I have never been within a mile
of a nervous breakdown, and I have not got one now, but if I went on
I should.' Well, she did go on. The personal magnetism which was her
glory had been falling to an all-time low, and the flow ceased entirely
and seemed to run into reverse. As if a lever had been pulled hard
over, she underwent a metamorphosis. Her relationships switched
from love to hate, from trust to suspicion. The malaise was peculiarly
hard to handle, for the fantasies accompanying it would capriciously
change. By the time the galley-proofs arrived from Macmillan, her
antagonism had centred upon Tottie, who became the target for her
sorrow. He took to sitting at the first tee on the golf course, just to be
out of the way. For the old obsessions had come back and she had
showered him with accusing love-letters:

> 'Dear – I don't want anything but for you to say in writing that I am the
> person you've cared for most in your life. You see, you'd never thought
> to care like that for anyone, as mistress or as friend. Your chief thing has
> always been to keep *yourself* intact. You weren't an "in-lover", nor was I.
> These soiled coins of speech were for neither of us. But love is another
> matter.
> 'So, when you came back from the Ras-el-Tin and began, as you got well,
> to get so excited about me, to kiss me and say the word love – it was the
> Lord's doing and marvellous in my eyes. You took every step of the way
> then. I never asked you to give out that we were married. You suddenly
> thought it would be nice and did it, and we sailed for the Castello. You
> tell me now if you die first I have my memories! Human beings, truthful
> ones, are not sundials, to chronicle only happy hours. The brain won't do
> it. Everything lovely you've ever done for me, you've spoiled. Our third
> anniversary, when I'd taken that horrid little house at Lymington as a
> headquarters, and you and I had the week-ends in *Gudgeon*, which I had
> thought was the only thing that was truly ours; we had a lovely night, and
> next day you gave me my earrings, and then you said: "Darling, you'll
> have to leave; I'm having people for the week-end." And I had to. How I
> explained it to May and the others, who were expecting me to be away
> until Tuesday, I've forgotten. You sent me a telegram every day. May
> asked nothing, she guessed. And I had my second miscarriage. And
> [Leila Fladbury] went back to London and, as usual, talked: "[Ben]
> was never so himself as at the helm of a boat!" She had taken her boy of 16
> into her bed and told him "what you really are to him, my dearest".
> 'I had never imagined such a thing.'

Driven desperate by this resurgence from the past, Tottie had then left the house and was staying at the Club in Manchester, from where he wrote:

'You want not only skilled but *mental* attention. If you will do what I have urged, and put yourself under a psychiatrist's care for five or six weeks, either here or installed at Melina Place with a nurse-housekeeper, I am sure we shall then both approach the future with a more normal outlook.

'It is no good further arguing about responsibility.

'I am perfectly willing to put all this behind us, but must feel secure as to nothing of the kind happening again.

'Do not think that I, in my way, do not suffer. But I am not going to allow my private miseries to interfere with my job, as they are doing now.'

He offered all sorts of suggestions for the future, should she prefer to sell Melina Place, buy a house in Cornwall, or a boat large enough to live on, and ended:

'If you will only do as I ask, you will realize that all molehills are not mountains. I have had the relief of my work. Far from tiring me, it refreshes me. What does break me down is the strain of the kind of thing we have been having, particularly for the last six months.

'I have made up my mind that I am going to die quietly.'

But Fryn was beyond entreaty. Over-activity had given place to a supine state in which she lay behind drawn curtains, refusing contact with anyone. She had conceived the idea that Crystal was poisoning her, or alternatively starving her; that May was her enemy and must be got rid of. Hostility emanated from her. Something had to be done. In his perplexity, and in the hope that work might be her salvation, Tottie put an advertisement for a secretary in the local paper.

Resentment had boiled up in Fryn, convinced that everyone had turned against her, even Stella. She would willingly have suffered Stella's cancer, but what she could not bear was her rejection. Shaken by this illusory injustice, she had reached another anguished conclusion: Tottie no longer loved her. Their learning to love had been a revelation to her. From the beginning they had seldom shared a bedroom; he had padded in to her room to pay his court, and she had rejoiced to find that they were rapturously happy lovers. Before the hysterectomy, she had feared it might impair their exquisite sensitivity and had doubted the gynaecologist's amused reassurances. Partly for that reason she had hesitated so long before returning to him, feeling herself mutilated. And then, when she did return, tentative strangers at first, they had found an ineffable tenderness each for the other. Yet now, she was to be deprived for ever of ecstasy, and by Tottie! Unhappiness overwhelmed her. Those she had loved had desserted her. The only palliative she could devise was to isolate herself more and more.

It was to this alienated household that Letty Cameron-Kirby came, to read the galley-proofs of *The Story of Burma*.

Letty was living at Wilmslow, from which neighbouring village her husband went daily to his office. She had a heavy baby girl, a slipped disc, and a selfish mother living with them. The obvious solution seemed to be to earn by her brain and save her back; but how? She had a degree in Modern Languages and was also a qualified secretary, so when she read an advertisement wanting secretarial help for an author living in Prestbury, she wrote applying. An appointment was suggested by letter, which she took to be from the author's wife, and only when the master of the house opened the door to her did her mistake become apparent. He explained that his wife, being far from well, was not engaged on any serious writing. There was a book with the publishers and she could scrutinize the galleys. There was a play ready for typing. Otherwise it would be mostly personal correspondence. She need not come until ten, she would lunch with the family, and she could leave by four. Letty was jubilant. This would pay for a house-keeper. Before the interview ended, she was piloted into the drawing-room to meet the author.

Fryn was standing up, one tense arm resting along the mantelpiece. She was facing towards them, and Letty's heart sank at the baleful expression in the eyes. Only gradually did she begin to recover from the dislike that had filled her. But by the time she had outlined her own background and problems, and had met Fryn's leaping intelligence and ready sympathy, it was tacitly understood that she should start at once.

During the weeks that followed, Letty assimilated all manner of contrary impressions of Fryn. Often when she got there the doctor had already given her an injection, the household was hushed, and Letty had nothing much to do. But when once they got down to work, Fryn seemed able to pull herself together, and would plan the next book she was going to write about her old nurse, or talk raptly about herself and Stella and Tottie. Between proof-reading and typing, Letty sat long with her in her darkened room, eating their meals from trays, talking, reading, or silently attentive to each other, while a bond was slowly forged between them.

Fryn told how she had hated living up there 'where nobody read or understood words', and how lucky she was that Letty did. She constantly mourned that Tottie was 'so old', which didn't make sense at first, for he played good golf and his mind was outstanding. She brooded over sex and desire, putting provocative thoughts into her letters, which shocked Letty with her puritanical upbringing. Young as she was, she had not found that ecstasy which Fryn seemed to be craving, and didn't know whether to laugh or cry. One phrase that struck her went: 'Though I've had three miscarriages, I'm still a good working model.' This, addressed as it was to a man, seemed to her almost lewd, yet she dared not shake the tenuous web of confidence in the making.

The lease of Parteen came to an end with the demobilization of its owner in the spring of 1945 and they had to move house. Woodeaves was smaller, on the crest of a hill towards Prestbury, and here the trouble with Fryn intensified. The migraines became more frequent, as did the injections, which put her out for hours, and Letty thought this was deliberately to get oblivion at any cost: 'In these spells of morbid depression her thoughts dwelt on unhappy things: how Tottie had kept in touch with the mother of his son; how she had never had a child of his; and that now he had turned away from her.'* Such bouts of black melancholy or *folie circulaire* poisoned her fondest feelings, so that she would speak to nobody besides Letty, casting her as a sort of familiar spirit.

A day came when May told Letty of her meeting with Fryn and their long affection, and of the recurrent crises that had afflicted her at Sabi Pas and at Hurlingham. She told of Fryn's unkindness to Crystal, who had been an angel to her; of how bitterly hurt May herself felt at being treated now as an outcast; and of how worried Tottie was that Fryn might remain permanently implacable. Then Letty, torn in equal halves, was asked to act as mediator.

Tottie wanted Fryn to go with Letty to London to see Dr Mackenzie and a psychiatrist. Fryn said she would, and wrote a number of

* Letty Cameron-Kirby in conversation with JC.

letters to men she knew. It was as if she were shooting off SOS rockets, almost at random, and they drew a variety of responses, from silence, to excuses, to advice, to a warm invitation to come and stay for as long as she liked. This was from a dear friend, a well-known character actor, to whom she explained that she was coming to tie up the loose ends of her official work for the Ministry of Information.

They set off for London in a hired car, Fryn in exalted spirits. And it was only then, remembering the obsessional harping on Tottie's great age, that Letty began to wonder what she was in for: 'It dawned on me that Fryn might be feeling sexually deprived and was subconsciously seeking a source of consolation.' But when they got to Bruce's flat and he had kissed her warmly, he let it be understood that he had his own consolation, who would be coming to spend the night as usual. Fryn had had plenty of homosexual friends, and had been known to say that they were among the most brilliant and talented people she knew, but she promptly developed a migraine and had to have a doctor in to give her an injection that night. It put her out for the next few hours, but when Letty surfaced the next morning, Bruce told her that Fryn had scared the life out of him by wandering into his room, her sensitive palm feeling along the walls. Her eyes without glasses had looked blind, as if sleep-walking, and he had steered her, sobbing a sad little story, gently back to her bed.

Fryn never stirred from the flat that week, spending the time just talking to Bruce, to Letty, and to the young medical friend of Bruce's who dropped in each day. Bruce did the cooking, at which he excelled. Letty and the doctor did the washing-up together, for he was sorely smitten. Fryn did nothing about her intelligence work and refused to allow Letty to get in touch with Dr Mackenzie, as Tottie had implored her to. Towards the end of their stay, Sybil Thorndike came to lunch – 'a dear thing, woolly-minded but a pet' Fryn said – and Letty had watched Fryn's own performance with apprehensive eyes. But she had held her own, and had swept out when the meal was over, leaving Sybil to scintillate over the coffee-cups, and calling gaily over her shoulder: 'To work, Letty darling, to work.' They had returned to Prestbury the next day.*

Then followed the worst time of all. Letty had had to go home for a while, and Fryn would have nobody in her room except the doctor;

* Letty Cameron-Kirby in conversation with JC.

ignoring Crystal's delicacies and threatening to dismiss May 'without a penny'. Why she had gone to London was a mystery, unless it was to escape from reality: the child with the Golden Secret had had her Royonex, 'a whole other life and world that you can step into when you like and that to you is real!' Of the several motives which may have surged through her sick head, stuffed as she was with toxic doses, the most likely is that she was 'tasting' a future without Tottie; the least likely that she had seriously meant to cuckold him as a punishment. But, if it were a punitive expedition, Tottie was at the wrong end of her stick. He cared nothing, so long as she came back to him safe and sound, and that she didn't do. Safe, yes, but still a crack-pot, who had evaded the treatment on which his hopes were set. It infuriated him that the ridiculous experiment had been for nothing.

On Sunday 12 May 1945, Fryn wrote a curt pencilled note addressed to The Coroner: 'Dear Sir – I am sorry to be a nuisance to you and my beloved husband, but my letter to him explains everything. Yours faithfully, F. Tennyson Jesse (Mrs H.M. Harwood)'

Her letter to Tottie lay beside it:

'Dearest – You did this to me, by your lack of self-control. I had hoped at your age to spare you everything. But May's temper is foul. Our cook is quite mad. I am so tired and weak because she has not fed me that I *can't* eat.

'I have loved you as more than myself, but now I am finished. Yours, who was never anyone else's,

'PS. I am terribly sorry for you, but you will have to tell the truth, not as you wish it but as it has always been. Point out to [Ben] that it has not been funny for me. Explain to the Coroner that my hand prevents me writing better. And I have six books still in me! If you have the money, please have them all reprinted, and vet them yourself. And spend not one farthing of our mutual money, when you sell the house or my furniture or my pictures, on any member of the [Fladbury] family. I should like all my share to go to the Merchant Seamen.'

She was resuscitated, of course. After the panic and the stomach-pump, she spent a week in a Wilmslow nursing-home, where Letty saw her daily. She had no specific treatment there, but it gave Tottie the chance to find a place where she could at last be seen by a psychiatrist. He had come to think that he might have lost her for good; that she had gone irrevocably out of her mind.

Letty, on the other hand, was not convinced that Fryn had ever lost touch with reality: 'Intensely depressed she had certainly been and furiously hurt that Tottie no longer desired her. But, both in the early days and at the Wilmslow nursing-home, she had been so perceptive over the tensions caused by my mother's presence in our house, and at the same time so pitifully vulnerable in herself.'*

Letty had then accompanied Fryn to a small mansion, away from village or town, where they took fond leave of each other before she returned home by the same ambulance. There she took up her own life, which was bristling with complications again, and it seemed no time before she had heard, in a buoyant letter, that Fryn was home at Pear Tree Cottage, working hard. Tiger was back with her. Plainly her relationship with Tottie was on a tender footing. How it had come to pass, Letty never knew; nor if any mental therapy had been involved. But the war was over. There was the prospect of making her home beautiful once more. A new book was in the pipeline. The weird wave movements that could rock her from the heights to the depths had come to rest. And gratefully the others acknowledged that it was dear unselfish Letty who had saved them all from a perilous abyss.

The history on which Fryn had been at work since the war began only appeared after it ended, owing to printing difficulties. In 1946 *The Story of Burma* was finally published by Macmillan, with eight fine illustrations including that of the lost painting. The dedication is: 'In memory of my cousin Captain Julian Tennyson of the Oxford & Bucks Light Infantry who was killed by the Japanese when fighting to free Burma: "The advent of death is like the coming of a great wind; no man knows whence it is nor where it goes. Its visitation is often without reason and its action without intent the understanding may perceive. One thing alone it shows. By his death man sets a seal upon his life and in the manner of his dying is revealed the strength of his spirit . . ." Penrose Tennyson (killed 7 July 1942) Fleet Air Arm.' For Julian Tennyson had died in 1945 in the Burmese jungle. A piece of shell had pierced his heart, killing him instantly, and the lines Fryn offered to his memory were those found among his brother's papers at his death in 1942.

Eric and Aunt Margaret had stayed on at Pear Tree Cottage for two

* Letty Cameron-Kirby in conversation with JC.

years after Stella died there. Then it was empty, till Fryn happened to read an amusingly desperate article by a man whose war-time flat in London was being reclaimed by its demobilized owner. This was Ernest Betts, erstwhile film critic of the *Sunday Express*, who was on the staff of the *Daily Express* at that time. Fryn knew no more about him than that, but she wired: 'If you still want a roof, have mine,' and that is what Ernest and Eve Betts did. They stayed till Fryn and Tottie came home to St John's Wood, when they left behind them two black kittens sitting in front of the Aga. Fryn kept them, of course, where they naturally considered they belonged more properly than did these interlopers. Ernest, and lovely Eve too, ate at her table at intervals ever after, becoming known as 'My Pettses, the Bettses'; and in his writing about the future of the film industry and the history of the British cinema, Ernest achieved three erudite books with the spice of humour in them.

Pear Tree Cottage had to be thoroughly renovated after these varied adventures. Then friends began coming in for lunch or dinner as before: the Greenes, or the Headforts, or Irene Ravensdale. A few fought shy at first, but even those who had witnessed Fryn's distressing *volte face* were unable to look askance for long. She had plumbed the lowest level of depression she was to reach and was pretty well herself again; a feat that called for more wonder than obloquy. Countless sufferers, known and unknown, have been cursed with similar symptoms. A tendency to transient mental collapse under stress ran in the Stuart blood and they called it porphyria. Something not unlike it ran in the blood of the Somersby Tennysons. Periodic manifestations of schizothymia had dogged the days of Fryn's maternal forbears; her mother and her mother's mother becoming semi-invalid and immobilized while still young, and at times showing schizoid traits. None of the victims was able to combat their scourge while it was upon them. To start afresh was all that any of them could do, and Fryn did that with might and main.

When the black cloud came down upon her and shrouded her radiant spirit, it would have taken a better diagnostician than any of the galaxy of medical practitioners who attended her through those times to say precisely what ailed her; whether she was mentally deranged, or psychologically disturbed, or physically poisoned by the panic measures she took. In the doldrums of morbid depression, the victim of excruciating headaches, unable to sleep, eat or work, she was in a state to try anything. Two or three injections every twenty-four hours was normal throughout the year 1945 to 1946, as entered in May's Prestbury journal.

But the bouts of drinking or of succumbing to morphia, the suicidal overdoses, were misleading symptoms of Fryn's frantic struggles to escape into the light. Inevitably she did wheedle prescriptions of the drug she craved; at such times the hankering for oblivion must have become insupportable, and everybody knew, though morphia was not mentioned, what the injections were at Sabi Pas, which she loved, and again at the marble villa, which she detested. She must have fought the addiction, for she got it under control each time, and probably only another addict can have any conception of how it was done. Recovery from it was like that after a long illness. But coming out of the black cloud without it was different. Then, the mood changed as swiftly as it had come and the cloud lifted spontaneously. Weak and exhausted, she was smiling and making lively sallies, the rasp and the drone forgotten, clear in voice and mind, looking at those about her with warm and friendly interest. May might glower at her, or mutter: 'Don't you dare smile at me; you ought to be ashamed.' But the relief was too great, the return to normal, then to positive infectious happiness was too welcome, to allow anyone to carp for long. Her family fell in with this and were as much at peace as they would ever dare to be. Only between her and Tottie there had to be an accounting, and they did it by letters. Tottie would not accept that the lapses were involuntary. He had to insist that sanity was the norm.

Yet, to those watching, one thing seemed clear; it was never Fryn who began the rot. It happened to her. The 'demon' that lay in ambush struck unheralded. She did not wantonly treble her dosages or injections, or deliberately cease to take solid nourishment, or start gulping gin in reckless abandon. There is no denying that she behaved abominably when it struck, as if she were drunk, or drugged, or crazy, which gave those who blamed her for the sad ruin about her justification for their censorious view, but her excesses were not the first cause. A few people took her to task, and those she never forgave. As she never saw herself as they had seen her, it hurt and angered her that anyone, particularly an old and trusted friend, should look upon her with the eyes of an enemy, and she treated them as such for their treachery. Other friends faded away reluctantly, too embarrassed by the queerly strident voice and inimical way of speaking to keep up the intimacy once dear to both. Fryn did not seem to know why they left, yet she did seem to know that they would leave. One simple guideline to mental states is said to be that when the person behaving abnormally is in touch with reality it is a neurosis; when not in touch with reality it is a psychosis. Sometimes the line can be too fine to tell where reality begins and ends.

The indomitable person who emerged after the war had not much vital strength to pursue her professional duties; somewhere she was deeply tired and battered, and looked it. But her spirited humour had revived and she proceeded to express original and incisive observations on any subject under the sun. If the delivery was a trifle repetitive, that was only towards the end of a day. And if the need for a stimulant began to show itself, Tottie now kept the cupboard-under-the-stairs stocked with half-bottles of champagne to serve as pick-me-ups. Sadly, the gynaecological surgery had not proved an artistic success, in that a more than slightly circular outline had overspread that of the sylph; self-mockingly she called it a 'cosy' figure. But the old capacity to take an interest in everything and everybody was there in full measure, and the loving-kindness to make others feel important to her. With infinite patience she laid siege to May's huffy heart.

No one could be more ardent in support of a cause she believed in than was Fryn; as witness her fierce protests at the hanging of Mrs Thompson, at the mindless opprobrium that drove Mrs Rattenbury to suicide, and at the belittling of the heroism of Hélène Vagliano. Her pen was poised to strike over the beaten child, or over the damage and indignity forced upon young girls and women in Africa and other Muslim countries, by the genital mutilation known as female circumcision. Against censorship, against cruelty, against race or sex prejudice, against murdering the English language, she was tireless in her campaigns, but she had always been too individual to be a 'belonger', and in *The Sword of Deborah* she had denied being a feminist.

Nevertheless she thought that women should be allowed to study any subject, and fill any post, of which they were capable. Her hairdresser, chiropodist and dressmaker were women. Her corsetière, cook and housekeeper too, and her secretary-chauffeuse. Her osteopath was a woman, also her gynaecologist and her oculist, as well as her literary agent for the greater part of her career. She had invented a woman detective and a woman pirate. But she did not care for hob-nobbing socially with her kind, womenkind, though they made up so many of her dearest friends. Once only had she been to a large all-women's luncheon, seated next to a woman who responded to no topic whatsoever. Finally, Fryn had faced her firmly and said: 'I'm a great believer in euthanasia, aren't you?' and with the first gleam of light illuminating her mind, the neighbour had replied earnestly: 'I'm a great believer in youth *anywhere*!'

In 1947 Fryn was elected by invitation of the Council to a Fellow-ship of the Royal Society of Literature. The proposer was the President, Lord Lytton, and the seconder was Sir Edward Marsh. Eddie Marsh was an old friend and favourite lunch-guest; a marvel-lously entertaining talker in that squeaky voice of his. He had a habit of absent-mindedly tipping the entire contents of the cream-jug over his pudding, which had given rise in the Harwood family to the expression 'doing an Eddie' for anyone who took all, regardless. Although she was a poor attender at meetings, the Fellowship pleased Fryn and made up for all the lost cream.

While her new novel was building up in her mind, she accepted Jim Hodge's proposal for another Introduction to his series. The body of a barman called Jack Mudie had been found by two landscape gar-deners on 30 November 1946. He had been half-buried in a Surrey chalk-pit, and round his neck was a cord tied with a half-hitch in such a way that it had only to be pulled slightly upwards to strangle him. Three men, Thomas John Ley, former Minister of Justice in the Government of New South Wales, Lawrence John Smith, a joiner engaged by him to convert a derelict house he owned, and John William Buckingham, who ran a car-hire service, were charged with the murder. When Buckingham turned King's evidence, Ley and Smith were left to face separate indictments. The trial was held within the Central Criminal Court, Old Bailey, on 19 March 1947, before the Rt Hon Lord Goddard, the Lord Chief Justice of England, and both Ley and Smith were found guilty and sentenced to death. As Fryn put it: 'Ley was the brain, if such it can be called, which designed the whole affair; Smith the hand which at least helped to carry it out.'

Accompanied by Tiger, she went to the chalk-pit. She talked to a detective-sergeant of the Surrey constabulary. She visited the boarding-house which had lodged Jack Mudie, of whom the landlady spoke warmly as a decent young man. Back in London, Counsel for the Crown, and for each of the accused, gave her of their time and knowledge at Pear Tree Cottage, as did the expert witnesses.

The interest of the case for Fryn was that Mudie had not even met Ley until the night he was sadistically murdered; a circumstance unique in the history of English Criminal Law. But Ley had an ageing mistress, of whom he was jealous to the point of paranoia. She had met Jack Mudie only once upon the stairs, but Ley had become obsessed with the preposterous notion that she had had an 'adulterous' affair with him. Rich, old and vain, he thought there was nothing he could not buy, and Buckingham and Smith were paid by him to lure Mudie to the derelict house, where he was pinioned and gagged and the half-hitch was strung from a beam to his neck. A young, strong man, with no idea of why this horror was befalling him, he was killed slowly by the cord from 'a slight degree of suspension'.

Buckingham had driven away. Ley had paid out the cash. He and Smith were left in the building, alone with the trussed man. Smith had disposed of the body in the chalk-pit. A fine mesh of links was carefully threaded together, till the chain of circumstantial evidence was complete. Some six days after the trial Ley was found to be insane and was removed to Broadmoor. Smith's sentence was thereupon commuted to penal servitude for life.

The *Trial of Ley and Smith* was published in 1947 for the Notable British Trials series, dedicated: 'To Moira Tighe – "TIGER" – My Fellow Worker in the Chalk Pit and Everything Concerned with it With Love and Thanks.' At the end of the Introduction there is this postscript:

'The Hon Thomas John Ley was sent to Broadmoor on 5 May 1947. He died there of a seizure on 24 July 1947. His brain, from early youth, bore the equivalent of the rotten speck within the fruit, which eventually influenced him far beyond his own understanding. Ley leaves behind him a trail of unhappiness, but which one of us is there who dares say that he was responsible for leaving that trail? We still know too little and those of us in full possession of our faculties are few who can say with truth that we have caused no suffering.'

In January 1948, 'Binkie' Beaumont wrote to Tottie, enthusiastic about a play-script of *A Pin to See the Peepshow*. Hugh Beaumont was still young then, but already one of the most influential production managers in the country and Managing Director of H.M.

Tennant. Thus propitiously began the fitful fortunes of Fryn's *Pin*.
By March they had the go-ahead in principle from the Lord Chamberlain's Office, and Eileen Herlie was to play the part of Julia
Almond. Tottie therefore got to work on it, clearing every scene with
Joe Jackson of New Scotland Yard. In the interval, Binkie had lost
interest; the banned play, *People Like Us*, by Frank Vosper, written
in 1923 and based on the same Thompson/Bywaters case, had after
numerous applications had its ban lifted, and was being produced by
Henry Sherek at Wyndham's Theatre.

By the end of July, Celia Johnson was writing to Tottie, very
interested in the part, yet wondering if the emotional treatment might
not be too unbearably painful to see, however enthralling to read. In
August, Ealing Studios asked for a twelve-months' option on the film
rights, which Fryn confidently refused, explaining that these were
not now available. For Peter Cotes was going to direct the play at the
Libraries Theatre, Manchester, with an option on a West End production to follow.

It was at that point that Mr Thompson, brother of the murdered
man, lodged a protest with the Lord Chamberlain, who after all
withheld the licence. The peculiar irony of his decision was that the
offending *People Like Us* had then been running for two months with
a licence and was free to continue, while *A Pin to See the Peepshow*
had neither been read nor seen by the protestor, yet suffered the ban.
As thirty-two actors had been rehearsing for a fortnight, and twenty
sets had already been painted, this was an expensive disaster for all
concerned.

Peter Cotes's introduction to Fryn had been by remote control.
Liz Allan the actress had said to him one day: 'If you're so interested
in criminology, you must meet a friend of mine, that little gargoyle
Fryn Tennyson Jesse. There's nothing she doesn't know about it.' He
and the Canadian actress Joan Miller had then gone to Cornwall for
their honeymoon, he having just finished his first book, *No Star
Nonsense*, championing the group theatre principle. In the train he
had chanced to read about a play based on *A Pin to See the Peepshow*,
a novel he'd read entranced as a boy actor. That was all the spur he
needed to write and ask if he might call.

The ban became a spearhead in an attack on the Act of 1843. Tottie
began it with an article in the *Manchester Guardian*, 'The Star
Chamber and the Stage'. Fryn followed with 'Why My Play was
Banned' for the *News Chronicle*, and the League of Dramatists used it

in their fight to ban the ban. Peter Cotes took up the cudgels inde-
fatigably.

During this publicity, the Club Theatres had begun to take an
interest. Sales of German rights, Italian rights, Swiss rights were
mooted. But the preference Fryn and Tottie now felt for giving Peter
the first shot at producing it, and Joan the first shot at acting the star
part, overruled all other considerations. It was the beginning of a long
and faithful exercise in mutual affection and trust, in which only the
element of luck was lacking. With typical delicacy of feeling, Fryn
never let Peter and Joan know about the rejected Ealing inquiry.

Before any more of her work was ready for publication, she had to
make new arrangements for marketing it. This was achieved in
America through the literary agency of Brandt and Brandt of New
York, who welcomed her as a distinguished adornment to their list.
Any number of stories, broadcasts and television adaptations were
negotiated, and the cry she heard was 'the more the merrier'. But to
come to an equally good decision about her home market was the
crucial problem. In the early days of the war, Constable would have
taken on Heinemann's existing list and all her future work, undertak-
ing to bring out a collected edition; but at heart Fryn did not want to
leave Heinemann. Nevertheless, after increasingly urgent petitions,
she put to them a final imperious ultimatum: either 'that a complete
list of my immortal works would *eventually* be done', or that they
relinquish all copyrights, which 'would be a very generous gesture
and one you would live to regret'. They replied in March 1948 that
they simply could not pledge themselves to so heavy an expenditure,
'and you may take this letter as a renunciation of all rights held by us'.
It was a tremendous shock to Fryn. She told nobody, but the letter
was found crumpled in the pocket of a cardigan. Her new crime book
was already in their hands, accompanied by the note: 'I am so happy
to be going to be a Heinemann author again.'

Comments on Cain was published by Heinemann in 1948, on
post-war paper and without her signet; the mould having perished in
the melting-pot of war. The British Book Centre, New York, bought
sheets in 1949, and Collier Books brought out a paperback edition in
1962. The three murder trials provided the contrast between how the
law works out in America, in England and in France.

The first concerns The Boy Harold or The Man Wolcott and is
sub-titled 'A Study in Alcoholism'. It is dedicated: 'To the dear
memory of Russell Gleason who took me every day to the trial at

Pasadena, RIP.' By a jury of ten women and two men Harold Wolcott was found guilty of the manslaughter of his mistress – 'the only verdict which the circumstances did not warrant,' in Fryn's view – and was sentenced to ten years at San Quentin.

The second case deals with Reginald Ivor Hinks, 'A Study in Classicism', and is dedicated: 'To the dear memory of Marie Morris, who attended the trial with me and was killed by a V.1. in Kensington Church Street London'. The accused was sentenced to death for the murder of his father-in-law and went to the gallows in 1934.

The final sample is that of Eugen Weidmann, 'A Study in Brouhaha', dedicated: 'To those members of the Bar at Versailles and my French fellow-journalists who were so helpful to me, and to Géa Augsbourg, who gave me his cartoon of Weidmann which is the frontispiece of this book. It is more than a picture of Weidmann, it is a picture of murder itself.' Six deaths were laid at his door, a shot in the nape of the neck was his method, and no sum was too small to put the method into operation. Extenuating circumstances were brought in, which were argued out of Court before the words *avoir la tête tranchée* were pronounced.

The crimes were all committed in the thirties, and the principals were all young men; predators, differing only in degree. There lay their fascination for Fryn. The opening words in her preface are: 'It would be well if we all realized that every one of us had committed an offence or offences punishable under the existing laws by fines or imprisonment, and punishable a hundred years ago by death.' She comes still nearer to the bone by ending it: 'Why murder is the greatest of all crimes is not that the life taken may be that of an Abraham Lincoln, but because it might be yours or mine.'

The *Birmingham Post* wrote: 'A vivid and scholarly narrative by an expert who can write pleasing English. All is mastery and rarest art.' Roy Fuller, however, in his article in *The Tribune*, 'Murder is a Coarse Art', winds up: 'She does not tell her stories too well, writes carelessly and ramblingly and is sometimes inaccurate. It is a pity that one has to say this about the work of one who elsewhere has written well and acutely about criminology.'

The Fine Cotton Spinners and Doublers Limited of St James's Square, Manchester, commemorated their Jubilee Year – 1898 to 1948 – with a Special Issue of *The Distaff*, their trade magazine. 'Our

Chairman, H.M. Harwood,' had written the foreword for it, and a drawing of him forms its frontispiece. He heads a list of twenty-two Directors of the fifty-odd mills, and it is claimed of him: 'In the days of Leonardo da Vinci and Sir Philip Sidney men were masters of many trades. It is fortunate that, in spite of standardisation, there are still men of versatility today; men of breadth of vision, wide humanity and the trained mind.' At the same time, the stockbrokers for the Association wrote that shrewd observers of the Cotton Textile trade considered that 'Harwood had put the Fine Spinners back on the map.' Across this letter Fryn has scrawled: 'Clever boy! But of course I knew it.'

Then, in November 1948, Tottie was invited by the Association to visit their large cotton holdings at Scott, Mississippi, to confer with the Delta and Pine Land Company on future prospects. He could hardly go without Fryn, cooped up all the war years, so she and Tiger were going too, Tiger as the Chairman's Secretary, and Fryn wrote: 'The thought of seeing American again is bliss.'

London was in thick fog when they left, and the Southampton dockers were on strike when they boarded the *Queen Elizabeth*. For a fortnight the travellers were blanketed in, while the faces of the strikers loomed through the swirling vapour at the prisoners in their cage. Wonderful food tasted like dust in the mouth, till on 1 December the sun came out brilliantly and they sailed past the waiting *Queen Mary*. That evening Martha Raye in a skintight frock did a terrific apache dance in the ballroom, but two days of gales stopped the usual nightly dancing and everyone except Fryn and Tottie felt queazy.

They booked in at the Chatham, off Fifth Avenue, Tottie creating consternation by asking the chambermaid for a potty. A battered tin one was eventually found and placed reverently beside his bed in their Louis Quinze suite. The dollar situation was so acute that Tottie wouldn't allow Fryn or Tiger any of their own pocket-money. But Tiger had thoughtfully bought a bottle of whisky, which they added furtively to the 'set-ups' of white rock and ice on the dry train journey from Washington to Mississippi. From Tennessee it was all flat sodden fields and broken-down cabins. At Memphis they were met by a lanky white-haired man who had come from England for the Alaska goldrush, and were driven through one hundred and fifty miles of cotton belt. They stopped at a red-brick hotel at Greenville, where the languid servants were straight off the cotton-fields.

Tottie and Tiger spent the days driving round the Scott estate, watching the mechanical cotton-picker in action while the negroes worked slowly alongside with eight-foot sacks, and Tottie predicted a social upheaval in the Delta country when machines completely replaced the share-croppers. They all lunched with the Managing Director on lovely cold meats, delicious vegetables, and hot cakes with ice cream, and did not rise from the table till four, the Manager's Meeting having been postponed with the airy: 'We needn't have that ol' Meeting today!' Their hostess was an old-time Southern beauty with a real drawl. But Fryn was feverish with some sort of local influenza when she gave an interview to the *Delta Democrat Times*, and it could not be said that the Mississippi gave her 'everything that you wanted'. The lack of wine was a sore trial. Her feet swelled up in the heat. And she suffered a major defeat in her war with the hotel room-service: having rejected a cold boiled egg, served decanted into a tea-cup, she overheard a maid in the corridor saying to the waiter bringing the new egg: 'Whe's you a 'goin', boy?' and his indolent reply: 'I's a 'goin' to Buckin'ham Palace.'

After their three-week stay, the entire staff of Delta and Pine Land lined up in the hall of their truly ghastly hotel to say goodbye, and they set off to see the plantation houses of Natchez on their way to New Orleans. They stayed at the Buena Vista in Biloxi, a huge white stucco building with a smiling young negro *maître d'Hotel* and real food. A note from Fryn to May in January 1949 reads: 'You can have Ye Olde South for me! Everywhere we go something is stolen, little things like scent and undies. We *loved* New Orleans, but all night the siren goes, for the police, the fire-engine, or the Mayor's mistress.'

They left New Orleans in February on an American freighter, the S.S. *Laetitia Lykes*. She was loading cotton bales and lying high in the water, so that Fryn had to negotiate a perpendicular gangway. They woke to hear fog-horns sounding, and remained anchored all day, logs lined with sea-gulls whizzing past like boatrace crews on the current. The next day was the same, thick white fog. Then huge storms followed, towering waves, the crash of crockery; Fryn's berth like a murder-scene, her sheets covered with nourishment torn from her grasp. When at last the fog lifted, the marshy country began to appear below it, with cattle apparently up to their knees in water, grazing off the Mississippi like strange amphibians. Then the pilot came on and the ships scattered into the Gulf of Mexico.

It became suddenly clear that the Captain was a darling, a charming

Virginian with beautiful manners and Italian brandy as smooth as silk. The ship, though due for a repaint, was beautifully comfortable, with shower and lavatory to every cabin, and wide berths. Everyone lay on deck-chairs in the hot sun along the Florida coast, and Fryn wrote: 'Among the eight passengers was a blonde, who looked as though she came out of Wuthering Heights. She was a nun, in civilian clothes because nuns were not allowed to wear habits in Guatemala as the President had an anti-clerical bias. "A nun, is she?" said Tottie, "Oh well, she hasn't missed much".'

When she learned that he was a doctor, she confessed with blushes that she was suffering from extreme constipation: 'Could Monsieur le Medicin come to the rescue?' Tottie sent along two enormous pills, known in the family as May-pills, but two days later – the whole ship agog – he asked her at breakfast: 'Comment ça va?' and the saloon burst into laughter as the nun gently replied: 'Je suis docile, mais je tiens encore.' However, all was soon well and the ship could resume its tranquil routine.

FIFTEEN

—••❊❊❊••—

An Egg Like Yesterday

SOON AFTER the family's return from the Mississippi in 1949, an anthology of poetry written by women was compiled by Clifford Bax and Meum Stewart under the title *The Distaff Muse* and published by Hollis & Carter. It contended that, since the taste of experience from the beginning to the end of life is conditioned by the sex with which we are born, women's verse ought to be as recognizably feminine as their handwriting, and if it isn't then something is wrong: that the last thing that should be said in tribute is 'she writes like a man'. Three of Fryn's pieces are represented, unusual in their delicate sensuousness. Of Fryn herself, the collaborators say: 'four lines in "Testament" indicate that she can steer her way through life without the lamp of religion. She is typical of her period also in her frank acceptance of the body's part in human love':

TESTAMENT

I will and bequeath
What — and to whom?
There is no child
Of my eager womb.
But if there's thought
Born of experience,
Teaching us lenience,
One should have wrought
Some knowledge to leave
To one who may grieve.
We die and all's over,
Love and the lover,
Fun of food and the sun,
Of the flesh that is one

For a few beating moments,
Of the soul that believes
In the notion of oneness
Ere again it must grieve
In the knowledge of loneliness.
We are what we are,
With children or none
Each soul is alone
Under moon or sun.
I will and bequeath —
Well, what did I start with?
Faith, hope and charity,
Youth, beauty, stupidity,
Total lack of cupidity,
No fear, but acceptance
Of life — in priest's vestments,
Gilded, ordered and blest
With a God to invest
One's tiniest movements
With cosmic importance.
I will and bequeath
My faith, hope and charity
To those who can still
Credit such rarity.
Youth, beauty, stupidity
I gave to my lover.
They are all gone
Now that love's over.
He gave in return
Lust, joy and security.
I will and bequeath
To those who believe
That there's life in maturity
My lust, joy and security.
I will and bequeath
My God to those fools
Who say in their hearts
There's a God and he rules.
I will and bequeath
My love to my lover,

Who'll be able to breathe
When my life is over.

For the remainder of 1949, Fryn gave her attention to the new novel. It progressed at top speed, for it was her own youth she was describing, and her own dear Nan she was remembering under the name of Nare. The whole edifice was built around that shapeless loving figure, who had been the vulnerable bulwark between her and her squabbling parents. The mortifying incident in the Guernsey bus of 'the monkey with the pea-green tail' reappears, and also 'a portrait of my father, not wholly unkind, for he became in his old age a lovable man'. Pin-portraits of Mama too pepper the pages, and Fryn is Ginnie, Genefer de Lisle. Her sister Silvia and she are one another's best friends and the tragic thing happens to Silvia 'with whom one never connected tragedy'. With many a divergence created by her fancy, the story is based on her beginnings, and springs fresh as the rose Ginnie puts between the curled fingers of a dying Frenchman at the last, a deep red rose in that alabaster cup of a hand.

With proposals from two or three publishers to consider, Fryn had decided with her agent's encouragement to sign a contract with Evans Brothers, who were newly breaking into fiction. They had agreed to bring out two reprints for every new novel she sent them; at least one reprint a year, all jackets and bindings uniform. She started by sending them Nan's life, *The Alabaster Cup*, and their reaction was ecstatic: 'I believe it to be really brilliant, and we shall be very proud indeed to publish it. It is not only delicate and full of charm, but has high-spots of real wit. It is a gem,' they wrote. The book was considerably shorter than full-length, which posed problems of layout and pricing, but there was to be a full-length sequel to it, Fryn assured them, based on Ginnie's own life. Meanwhile, arrangements were put in hand for reprinting *The Lacquer Lady* in 1951.

In collaboration with Dr Harold Dearden, Fryn had adapted one of her unpublished Solange stories as a melodrama. They called it *Birdcage*, and the business of the chief characters – an Englishwoman married to a Levantine whom she jealously dotes upon – is murder. They adopt young people, insure them, and kill them in such a way that they appear to have stumbled over a cliff-edge after an escaping cage-bird. Fryn had found the original case in an old volume of French memoirs and the play was produced by Peter Cotes on 15

May 1950 at the People's Palace, with Joan Miller as the daring girl
who plays a decoy-duck and exposes the unscrupulous pair. They
took it on tour through England, but in spite of good notices the tour
lost money and radio expectations were not realized. In the stress and
propinquity, Harold Dearden confided to Joan and Peter the history
of Fryn's morphia addiction.

For her part, anxious over their financial sufferings, Fryn ploughed
in an extra £400 as her share of the production costs, on the pretext:

> 'Money means nothing to me, petty pies, because I haven't any. This
> penny has just come to me from one of my very few fans, so it hasn't cost
> me anything. And as it was by way of a legacy, it hasn't cost him anything
> either!
> 'Alas, I have not been out of the house, as my head began to swell up in
> large bumps, which kept on pulsing up and down like the lifts at
> Selfridges. It turned out to be "oedema of the soft tissues". I can only just
> get my specs on, but as I'm not allowed to read that doesn't help much.
> Your little friend in fact looks absolutely repulsive, but she loves you just
> the same.'

Following the publication of *The Alabaster Cup*, Fryn was invited
to attend a Foyle's Literary Luncheon, at which Joan and Peter were
also present, his book on Charlie Chaplin, *The Little Fellow*, having
lately appeared, and Joan has described how, looking terrified and
somehow frail and pretty, Fryn made a marvellous speech as guest-
of-honour. Afterwards, Peter wrote to her: 'You made rings round
all the other speakers. When you were talking, a great big warm glow
seemed to be present in that room.'

At the end of the year, Tottie's Chairmanship had come to a natural
end. He was seventy-five and younger men were being slotted in to
fill the senior vacancies on a peace-time basis. As part of their tribute
to him, the Fine Spinners & Doublers laid on a cruise on the
Alcantara, to include his chosen companions as before. The ship was
bound for Buenos Aires, but by their desire the party of three would
disembark at Rio de Janeiro. Tottie was like a boy let out of school,
and Fryn was his worthy playmate: A strip from Tiger's diary,
written off Vigo on 13 January 1950, gives a glimpse of her:

> 'There have been four days of the most fantastic gales. Fryn received a jug
> of ice-water straight over her shoulders on lurching through Tottie's
> cabin with sodden pillows. Through all this she has been the life and soul,

eating heartily, sampling vintage wines, while the saloon tables leant over at an acute angle.'

Of 16 February the diary reads:

'Fryn and I went ashore at Lisbon. It is a queer feeling to land at a gay-looking city full of shops and be able to buy nothing; it must be torture to the shop-keepers to see an English ship arrive.
'Our driver took us up to an old Moorish castle, saying: "The Moors conquer long ago – maybe hundred year . . ." but Fryn patiently contradicted this and gave him a brief lecture on Portuguese history.
'The view from the castle battlements was of pink, blue, red and green houses slipping in terraces down to the harbour in brilliant sunshine.'

On a cinema poster there, Fryn had been entranced to see, written large across the magnificent torso of the sultry hero: 'He was hurted in his proud', and she gleefully took the phrase into her vocabulary. When outside Lisbon they ran into a gale again, she continued to flourish and Tiger wrote:

'Tottie is bearing up very well, despite occasional moans that his right leg is falling off.
'Fryn is wonderful, completely her old self again, looks ten years younger, walks about everywhere unassisted, talks amusingly and perfectly clearly at any time of the day or night. It is really a miracle!'

And from the Copacabana Palace Hotel the diary continued:

'25 February, Rio de Janeiro: This is the most beautiful place I have ever been to, and everywhere you look are the most fabulously beautiful women in white and green and magenta bathing-suits.
'Miles of bright blue surf with enormous breakers. Pale yellow sands. Dark brown bodies. Never, since the early days on the Riviera, have I felt such an atmosphere of money.
'Fryn is now the hearty member of the family, and eats more in a day than she ate in a month at Melina Place: frogs legs in garlic, stilton and guava cheese, *moules marinières*; European cooking such as can no longer be done in Europe.
'Last evening we all went for a drive above Rio; rather like Ceylon, jungle and hills, with mangoes, bananas, hibiscus, orchids, jacaranda growing wild, and beautiful trees with large purple flowers known as Easter trees because that is when they bloom.'

Fryn had a birthday in Rio, and wrote thank-you letters to May and Aunt Margaret on the day:

'No, I won't buy a little present from you here darlings. It would cost £50 to get a handkerchief.
'I had a pick-up in the swimming-pool, where I was peacefully reading an entrancing book called *The Sons of the Eunuch*: he wanted to take me to Sao Paulo.
'We are lunching with the American Ambassador on Saturday. This is the hottest place I have ever been in and our feet have swollen out of all knowledge. I had brought out for the ride, so to speak, all my beautiful Faulkner shoes made to my new last, and it is impossible to get into any of them. My shabby old black-velvet slippers *will* look swagger at the Ambassador's luncheon!'

To May she added a postscript:

'The most terrifying thing has happened; one of my only two pairs of reading-specs has got broken. Take my prescription and apply pressure, for your own sake, so that they are ready for me when I get back.'

At sea, on 23 March, she wrote to May again:

'Darling, we've all had a grievous infliction; the whole ship has a sort of Gippy Tummy. I enclose a prescription for Med, which perhaps you could have made up ready for me, as I don't want to ask Jock for them the moment I arrive. Your thin Fryn.'

Fryn hadn't been taking Medinal for years, but on board the *Alcantara* a sea-change had taken place so desolating that Tiger could scarcely credit it, and she it was who failed to recover. For Fryn, from playmate, had switched half-way home into a fiend. Her feet swollen, a virulent germ ranging round her susceptible person, her glasses broken, she had fallen into a pit of depression and had turned and rent the unoffending Tiger. Inevitably, some inkling of the Prestbury ordeals had reached Tiger's ears through Virginia, and she had privately resolved to treasure her independence. She had only been brought back into the fold by Tottie's imploring entreaty; that and her broken engagement. But she had come to rate her own worth too high to risk being absorbed into Fryn's cycle of derangement, where she was liable to be used as a whipping-boy. 'I can't begin to explain how painful it is when a loved and loving friend becomes instead consistently unkind,' she said, 'and the worst of it was that we couldn't get away from each other, as we had been allocated a grand suite of intercommunicating rooms. It got so bad that Fryn had to be carried off that pleasure cruise upon a stretcher.'*

As soon as she decently could, Tiger made her escape. Fryn, on recovery, saved everyone's face by telling friends like Rosie Head-fort: 'My beloved Tiger got asthma so badly when we came back from Rio that an English winter is out for her and she is going to Kenya.' Whether she knew or divined that she was the cause, she loved Tiger enough to let her go with her blessings and a cheque towards an outfit. It was to a thatched mud-hut in the garden of Noreen's house in Nairobi that Tiger went. That ebullient school-friend who had brought Fryn and Tiger together eighteen years before was married for the third time, to Roddie Antrobus a racing driver, and they had settled in Kenya. Later, when the Mau Mau violence exploded, Tiger had to move into a flat with lock and key. She was by then secretary to the President of the Court of Appeal for Eastern Africa, travelling on circuit with the judges, and happy as a lark in her work.

Fryn had set about filling the unnerving gap by first telling her friends, and Peter Cotes found someone temporary almost at once, which gave her the peace of mind to await what the Fates would send. Apparently the first half-dozen candidates were so comical in her eyes that she wrote an article intended for *Punch* on the interviews. But after the ancient in a shovel hat, and the one who had to play the piano for three hours a day to keep herself calm, I, Joanna, walked in, reaching the wrought-iron gate as the sun was setting. The fountain from the lead boy's conch was still splashing into the gold-fish pool, and a little grey poodle cavorted up to me, light-footed and inquisi-tive. Fryn was standing at the open front door, wearing a suit of red-flowered wool, and she seemed to pulsate with warmth and light. She stretched out her left hand to mine with a peculiar slow grace, more like a benediction than a clasp, and there was never a moment's doubt that I would stay.

Still, we held a colloquy of sorts. Sitting together on the long, curved sofa in the drawing-room, each nursing a glass of 'my fan's Amontillado', we talked about love, marriage and divorce, about poor Cousin Hebe who had embroidered the rugs and put her head in the gas oven, and about the First Aid Nursing Yeomanry of which Fryn had written and in which I had served. Then I was led upstairs to

* Moira Tighe in conversation with JC.

meet the man of the house. He was spreadeagled in a large red armchair and his tanned fist gripped a folded *Times* against his cherry-coloured corduroy slacks. The majestic head swivelled my way without haste: 'What is a scarlet flower that saved many lives in nine letters?' he boomed softly. 'Could it be a pimpernel?' I suggested, startled. 'Hmm! I do believe you are right.' He nodded judicially, flashing a seraphic smile at his wife, and as I followed the cap of golden waves down round the little staircase, Fryn's words fluted up to me: 'Isn't he adorable? I got him cheap because he was born without a tail.' For on that day, as on many of the thousands that made up the next ten years or so, the poodle in question, poised on his hind-legs, escorted me to the wrought-iron gate; a manly duty for which his frame seemed purpose-built.

Born in Midlothian of Scottish parents, I was the fifth of a family of eleven settled in London since the First World War. I had been at a girls' school in Highgate for the eight years before going out to Northern Rhodesia – as Zambia was then called – to keep an elder sister company while her husband was in the bush recruiting native labour for the mines. There I had met and married another Scot, and had lived in the West country until the Second World War sent me for six years with the FANYs, driving ambulances and desert convoys and training Israeli and Cypriot recruits for the ATS Motor Transport Companies in the Midde East.

My life had split in two when I found myself, on demoblization, unable to return to the husband of my youth. Still scarred from the self-inflicted wound of divorce I was learning to find my feet and earn my keep, for alimony was the last thing I wanted. Since doffing uniform and pips I had been working in Harley Street, and at the Chelsea Hospital for Women, for a brilliant obstetrician and gynaecological surgeon, but he had himself lately succumbed under the knife.

Fryn's advertisement was the first that my old Secretarial College had thought fit to offer me, and it chimed with the exhilarated mood that had come to me on discovering that life and love were by no means behind me. I was forty-one then and Fryn liked that; it made us seem contemporaries. She liked my size and strength too, and started right away on a campaign to get me to curl my brown hair and wear bright lipstick; a futile campaign she was never to despair of. Naturally she responded to my latent happiness and I to her verve. The Fates had been kind to us indeed.

My first task was to despatch the thirty to forty personally inscribed copies of the new book to the dearest of Fryn's friends. Evans Brothers had published *The Alabaster Cup* early in 1950, and it was dedicated to 'Margaret and Robert Gore-Browne with love and friendship'. May's copy bore the inscription: 'For darling May, whose childhood, in a different way, was about as gay as mine'. It was hailed everywhere as one of *the* books about children, but gone were the earlier transports of excitement. The *Daily Telegraph* found it 'a touching, poetic book, beautifully truthful, with real strength and wisdom,' while the *Evening News* wondered if this was the best of all her novels: 'It's chief trait is compassion – compassion towards the young and forlorn, and towards the old, the helpless and the abused. Her method is sharply, plangently impressionist. But what matters about her book is its code of values; she is a passionate humanist.'

Towards the end of 1950, Peter Cotes Productions had decided to open their own New Boltons Theatre Club with a three-week run of *A Pin to See the Peepshow*. In the event, the play did not open till the first week in May 1951, and it was overshadowed for its first night by the many big London openings in the early days of the Festival of Britain, so that few important critics could attend. Yet those who came gave a glowing account of it, the *Evening News* saying: 'Try hard to see that brilliant performance by Joan Miller,' while Kenneth Tynan wrote: 'There was a tumult going on inside which had to be let loose. So, in a strange, possessed way, I shouted my thanks. No performance in my memory has broken down so many of the barriers that hide the last deepest wrath of the human heart.' To this Joan replied: 'filled with a deep sense of well-being for one of the kindest and most generous tributes it has ever been my good fortune to receive.'

Joan had recently had an operation to her back and, believing that Fryn's affection was more towards Peter than herself, she was touched when she came specially to see her. On leaving, Fryn whispered: 'Darling Joan, you must get well soon. You know, a man cannot stand a sick wife.' Now, Joan had often been ill and in pain since their marriage, and had found Peter gentleness itself. Surprised, she said: 'But he's even more loving then!' But Fryn persisted urgently: 'Believe me, pet, he will tire of it.' And she contrived to leave behind a consultant's fee, pretending she had come by an unexpected royalty.*

* Joan Miller in conversation with JC.

But for the ban, no less than five West End managements showed their eagerness to negotiate a transfer from the Boltons, and the run was twice extended. So Peter and Joan, who believed passionately in the play, began to lay their own plans for a Broadway production. Already a producer who had seen Joan's performance had applied for an option, and Fryn hastened to arrange that a Penguin paperback edition of the novel would be ready for sale in the New York foyer.

There is no escaping the fact that Fryn could lead a publisher a pretty dance by this time. She put it to Evans Brothers that she had a collection of poems ready for them. And when they explained that they never touched the poetry market, but to please her they would print, say, a hundred copies at her expense in the 'uniform' binding, she expressed pained contempt and quietly arranged in 1951 that dear Jim Hodge of Edinburgh should publish *The Compass and Other Poems*. Several of the eighteen chosen had appeared in the *Observer* or elsewhere and the book was dedicated: 'To HMH in love, war and peace'.

At the same time, she faced Evans Brothers with a new poser: her Prison Anthology was well under way, together with an enlarged *Murder and its Motives*. 'But,' they protested, 'we don't like murder!' – 'Nonsense,' said Fryn, 'everybody loves murder and, I promise you, murder sells!' – 'No, thank you,' countered Evans Brothers. 'Crime is not in our line. And *where* is our beautiful sequel to *The Alabaster Cup*?'

Fryn had been by-passing her agent, A.M. Heath, in all this correspondence, partly because Audrey Heath had broken a thigh which would not mend, and partly because she could thus feel her way through the tanglewood before her. For she was coming to the conclusion that she could not write that novel – yet. *The Alabaster Cup* had ended with her own, and Ginnie's, marriage. The breaking-point was still ahead. But how could she write Ginnie's life without laying bare the intimate history involving Ginnie's husband, his son and the mother of his son? It would be a torment and a madness to probe further now. That is the impasse she had had to accept. The half-dozen drafts, typed by herself as by a drunken mouse on the red ribbon of her typewriter, showed how frenziedly she had tried to break a way through it. But there was Tottie to think of; her conception of that novel would pillory him. Perhaps one day, if in the nature of things she should outlive Tottie, she might be able to put it all down, and thereby might outlive the woe that still haunted her? For this reason she had allowed the drafts and the folder that hid them, labelled *Sequel to the Alabaster Cup*, to silt down to the very bottom layer of her work-chest.

The Lacquer Lady reprint had already appeared under the current contract, with a new vermilion drawing of the Golden Palace as end-paper design. She had gladly agreed to forego her royalty for this and for *Tom Fool*, since the kudos was infinitely more important to her than the money. However, if her side of that contract for a uniform edition was to be fulfilled, it was essential that she should now provide a novel, even if not the one Evans Brothers had wanted. Nevertheless, she wrote to them: 'I am as little temperamental as any writer can be, but the feeling that you are waiting for a new novel is really paralysing me. I have got to have space round me in time to write a new book!' It was then that Evans Brothers announced that they were withdrawing entirely from their experiment in the fiction field. Thus author and publisher agreed amicably to release each other from proceeding beyond the coming reprint of *Tom Fool*.

Relief at this solution made it not immediately apparent to Fryn that she must give up her dream of the Collected Edition. No new publisher could be expected to reprint the reprints, and three of her best titles were among them! With this disillusionment she withdrew herself from her agent of countless years' standing, feeling that some at least of the responsibility clearly belonged to them.

At about this time, Tottie's literary company, Regency Productions, took over the contracts of all Fryn's writings, past and to come. Tottie was now a retired man and, to fit himself for a life of leisure, he went away to Droitwich, but only stayed for a bored fortnight before pining for home. He came back a size smaller, but disgusted at not having been restored to youth. Philosophically then he rifled Aly Khan's bedroom and lay in the sunny garden, a sheet of *The Times* at hand to cover his nakedness in emergency.

Fryn took to joining him there towards noon – a handful of Bemax ready to sprinkle for the goldfish while she glared at her marauding Pussums – and they were so engaging together and took such pleasure in each other's presence that it was not credible that it had ever been otherwise. 'But he knows nothing about gardens and less about religion,' she would scoff. 'He doesn't know the difference between a flower and a weed!' – 'There is no difference,' he would counter. 'A weed is only a flower in the wrong place.' She would be protected by a huge straw hat, having undergone 'the care of the boady' in the comfort of her bedroom. Although the Church did not come to Fryn, just about every other service did; from doctor, osteopath, face-lady, toe-lady, hair-dresser, corsetière or dress-maker, in which regimen Tottie took as much interest as she.

Their earlier hours would have been spent sitting up in Fryn's French bed, surrounded by newspapers and post, while his elbow ground into 'Beaty and Babs'. There, on one such morning, when the housemaid came in for their breakfast orders, Tottie had essayed tentatively: 'Give me an egg like yesterday, will you?' But this was too much for Fryn. 'No, my darling, you can't mean that,' she had protested. 'An egg tomorrow and an egg yesterday perhaps, but never an egg today. And never again an egg like yesterday. Just think of it! Playing human chess on the tiles at Cut Mill, or drowsing on deck in the Dollard Sea. You can't want all that over again.' He glanced kindly down upon the round crown tucked underneath his arm, then stuck out his underlip. 'I'm game, if you are,' he said.

So, when one of his investments declared a double dividend, he invited Fryn to choose whatever spot on earth she fancied, to hibernate in for the winter of 1951. Only after they had mutually concluded that everywhere was precisely the same nowadays, a message came through the friends' grapevine: the actress Gabrielle Dorziat's villa outside Biarritz was available for the first three months of 1952, complete with *major-domo*, cook, maid, car and chauffeur, and all payable in sterling. Who could argue against such expedience? And just then Fryn had good reason to go to Paris, for there was an unwritten novel stored in her cranium, whose venue was the Ile St Louis. She could quarter the Paris pavements *en route*, and she could be writing the book in the villa.

A familiar pattern was repeated; May invited Marjorie and Fryn invited me. Virginia Vernon, French-born and presently in Paris, would make the bookings, would bespeak dinner for six at Drouant's famous restaurant and bring Pierre Comert of the Quai d'Orsay, who knew and would remember the France of 1914 and of 1939. The party left on New Year's Eve and stayed at the Plaza Athénée, in a suite of state-rooms banked with red carnations. Fryn talked deeply to Pierre. The restaurant's mirrored walls and copper-coloured velvet hangings were the authentic background for reincarnating the

tortuous love-story they had once enfolded. Then Fryn and I paced
the quays and lingered beneath the rose-window in Nôtre Dame and
drove out to Bougival, Fryn's memory stimulated by the sun sparkling on the Seine.

Once ensconced at the villa, however, gloom descended. The
mimosa trees lining the steep drive did not compensate Fryn for the
sighing of the pines in the sharp winds from the Bay of Biscay, which
tore across the rocky hillside on which she dared not set foot. For the
legs which had refused to support her as a child were refusing to
support her again, and the eyes with their severe astigmatism were
confounded by the precipitous garden-paths. Turned into a prisoner,
soon a prey to insomnia, she took to reading through the night.

Only the staff were beyond praise. The *major-domo* was a Basque
who ran everything to perfection, from his first *'bon appetit!'* with
piping-hot coffee and croissants on waking, to the great wood fire he
built after dinner. Madame Pétriarte contrived to cook on a tiny
charcoal stove such dishes as can only be dreamed of. And Marie ran
the bath-water, laundered our nightgowns into goffered pleats, and
told Fryn monstrous tales of the Wicked Baron in whose hovel she
and her babies dwelt; a manger, waterless and unlit!

Leaving these two to comfort each other, the rest of the *ménage*
would pile into the car on market-days, where Tottie would select,
Madame would bargain, I would pay, and the chauffeur would load
himself with the birds and fruits so temptingly displayed. Later, after
Fryn and Tottie had exchanged some secret *billets-doux*, there were
happy days for all, tasting wines on the verandah, watching a pelota
game, or driving down into Spain or up to the Dordogne through the
Landes, past rose-painted houses, and discovering a white farm with
white peacocks and turkeys and a stupendous white bull. The book
began to grow apace. But, when George VI died, Fryn's spirits sank
once more and it was time to go home. As Tottie entered the gate of
Pear Tree Cottage, the prophetic words burst out of him: 'Never
again! From this day forth I travel no further than Lords!'

The dramatization of 'The Mask' had never ceased to draw the public
eye since 1912. In 1949 it had been included in an anthology in the
USA, as well as appearing on television in England. In 1951 it was in
the last Grand Guignol programme at the Little Irving Theatre, and a
music hall version was staged at the New Cross Empire. Now Peter
Cotes produced it on BBC television, with Yvonne Mitchell and

Robert Brown, and Fryn wrote to him: 'I suppose if I had been writing it now, I would have called it "Black Silk", but in those days I was as innocent as a daisy and it was about a mask! What puzzles me is how I knew what I was writing about, but I projected myself into this fiery girl and wrote through her.'

In October 1955, I married Sybout – the Friesian name of a Dutch history graduate who during the war had run errands for an 'underground' newspaper, and had been astonished to find himself on Boxing Day 1946 as that paper's first London correspondent. Fryn and Tottie were at the reception. In her red cape and feathered toque, Fryn sat enthroned in the midst of the standing throng of wedding guests, and at her feet knelt Gustave Renier, then Professor of Dutch history at London University. They were excitedly toasting each other instead of the bridal pair, at the revelation that she adored his *The English Are They Human?* as ardently as he adored her *Murder and Its Motives*.

Fryn had not been very well since Biarritz. She was making an effort to work, but there was an uneasy air about her. Then one day she made the discovery that she was seeing with one eye only. In rising panic she demonstrated it again. At the threat of blindness, all sense of confidence and security deserted her. She craved reassurance, not only on this new terror but on the old doubts. Obviously, her trusted oculist could and did help with improved lenses, but the examination had only confirmed the dire fact that a cataract was forming, and on both eyes. It might take years to reach the stage for operating, but working would make matters no worse for as long as she could see to do it.

Though the relief of that advice was enormous – for the thought of twiddling her thumbs till each eye was obscured was too frustrating to contemplate – yet the other doubts persisted, and she wrote a shaky letter to Tottie:

'Darling – I enclose a letter which I wrote you earlier – so many years too late, but not too late to bring you to my side. If [Ben]'is still alive – you won't get this till I am not – I beg of you to tell him what you tell me; that, since we became "us", I and no one else was the love of your life. Neither she nor he. And that she ought never to have told him. And that it was your weakness in wanting to keep everything, and stay friends with everyone, which made my life so unhappy. But for that, what a life it might have been! Don't let Maggie come to comfort "her dear one" at my funeral. It will be the first time I ever refused her my hospitality.'

This time, Tottie was watchful of her mood and she was circumvented. No harm came to her, and he replied instantly:

'Dearest – I will try and write soon about your earlier letter. Try to fix
your thoughts on what we still have *now*. How can I help? It's done and
no talking will alter that. I did think you knew there had been a complete
break long ago. There was nothing definite said; it just stopped by mutual
consent. But you're wrong about my wishing to stand in well with
everyone. My trouble is with myself. The iron of my first experience bit
too deeply. It was that – not the later one – that set my course on the road
to disaster.
'Am getting very tired just now. Amen to what you say about life. x. B.'

That earlier letter of Fryn's, written at Biarritz before they had
made peace, had lain in her handbag since. Now here it was again,
chock-a-block with lamentable thoughts:

'Don't do anything to spoil this last home we have.
'Don't shout and get cross.
'You spoiled *Gudgeon*.
'You spoiled Cut Mill when you lost your temper with me at Eze and said
it was all the money spent on Cut Mill that had ruined you. I had so loved
the summers at Cut Mill and our lavish hospitality, and now I can't bear
to think of it.
'You did write that I ought never to have been told that, least of all by
you. And so we made it up, but Cut Mill was still spoiled. Unless it is as
impossible for you to live happily without me as it is for me without you,
we must part.
'For what has gone before, I take my share of blame; I let things eat me
too much, throwing what might be present good times after bad. I have
never blamed you for my miscarriages but, knowing how body and mind
are bound up together, the circumstances didn't help. What I suffered
when you used to go and stay at the [Fladburys] you cannot guess; nor
what it meant to me, your having hung that photo in the bedroom where
we made love. So it went on, thing after thing! But you were very kind to
me when I grew my eleven billiard-balls, and when I had to have my
hysterectomy.
'I blame you only from when [Leila Fladbury] told [Ben], and you
did not then cut off everything except financially.
'Oddly enough, I think – though I may be wrong and it doesn't matter –
you have been faithful to me.'

To this was added her pencil note:

'When I left you with this letter, in France, you came after me where I stood trembling and said: "Darling – I'm a bloody fool, and it's all been my fault."

'And I said in tears of happiness that I'd like to have that in writing; but of course that was only a joke.

'Now, what I want you to do, is to wire St John Ervine to do my obit for the Times. You know how awful they are to me now. And please tell [Ben] it was I you loved. You see, his mother told him our marriage was so right because *I* was so in love! And she seduced Maggie, who loves being confided in. I know all this sounds very egoistic, but my love is all I have had in my life except my writing, and I love you so terribly it hurts me to look at you.'

Tottie's letter followed the next day:

'Dearest – whatever happens. As you asked, I have not hurried to write. I tried in bed last night, but couldn't manage it. At Eze, when things were at their worst, why did we agree to go on trying? Because behind everything was the knowledge of what bound us together – that there was for neither of us a separate existence. Without that, would either of us have submitted to the recurrent miseries? There is no other woman – alive or dead – for whom I would have gone through these things. And I would not have faced it then if I had not thought it agreed that whether the ghosts were laid or not they should not reappear.

'There are few if any people with so many worthwhile memories, even if not entirely happy ones. There are probably no two people whose minds are so closely interlocked. There is no one – I speak now for myself – whose "glow" – yes, that is the word – is so dependent on another. I told you a short time ago how much more I loved you than ever before, and it is true. The flame may not be there, but the warmth is, and it will surely last my short time.

'Now, at some risk and only because you ask it, I must refer to some of the "old" things: First, as to your not knowing that communications had been cut. I cannot remember the date; I think it was in the middle twenties, but anyhow before our second visit to Burma. I told you this was so, and that if it should not continue that way I should tell you. It *did* continue. After then, there was neither meeting nor letter, nor was there any attempt on either side to alter that. Was I to keep reporting that there was no change?

'You say it has never been cleared up. *What* has not been cleared up? That I had a mistress? Everyone, as you say, knew it. So did you. Did I ever try to disguise it? You seem now to be going back to the origin, nearly 40 years ago! About 10 years before *we* even met! You can't mean that there is something about *that* to be cleared up? That you might want some light on why I behaved as I did later is natural, but you have already fathomed that; unjustifiable, stupid as it may seem. The reasons for that go even farther back in my history.

'You say that to compare ourselves with others is of no avail. I cannot agree to that. In a world where half the people have lost all they live by or for, I think it not unnatural to do a little private stock-taking. The last time you spoke of these things was on the day that I knew about Stella. I longed to stop you but, not being then absolutely certain, couldn't. It seemed to me that when you knew you would feel the incongruity.

'But the ghost still walks, in spite of fifteen years of silence and death, and if neither our private nor our general griefs can put it in its place, what hope is there?

'As to our writing, it was your illness and all that came out of it which did the damage, not the other thing. *Tom Fool* was conceived and born during what by your own reckoning were the worst years – between 1921 and 1924. *Lacquer Lady* was written between 1927 and 1929; ten years after our marriage. What happened in 1930 and after was what knocked out the creative urge and, though I would not dream of comparing them, it ended that phase for me too.

'Does this break the crust? If not, what more is there to say? You ask me what I should feel if you died before me. I cannot tell you that, any more than I can tell you what I should feel if I were blind. You also ask me what *you* would have under the same circumstances. I think I know the answer to that one – Peace!

'I agree with all you say about our chances. I see everything in its favour. But the ghost must walk no more. x. B.'

And to this Fryn bowed:

'Oh dearest of all. You must have known I have been longing to write to you ever since reading and re-reading with such joy your own letter. I didn't necessarily want you to stress how wrong you'd been, which you most generously do; only what I really knew to be true, that I was the only woman you'd loved. But, having destroyed every one of your precious letters at Hurlingham, I hadn't got it in writing!

'My only love. I think I knew I would love you from the moment when you came back from Alex and, on my way home in the 'bus, I began to know you were there. Is it not wonderful that we are together?'

Fryn had by no means retired. While trying to accommodate herself to the new lenses, which made her eyes look like gold-fish bowls, she got on doggedly with the novel. On climbing up to her work-room, she would settle down at the gate-legged table each morning, panting gently. This room was both sanctuary and arsenal, never invaded. The type-writer desk faced the only window, overlooking the garden, and the entire walls were shelved to the ceiling. Poetry surrounded the window. History occupied the eastern wall. Wonderful maps, books and prints of the sea and ships lay to the west, together with the shabby old globe. And 'the finest private crime library in London' stretched across the wall known as the back-to-back, including the immense series of Notable British Trials, of which only one volume was missing. Downstairs, the first floor housed literature, drama and biography; while in the long drawing-room were the shelves dealing with religion, mythology and fairy-tales.

After reaching for her only cigarette of the day – she smoked as if she were a learner and didn't much like it – Fryn usually began dictating at once, expelling her night thoughts first. She would dabble in a tray of oil paints and add a bright corner to the box or bowl she was currently decorating. Then, plunging into a half-developed sequence, she would link the chain of events infallibly in its place and time. The room was a little factory in its way. A large inlaid chest-of-drawers held the manuscripts of everything she had ever written.

Their stint over, both operators would gravitate to the dining-room, summoned by the dim boom of the Burmese gong. Now everyone's adventures and thoughts were munched over at leisure with the excellent food and wine. More often than not it was good talk, and Fryn's *bon mots* were as likely to trip off her tongue with only her familiars to hear as in illustrious company. There were days when visitors took over and days when migraine took over. Mira Crosse might arrive from her sheep-farm in North Island, big and beautiful, releasing cascades of memories of the ADA with Stella. Or Sam Behrman might fly in from the other direction: 'a will-o'-the-wisp, a moth in a lamp-globe, an angel, but no present help in time of trouble,' as Fryn summed up affectionately; herself so wise, witty and withering. When migraine intervened, there would be the silent curfew signal of the closed door to her darkened chamber.

In addition to the *Alcantara* cruise, the board in Manchester had rewarded Tottie with a fine Chippendale chair; but his well-beloved Queen had not rewarded him as Fryn had hoped, for had he not jettisoned ten writing years for the sake of Her Father's realm? Prone on the couch in his study, she mused aloud in the freedom of his deafness: 'A first-class brain is rare indeed; we are lucky to have known a few who had it. Darling Edwin Hubble certainly, and I think Wilfrid Greene. Tottie had and has a good second-class brain, and that's uncommon enough. What I had was something different: a tiny spark, a visionary gleam, and I threw it away. That is what is so unforgivable. I could have been so much more. But we chose the flesh-pots, and Tottie's talents suffered by that less than mine.'

And now she was terrified of losing him, for he was ageing fast. His hip hurt; to save crouching in the wine-cupboard he had to appoint me as butler. He had to have five teeth out. He had to be fitted for a hearing-aid. He had to confess to Fryn that dinner-parties were beyond him. Fortunately she admired him for that, and even more for making no apology: 'Never mind, my darling, we will just have lunch-parties instead,' she agreed. Enormously relieved, he took to wandering off to his room with a whisky-and-soda when the evening papers arrived, and having his favourite cocoa and sardines in bed. He would have his favourite smoke there too, regardless of her fears: 'One day you'll set yourself on fire: look at your beautiful cashmere pullover, covered in burns!' He would grin imperturbably: 'There seems to be an awful lot of it left.'

The old jibe: 'Waited on, hand and pot!' first levelled against him by Mack McCall, became truer than ever. And Fryn had her French dressmaker fit him out with giant one-piece pyjama-jackets in red, orange and green, with initialled breast-pockets. 'Turn that damned radio off,' he would protest. 'I can't understand a word. The world has passed me by.' A process of withdrawal into their all-absorbing, delicious, unassailable and deeply satisfying love for each other and for their home had begun. With an occasional foray in my veteran Daimler, for him to the Number 1 Court at Wimbledon, for her to the Number 1 Court at the Old Bailey, they receded like hermit-crabs into their one-ness, their us-ness, their increasingly contented hibernation. Disturbed by no more than the gentle play of little Brother, the stimulating lunch-sessions, or the twice-weekly load brought in by May from the Times Book Club, they consciously luxuriated in the strange new peace that had entered their hearts.

Notes would pass between their two bedrooms, via the corridor known as 'Tottie's back passage'. From her: 'Happy birthday to you, my heart. I am so thankful that you were born and that we met. It is odd how love grows when it has had nearly everything to destroy it. I suppose because it has always been a living thing for us; never more than today.' And from him: 'Over fifty years ago, I was told that I was incapable of love. I thought it probably true at the time, and it remained true for over twenty years. If during that time I had been told that I should come to share a personal relationship which made all else insignificant, I should have been incredulous. Yet that is what has happened. I tell you this to try to persuade you that your only rival has been my own egotism, which has been responsible for all my sins of commission and omission and which I deeply regret. If there is such a thing as the marriage of true minds, surely we are in the running. And we've had fun too, the memory of which is precious.'

Meanwhile, the little factory went on. The Introduction to an enlarged version of *Murder and Its Motives* was almost ready. Fryn had met J.H.H. Gaute of Harrap at a party in honour of Bernard Spilsbury and by mutual attraction her new *Murder and Its Motives* was published by George G. Harrap in 1952 and in paperback by Pan Books in 1958. The British Book Centre New York bought sheets. Fryn dedicated it 'to Edmund Lester Pearson, Alexander Woollcott and Harry Hodge, who became my friends because of this book', and the Rt Hon Sir Norman Birkett, in a full-page review for *Books of the Month*, wrote: 'It has now become a classic in its own right. She writes with a complete grasp of the essentials of criminal law and with a wonderfully comprehensive knowledge of human nature. Her writing moreover bears the unmistakable hallmark of style. This new edition will be widely read for its wisdom and the light it sheds on one of the dark places of national life.'

SIXTEEN

—••€)(ϡ••—

The Half-Open Door

AMONG the library books Tottie had been reading was a first novel, *The Thin Line*, written by a Christian Arab called Edward Atiyah. It had fascinated him to such a powerful degree that he had begun to write again in one of those little note-books of his, cupped in the palm of his hand. Anticipating that it had the makings of a play, he had petitioned Fryn to invite the author to lunch. Edward Atiyah came, bearing contributions to the meal from Fortnum & Mason. But, when he saw the style of Fryn's hospitality, this gloriously extrovert man was abashed and tucked the carrier under the table, where it clanked if any foot strayed too near. On a later visit with his Scottish wife Jean he confessed, but by then they were firm friends and collaborators, and Fryn and Tottie had both read his splendid biography, *An Arab Tells His Story*.

Apart from the dramatization of the *Pin*, not since their gruesome one-acter *The Black Mask* had Tottie veered from the pungent dialogue of comedy. Here instead was the compassionate killing of a loved but insane marriage partner. After submitting the script to Lionel Hale, to Peter Cotes and to Gorey, he came to the conclusion, despite their doubts, that he could add nothing to it, and that his play must take its chance as it stood. So it was decided to try out *The Thin Line* at the Whitehall Theatre on Sunday 8 March 1953, as the opening production of The New Edward Terry Players; a group of ex-professionals named after the famous grandfather of the leading lady, Iris Terry.

Long before evening came, Fryn had been suffering from nervous dyspepsia. In fact, both were several skins short on such occasions, and unfortunately it was justified this time. The reviews were too discouraging to take the production any further, *The Times* deciding: 'The thin line of the title is that tenuous elusive division between sanity and insanity. But there is another thin line lurking in the play unknown, apparently, to author and producer; it is that which separates drama from melodrama and, like the thread of the Fates, once broken it cannot be joined together again.'

Although the play was a failure and Tottie never wrote another, a different version of Edward Atiyah's book was filmed. It was followed by several other novels, and Edward told Fryn: 'You write with such superb and infectious gusto that it is an inspiration to me.'

On 9 July 1953, Peter Cotes and Joan Miller sailed on the *Queen Elizabeth* to launch *A Pin to See the Peepshow* on Broadway, having been persuaded by the producer that her contract for the theatre was signed and that the capital could not be withdrawn by her backers. But the instant they arrived trouble began. What they found was a middle-aged neurotic woman who had joined the great army of 'shoestring' producers. She wouldn't allow Peter to engage the good actors he chose, because their salaries were more than the Equity minimum. She would take advice from nobody, even when the top theatre lawyer, Arnold L. Weissburger of New York, warned her that she was steering everyone to disaster. The scenery was inadequate, the lighting too dim, and again and again, contract or no contract, Joan and Peter debated unhappily whether to take the next boat home.

The play opened at the 48 Street Playhouse on 17 September, with a cast of twenty headed by Joan, and it was withdrawn after the first night. The *Daily Express* of 19 September wrote: 'Murder has been committed and I was at the scene of the crime; the butchers of Broadway assassinated *A Pin to See the Peepshow*.' There had been three previews to invited audiences, and great numbers of the theatrical world saw it and applauded it enthusiastically. Peter wrote to Tottie: 'After the first night we were taken to Sardi's, and as Joan walked in the entire restaurant rose and clapped. This had only happened twice before in thirteen years. But the next afternoon the business manager telephoned to say there was no money to pay the stage hands for even one more performance.'

Abbott van Nostrand, Tottie's New York agent, wrote to him: 'The applause from the audience was vocal, warm and spontaneous, but the critics, as usual so early in the season, were rather "cold". However, the quotes for Miss Miller alone would have been enough to keep the show going, but the producer had banked on such a rave press that the box-office next morning would have been besieged and she could have paid her oustanding liabilities. But she got cold feet.

Poor Joan and Peter are quite broken up.'

This was a brutal end to a bold adventure, but it was simultan-
eously demonstrated to the victims that the Harwoods were not as
others are. 'Alone in our experience,' said Peter, 'they treated us in
adversity as allies, rather than as sudden opponents who had let them
down.' 'Indeed, they were adorable to us,' agreed Joan. 'And we have
heard the very same from Ernest Betts and others.'* Just then a
request reached Fryn from the National Institute for the Blind to
produce a 'talking book' of the *Pin* and with that ironic success she
had to be content. *The Alabaster Cup*, too, had been transcribed in
Braille.

Her sight was deteriorating all the time, and made her giddy and
more unsteady on her feet than ever. Her dear and faithful osteopath,
La Wareing, who also tended the joints of many of the dancers from
the Royal Ballet at Convent Garden, now came almost daily by
taxicab straight after breakfast, to relieve the lymphatic swellings of
the joints of her feet caused by saturation of drugs and alcohol; an
extremely painful condition which had also produced the lymphatic
fluid around the jaw and hairline, spoiling the outline of her once
heart-shaped face.† And Fryn conceived the idea that, if she pre-
tended to have a sprained ankle, nobody need know that she was
going blind, nobody need know that she was crippled, and nobody
need assume that she was 'tight' either! 'You see,' she wrote to Grace
Hubble, 'if I were to walk in the street, I should be taken for a drunk,
or for an old lady of eighty, or perhaps even for a drunk of eighty.' To
keep her dignity therefore, should she totter, she decided to wear a
bandage round one foot, calling it Alibi Alf.

The need for such a subterfuge had not prevented her from coaxing
Sir Norman Birkett, Lord Justice of Appeal, into giving her and me a
special pass for the City Lands at the Old Bailey, to enable her to
assess the personality and demeanour of John Reginald Halliday
Christie in the box. As long ago as Janaury 1950, the dim young
Welshman, Timothy John Evans, who had lived at the same mean
little house at 10 Rillington Place, and whose wife and baby daughter
had been strangled there, had been tried and found guilty of the
murder of his child. He had been executed without public protest,
after futilely claiming that 'Christie done it'. Having made many

* Peter Cotes and Joan Miller in conversation with JC.
† Elsie Wareing in conversation with JC.

confessions and told many lies, this one was regarded as despicable, for Christie had been chief witness for the Prosecution and was above suspicion. Yet here was Coronation year, and Christie apprehended, having left behind in his 'larder' the trussed and sexually assaulted bodies of three young women, as well as that of Mrs Christie under the floor-boards. The bones of two more were yet to come, but Fryn was not slow to recognize a monster. As she sat at her lunch-table, picking delicately at some tasty morsel while apprising the company of the latest 'finds' by the police, she explained that these were 'not to be confused with the Feast of Corpus Christi'. She had written to Jim Hodge for the go-ahead to do the Introduction for his series as soon as he could get hold of the transcript of the trial.

In 1954, Tiger came home on leave, first to stay at Malahide with 'the iron-willed *petite blonde*,' her mother, and then to London. There she spent long days with Fryn, who declared a holiday for herself as well, while they mingled happy tears and talked until the four-year gap was sandwich-packed between them.

Fryn also busied herself with numerous true-crime studies. But not until A.D. Peters had become her literary agent – with the blessing of Audrey Heath – did a lively market open for them in England. Some of her short stories were televised too, and she wrote several new ones for inclusion in a collection to be called *The Burglar*. By then the novel was finished, and A.D. Peters offered it to Michael Sadleir, who accepted it for Constable. At last, Fryn could feel that she was in good hands again, and the proposal that she might follow up with her autobiography was warmly encouraged.

The first intention had been to call her novel *Here Are Dragons*, and she had written to the National Maritime Museum and to the Peabody Institute in Baltimore asking for their help. For her theory was that cartographers used to write something of the sort over the unexplored areas of the earth, and that such uncharted places exist also in the heart of every human being. By chance, Stella Gibbons published a book just then called *Here Be Dragons*, so Fryn had quickly changed hers to *The Dragon in the Heart*.

The writing was complicated by having to keep two secrets almost to the end, which meant relating events through the medium of someone outside the story instead of through one of the principals. She chose a young woman painter, and the characters move between their *rendez-vous* at Drouant's and the Ile St Louis where the painter has her apartment, or to the river bank at Bougival where the lovers meet. It tells a true story about a 'cousin' of Fryn's on the Tennyson side, whose real name was Psychette and who was 'pursued by the Furies'. Not only is it set against the background of two of the greatest calamities that have befallen the human race, but the heroine loses her baby son (he belongs to the lover who cannot marry her and not to the hero), the hero is wounded at Ypres and made impotent, and the heroine dies of a wasting disease. It is reminiscent of the six-year-old Fryn's story about little Mary, who was orphaned, and lost, and who died too, but Fryn's own comment was: 'It is a sort of spiritual who-dun-it. It is also my very first love story, and of course I would make my hero impotent! My second theme is that there are other paternities than those of the flesh, and this is the essence of the book'. Though Brandt and Brandt thought it would be too quiet a book for American publishers, Constable held that that was the heart of it. They published it on 20 September 1956 and Fryn dedicated it to 'my French and Italian friends with love and faith'.

It was quietly received, but did manage to justify the publisher's confidence, neither they nor Fryn having had exaggerated hopes for its appeal to the public. Michael Swan wrote in the *Sunday Times*: 'Novels confected for Woman by Woman about Woman; Miss Jesse seems convinced she is writing a very serious novel, but in fact she has written a tear-jerker in an old tradition.' But St John Ervine thought otherwise. Though he had barely recovered from an operation for a detached retina, he wrote post-haste to Fryn: 'I am baffled by Swan's review, because I can see nothing in it that is relevant to this novel, and anyone less entitled to that description than you does not exist. I take it however that he wished to wound you for some reason. My view of the novel is that you have here the makings of your master-piece. Ignore the summary and write the amplified book and I am positive you can do it.'

He had hit the mark, of course. The sense of time pressing and darkness closing in could not have failed to leave its imprint. In fact, Fryn did not see the destructive review till later, for she was in St John's & St Elizabeth's Hospital, having the operation on the first eye. As stillness was essential for a successful result, Tottie had been advised by Jock not to come and see her, but he had written: 'My thoughts are always with you. Will it help in the hours of darkness to know how dearly you are loved? I shall be waiting, straining at the leash!'

It was six or seven weeks before recovery was enough advanced to fit the new spectacles with the artificial lens, but she did reply to St John, adding: 'I creep about the house as blind as ever, only no longer terrified. We must face the fact that it was not a Christmassy sort of book! Tottie has been quite ill while I was operated on, and worried sick too about Suez. He is well again, but I never look at him now without expecting him to drop dead. When I told him so, he said: "Let us look on the bright side; let us consider that it may be you who dies first!".'

The balance of power in the house had shifted. As the habitual helplessness of both her charges increased, May's tongue had grown an edge. To crow over Fryn had been a part of her attitude ever since she had rescued the five-pound note from the curling-tongs. Affection had overlaid derision in the good years, but had worn thin at Prestbury and resisted all Fryn's blandishments since. That some harmony was now restored was due to the arrival of a ministering angel. She appeared in the guise of a retired theatre-nurse, who lived in the cul-de-sac parallel to Melina Place and took up her duties the day Fryn reached home in her black eye-shade. Before that day was out, she had been nick-named Minnehaha Laughing Water, Minnie for short. The laugh was part of her. While she powdered Fryn's nose, or brought in her glass of 'sweet white porty'; while she shaved Tottie or gave him a high colonic; she scattered melodious notes like a skylark. She had the fluffy white hair of a dandelion in seed and, as well as being an excellent nurse, she knew everything there was to know about racing: every horse that ran, its owner, trainer, jockey, and the odds that day. To hear Fryn's exquisite speech sprinkled with the jargon of the turf as she chatted to Minnie was comical to the point of pain.

Temporary nurses had often come and gone, as Fryn's ailments dictated. May had not had anything to do for her intimate bodily care. May feared illness, shrank from the touch of flesh, and fainted at the sight or mention of blood. She might, all the same, have resented the intrustion of Minnie, and in fact she did. For this was no temporary; this was a God-send, come to stay. But she settled for it, relished the daily betting sessions as did everyone else, and she was the lucky one.

Fryn had been back at home for only a few days when an inquiry came from *Woman's Own* for the first British serial rights in an article on her eyesight. Momentarily she was indignant at the very idea, but when A.D. Peters had reminded her that something like five million people would read it, and that it might conceivably be helpful to one of them, she decided that the generous sum offered was 'better than a slap in the belly with a wet fish.' In 'My Fight Against Blindness' she told of the dizziness and her recourse to Alibi Alf. She explained the nature of the film that forms within the lens of the eye, causing it to lose its transparency. And she described the brilliantly-coloured panorama that passed incessantly against the black background of bandaged lids and calmed the fear of never seeing again. 'The only possible way for me,' she concluded, 'was to set myself a difficult task, and to keep the knowledge of approaching blindness within the four walls of home.' The article was published while she was still blind-folded, which gave an added relish to the fee.

The task she had set herself had begun when she had petitioned Jim Hodge for the Christie case. She had had no idea then that it would proliferate to include the Evans case, as well as the Scott Henderson Inquiry into the verdict thereon. All this, and the delay in the release of the transcripts of both trials, took longer than anyone had expected and, thoughout the year between the finishing of her novel and its publication, Fryn had invited a number of experts, one by one, to lunch at Pear Tree Cottage. Joe Jackson came, and Mr Malcolm Morris who had defended Evans, and Dr Francis Camps the Home Office Pathologist, with his rollicking humour which must have been such a blessing to him in his grisly work. 'Everyone connected with either case – barristers, solicitors, police, prison governors, psychiatrists and pathologists – came to me at my home,' she wrote, 'and spared me many arduous expeditions.'

In pursuit of such first-hand information as was still available, with a pass from Scotland Yard, and with Alibi Alf *in situ*, she and I had visited Rillington Place, where a courteous Jamaican occupant showed us upstairs and down, and into the wash-house where the neat parcels containing Beryl Evans and her baby had been hidden, and out to the wretched garden where a thigh-bone had propped the fence. We had called on Mrs Probert, the mother of Evans. We had been to the Notting Hill police station where Detective-Inspector Black and Chief Inspector Jennings, CID, had taken Evans' last confession, and to the Putney police station where Christie had been brought in by an observant young constable. And we had called on

Dr Desmond Curran, who had examined Christie at Brixton Prison.

Fryn had finished the writing by working until seven in the evening for the last month, and when Jim received this Labour of Hercules he wrote: 'It is a truly marvellous piece of work,' and he sent her a cheque for double the normal fee. It made her smile, for it totalled exactly half what she had earned for the cataract article, but the smile was a proud one. The book came out in mid-summer 1957, and Sir Theobald Mathew, the Director of Public Prosecutions, wrote to James Hodge as publisher, praising 'this admirable Introduction, a concise and objective statement of the facts and issues. An eminently fair and masterly study.'

In his review in *Books*, Sir Norman Birkett wrote: 'It would not be too much to say that Miss Tennyson Jesse has rendered a great public service in her dispassionate account. It is a notable addition to a series already notable all the world over. It is first class in its arrangement, in its acute analysis, its judicial temper, and its powerful and effective writing.' Later, when he reviewed Ludovic Kennedy's *Ten Rillington Place*, which set out to show that Evans had been wrongfully convicted, he wound up by saying that further inquiry 'could not *establish* or *prove* that Evans was innocent' and 'the truth was perhaps best stated by Miss Tennyson Jesse when she wrote in 1957: "It seems to me more likely that in the pursuit of his lust and under the guise of performing an abortion, Christie murdered Beryl Evans, and that he murdered the baby. There are objections to this conclusion; it does not satisfy all the conditions or resolve all doubts. No explanation I have thought of does this".'

There was adverse comment too. The *National and English Review* called it 'turgid stuff', and Ian Gilmour in the *Spectator* was so scathing that Sir Theobald Mathew confessed to having been 'roused to savage wrath at this irresponsible and deliberately offensive attack.' The *Trials of Evans and Christie* is dedicated to myself 'with gratitude and affection,' and the preface gives thanks to the mighty list of those who helped so generously in its preparation.

On 5 August 1957, while the reviews were still coming in, Tottie had a haemorrhage and was taken to 'John's and Lizzie's' – St John's and St Elizabeth's – for a barium meal and X-rays. He had broken an artery in his duodenum. Fryn followed a couple of days later to the floor below him; the operated eye was not adjusting well and was to be 'needled' without an anaesthetic. In a note to her there, Tottie quoted from the French that it was more than a question of two similar minds, or a rubbing together of two epidermises; that even when she was not touching his hand and he could not see her, he knew she was with him. As she wrote to Jim:

> 'This makes life worth living and makes me almost believe, what I have heard some people say, that life is sweet. I write this quite calmly. It is a nightmare that has to be coped with. But of course he is doctor enough to know that this is probably the beginning of the end; it is the warning bell.'

After completing the trials, Fryn had begun writing a great many letters, as always between books. She had also collected her essays for publication, though A.D. Peters had not yet found an outlet for these, nor for her short story collection. One story, 'Lightning Strikes Twice', had been adapted in collaboration with Patrick Campbell as a play for ITV under the title *Not Proven*, and this was produced by Peter Cotes in November 1957.

Tiger was back again on leave that winter and found Fryn alarmingly frail, having despatched Minnie to the West Indies for a cruise in gratitude for having nursed both herself and Tottie through their crises. The house was so quiet without Minnehaha Laughing Water that Fryn said: 'Now nothing is heard but the voice of a Harwood coughing to its mate.' Still scorning television, even for the sake of watching cricket, Tottie had made frequent use of the ancient's privilege of being driven by me through the Grace Gate right up to the MCCC stand. He wrote to Fryn then:

> 'Sometimes I wonder whether my many stupidities may not have helped to form the cement which joins us. When I say, as I do now, I love you, you must try and guess at all I want to mean. One thing, my pet – don't let me be mothered to Golders Green. So long as you are alive – and after that it doesn't matter – you may be sure that I shall do my best to go on breathing. Whatever else has happened to you, you have not "dwindled into a wife".'

Rising from table one evening when Tiger was there, Fryn fell flat on her face. She lay there weeping silently, not because she had fallen but because she had not the strength to rise. May had detested sitting through those evening meals, ever since Tottie had ceased to be there. Listening to Fryn's monologue, watching her interminably sipping, drove her nearly frantic. The champagne cure, effective at first, had begun to produce acid side-effects and had been replaced by a sweet white wine, which had come to serve as Fryn's staple nourishment. But, to May the abstainer, despite forty years of urbane living, a glass of wine was 'drink' and to fall on your face was to be 'drunk'. She was rigid with disapproval. Tiger sat down on the floor beside the toppled figurine, her heart bursting, and gently raised her up. She had a simultaneous image of Fryn then, as she had seen her pressed precariously against the tall side of the ship she wrote *The Saga of San Demetrio* about: it was in ballast, high in the water, and she was coming down one of those slatted rope-ladders behind the Captain, in her high heels and with her one hand.

That Christmas, Fryn managed as usual to dash off by hand her four-hundred cards, each with its personal message, and to despatch to her eleven honorary God-children their due money-present. But twice only in 1958 did she climb to the top of the house: once on a mercy visit to May, who was lying scared stiff on her bed with vertigo and who wailed irritably: 'Don't pant so!', and once to caress and steady the trembling body of little old Brother, who had had a series of uraemic fits, while kind Mr Evans the Hampstead veterinary prepared to give him his quietus.

All through those weeks, friends had been reappearing in great variety: Mack McCall and Alison Settle, the Hubbles and the Balderstons, and Enid Bagnold, her dream of becoming a successful playwright splendidly realized in *The Chalk Garden*. Damit, ten years a widow, who had designed the sea-horse book-plates for Fryn's library, arrived bearing a cheque for the thousand pounds, from a family legacy, in honourable settlement of Percy's bad debt. And Fryn had taken it, astonished and much moved, with the proviso that a percentage should go back to Damit on her birthdays. Auntie Margaret had had a stroke and was in the Sandwich Nursing Home, but Eric travelled up from Ninepins, still maintaining with Crossauntie what Fryn called their symbiotic relationship through mutual memories of Stella.

A correspondence had begun with Alethea Garstin, painting still in Cornwall though both her brothers had died, and through her came other Newlyn news; of Phil Gotch, three times married since the giggling escapade she and Fryn had indulged in; of Dod Procter, many years a widow, whose powerful paintings duly appeared in each year's Academy; also of the Jesse cousins at Torcross in Devon, bringing visits from Cecily's daughter, Andolie Luck: 'I'm told how they all washed each other's hairs,' smiled Andolie, 'and if Fryn wanted hers washed, everybody vied to do it for her; she was so delicate, and so dominating, and her hair was so very lovely.'

There was nothing random about this spate of visitors, these sheaves of letters; each and every one was bringing back messages, like carrier pigeons: Guernsey, Newlyn, New York, Brussels, London, Burma, Bosham, the Côte des Maures, Hollywood, Fryn was re-living it all in the mind. And while she was as pregnant with ideas and impressions as the portfolio she had brought from Cornwall so long ago, the summons came in March 1958, calling her in to hospital again for the operation on the second eye.

Though this operation was pronounced successful, the sight failed to return. Obedient as she had tried to be, she must have rubbed the eye while half asleep, for it had suffered a set-back. Home again, she was gentle in manner, allowing Minnehaha and La Wareing's devoted skill to care for her, and for Tottie's increasing distress, with patient gratitude. He had sent in a pencilled note: 'How are you getting on, dearest? Too sad we have this drawn colon between us.' For the spasmodic pain, which had begun with the haemorrhage the year before – that and the pain in his hip – was keeping them islanded from one another, unless she could make her way to his bedside.

So, every day, uneasily balanced, she would drift along the corridors and through the study, with a languid wave to the inhabitants, as though she were a tight-rope walker nonchalantly passing by, and sit beside him, holding hands. Then she would return, completing the tight-rope walker's act with a courteous bow, her mind exercised with dread of his cancer, as his was exercised with dread of her blindness. A pensive melancholy hung palpably over the house. Sheltered in its cul-de-sac, Pear Tree Cottage was insulated from traffic sounds by a barricade of tall flats. It basked in the heat, its walls aglow like sunburnt skin. Charles Turner geraniums trailed from the flower-boxes along the roofs, and along the garage and the loggia, gleaming rosily. Pale water-lilies floated in the pond that was wired like a meat-safe against the 'torts' of prowling cats. As evening fell, the scent of phlox wafted in at the open door.

For some time, Dr Jock Mackenzie had been staying to lunch after his daily visit. When his wife had died, Fryn had promptly prescribed a meal-ticket for him and, on the expansive principle that what was enough for seven was enough for eight, eight then sat down to table, not counting guests. Only the providers of the feast might sometimes be out of sight. And then Jock had had a heart attack and came no more. Fryn was accustomed to charming what she wanted from him in the way of prescriptions. He knew she had to have some drug, and had tried always to keep her to the mildest kinds, thus modulating her condition for years. His collapse might have been crucial for her. Instead, docile as never before, she did without, taking her chance of sleep, too weary or too sad to appeal to the stranger who took Jock's place and who spoke sharply of and to her. There are doctors who can treat someone in great need of help with this easy contempt.

She returned to ruminating upon her life's beginnings; upon the Island game, that Golden Secret shared only with Stella. She let me prise out her Guernsey memoirs and her Newlyn diary, and gave them to me to study, along with the scissors-and-pastepot tomes of her Papa's. And she began to talk of two volumes of autobiography at least.

Dwelling among these old familiar things, it was as though she were conscious of being born again. This was something she did not need sight for. The intractible eyes that refused to learn new tricks were seeing the days of her youth as a bright panorama behind the lids. And she took to having someone read to her again, as her mother had read to her. It gave her the respite she could not get while her mind was churning, and it gave May, a tireless reader, the balm of a renewal of their old companionship.

Fryn had always enjoyed making a Will, refusing to give lip-service to legal language for what was in her heart. For her, a Will was a way of giving presents when she could best afford to, and she loved giving presents. She never forgot living on a shoe-string.

Tottie's way with a Will was far more sensible. Instead of dividing and spreading as Fryn did, he liked to gather all his resources together. He had respect for what was proper in the treatment of money, while Fryn had none. But his respect for Fryn was such that he did not dream of interfering with what she did with her own.

The fancy had taken her to answer an advertisement offering to value Victorian and antique trinkets and jewellery 'at your own home'. She invited the valuer to come by appointment, and he came: a small Jewish gentleman, well-dressed and well-mannered. Having been more than half prepared to defend Fryn's life or property, I felt reassured; this visitor did not look like even the thin end of a blunt instrument. It was a glorious afternoon, and Fryn received him in the drawing-room and sat him beside her on the window-cushion of the wide bay. They talked easily of London and Vienna, Amsterdam and Paris and Rome, and she sent for tea, though she never touched tea herself. Then she produced the little leather box and the big carved box, and turned all her pretty things out on to the round inlaid table and began to discuss their merits and their history.

She was gay, if a bit light-headed; for the last few days there had been something capricious in her moods. Gradually the jewels formed themselves into two piles; one reserved for 'my Godchild' or 'my darling Grace', and one to be assessed. Then, as if they were playing some game of chance, the visitor abruptly swept the second pile to one side and called out a figure. Like a delighted child, Fryn cried 'Done!' and gave him her hand. It was the left one of course, the one she always gave. He kissed it and then, saying 'May I?', he tilted it this way and that on his palm, studying it in the light from the window. The solitaire diamond on her engagement finger flashed, unnoticed. 'How incomparably beautiful,' he murmured, and it was the hand he was talking about. He didn't ask what had happened to the other, curled out of sight beside her in its fresh mitten.

When he had gone, leaving the unconsidered cheque on the table with the boxes, Fryn said: 'Nice, wasn't he? I do like intelligent Jews.' And she recalled with deep affection the Monds and the Readings; their infinite kindness and generosity. But she was shivering, and had to be almost carried upstairs and tucked under the eiderdown for Minnie to put to bed.

Still feeling vaguely uneasy, I went along to see Tottie, for several of the ornaments had once been given by him. He lifted an eyebrow and asked: 'And what was all that about?' but when he had heard he said very quietly: 'Don't worry. As long as she has her diamond, which will one day provide for May, I don't mind what she has done with the rest. It is her good right. It was all hers.' He stared up at the ceiling: 'You see, I believe she is beginning to wind up her affairs.'

There was an enervating breathlessness about the days that followed and Fryn kept to her bed, though inside the house the brilliant sun was banished. One afternoon, I was reading aloud to her a letter from Sonya Levien Hovey in Beverly Hills. It was about that first visit of Fryn's to New York with Susan her nurse. The room was dim and hushed, scarcely disturbed by the rhythmical words and the turning of the flimsy pages, yet profoundly disturbed by a fainter sound, the trembling flutter of the sheet that was Fryn's only covering. Drawn up to her shoulders, it vibrated like a sail as it turns into the wind. Yet the face above it looked composed enough with its magnificent leonine brow, and the voice that broke through as the letter ended was strong and resonant: 'Now, my pet! Fetch your notebook and sharpen your pencils. We're going to get down to the story of my life.'

Steadily she began to dictate, and by the time a draft was ready for her that evening, young Whiny Fee was in the rickshaw at Cape Town, crying: 'Faster, boy, faster!' It was late, but she was able to raise a smile for Minnehaha, who came on duty hoping to wheedle her with a beaten-up egg in brandy and having won herself a nice 'double' on the afternoon's races.

The next day it was the same: the August sky and the unsparing will. Every now and then she had to rest, and then her hand would waver out before her face as she pulsated like a trapped butterfly. 'Flowers!' she whispered. 'How strange. Little bunches of flowers are floating all around me.' And then the concentration would begin once more. Towards evening Fryn took the typescript from me, focussing on it with hard deliberation, and when she put it aside the stamp of beauty was on her face. She could still glow. 'You know I love you, Joanna,' she said slowly. Then smiling: 'I'm thinking of calling this life of mine *The Open Door*. Or do you think perhaps *The Half-Open Door* should be enough?'

She was found by May in the morning, on her side as if in sleep, but ringed about with that unearthly stillness which is so far from sleep. Then Tottie had come and cradled her in his arms in a passion of grief and rocked her against his heart. He had lifted her up and held her high on his chest. And he had started walking up and down, up and down, on and on between the mirror and the door, his face drenched in tears, jaw jutting, eyes wide with pain. She lay across his arms and her feet stuck out stiffly. She looked like a little sawdust doll, her pretty nightgown fluttering at each turn. Up and down he walked, till the doorbell told of the doctor's coming. May watched, propped against the doorpost for support, frozen like a hare, while he crouched down and tilted his small burden back into the bed and drew up the covers. As he limped past the doorway, his face turned towards May's and he paused: 'It's been a stormy passage,' he said hoarsely.

That was all the recognition he ever gave her of their joint guardian-ship. Behind the hollow feeling of loss and fright, she was conscious of relief that they had not ignominiously failed in it; if they had had a part in it at all, that is. Without drama or headline; without anything embarrassing or disgraceful, Fryn had weathered the storm alone. The evening papers of 6 August 1958 had reported: 'She apparently had a heart attack early this morning.'

Fryn was cremated at Golders Green without a service, and Tottie did not go. What was necessary should be done with the minimum of fuss and he did not want to hear about it. 'Funeral private. No letters or flowers please,' he had announced. Those who wanted to go did so: Gorey in his top hat; and Peter, of course; May, who had never worn black, in black from head to foot; and Cousin Charles in his summer flannels, having walked down from the house he shared with his son Hallam. In his last book about the family Tennyson, he was to describe his kinsmen as 'a unique blend of childlikeness and gran-deur'; a perfect description of Fryn. Hallam, a writer too, had written to Fryn not long before about the review of a new book of his, and had said: 'I don't worry too much, and can keep the "blackblooded-ness of the Tennysons" at bay. Do you have it, Fryn? But perhaps, since my father is so gloriously free of it, it isn't Tennysonian at all?' To this Fryn had made no reply, ignoring the blight that had some-times dimmed her soul.

To Tottie now, nothing mattered but the bitter pain of Fryn's bodily absence. It merged with that other pain that tore at his guts, and his only relief was the practical task of rearranging financial matters with the utmost speed. For the whole tenor of these had been based on Fryn's being left as well provided for as possible within the terms imposed by the Trust. Her gifts and bequests must be carried out in his lifetime, he said. Her affections must be given instant expression. For the rest, all must be as she would have had it. He wrote to me: 'I have an idea which may enable us to continue working together as she would have wished, while giving me the excuse for your services. Details when we meet. One is carrying on. Love T.'

And carry on he did. Letters poured in from friends and fans. He looked at them, entertained, and took pleasure in the words. They were true words and part of Fryn: kindness, beauty, fun, genius, courage, generosity, wit, warmth . . . he played with them, dis-tracted and curious, seeing their bright images as through a kaleido-scope, recognizing her in them. Then he let them go, returning to his inner vision of her and to a capacity for suffering, a consciousness of desolation, that drifted him away from the world in which he still took up space, so that he saw everything there as from a long way off.

The Times, the *Manchester Guardian* and numerous other papers published obituaries, and that of Ernest Betts praised 'Her passion for facts and a stinging epigrammatic wit reminiscent of Oscar Wilde'. Peter Cotes found her 'unique among friends.' And Rebecca West added in *The Times*:

'There is one fact about Fryn Tennyson Jesse which her old friends would like to be remembered. In her youth she was one of the loveliest girls of her time, far surpassing all the more advertised beauties. Many people knew her later as a charming and clever and kindly woman, but it would be a pity if the girl that she was should be totally forgotten. Though she was always ambitious, she never knew the meaning of the word "rival". She would lend her best evening-dress to a poor and pretty young actress. If she liked a book, she would sit down and write a stream of postcards telling her friends to read it; and it was all done gaily and volubly against the picturesque setting she could make for herself in the smallest house. It was then more than her sense of humour could take that an old gentleman well known in literary circles insisted on calling her his "golden lass". But today that name seems not inappropriate.'

The dispersal of Fryn's personal possessions involved May in furious activity on the telephone, and in the tying up of dozens of packages, at which she was so expert. Work eased her and, in the first sufficient gap in her days, she bearded me in the workroom, from which most of the treasures had already been stripped for beneficiaries. She brought with her a sack, a key, scissors, and a variety of tools like a burglar's outfit, and tugged out a small tin trunk. It had stood padlocked behind the rows of files for years, and was labelled: 'Letters to be burnt unseen on my death.' For the next four hours, bundles were withdrawn, ribbon-bows were removed, and one by one the letters were demolished. Often May knew what style of writing or of note-paper belonged to which of Fryn's old love-lives, and a reminiscent mutter would escape her. For they were all love-letters, sometimes hundreds with the same letter-head. There was no mistaking their nature, even with senses numbed with repetition. Doggedly the work went on till the trunk was empty. Only the worthless ribbons were salvaged and folded away in the house-keeper's drawer.

Too tired to speak, with sore fingers, and not sure whether we were criminals, or witnesses to each other's crime, or just victims, the demolition-workers watched the thick layer of ash collapse. Was the order intended literally to be obeyed? Why had Fryn not done it herself? Had she visualized that the man responsible for a great number of those vanished letters would be propped up in bed reading, only a few steps away, while countless pages of his fine light script went up in smoke? And would he have interfered, if given the choice? Surely not. He had not forgotten anything.

Visitors had ventured to call; dear friends, Cathleen Nesbitt, Virginia. And at first he saw them. Willie Somerset Maugham spent an afternoon with him, their voices reverberating animatedly together. So did Laurence Olivier and Archie Batty. Robert Gore-Browne came often, and it was a proposal of his, that they should collaborate again on a sort of commentary about the direction the theatre of tomorrow should take, that had prompted Tottie to consider putting himself to work again. All too soon he withdrew, rejecting the idea that he could have anything more to contribute to this world. As to tackling the work Fryn had left undone, he consented to think about it overnight, and then utterly dismissed it, his face ravaged. 'If you have the heart for it though,' he said to me, 'you do it. But how extraordinary that it should be you, who only came in at the sad end. You never saw it at its peak: the wonderful, wonderful life we had, she and I. Cut Mill, Sabi Pas, Hollywood . . . such unbelievable happiness she gave me! Tiger could tell you, or Robert. But yes, you do it Joanna.' A faint hint of pleasure at the thought brightened his eyes, before he flashed: 'Only, don't make it one of these damned boring literary criticisms, will you? Just tell what happened. Make it live again. Write about the woman she was.' He sank slowly back against the pillows, and a queer groaning sigh came out of him as from a blacksmith's bellows. If Fryn had heard it she would have protested: 'No moany, my darling!'

He answered his letters in the minimum of words. He cried off from all further visitors. He engaged the firm of Carter's from St John's Wood village to bring Fryn's house into good repair and to repaint it in her colours. Then he set himself to get through the days, conceding that there was still something the world could contribute to him: he would read everything worth while he had missed and everything he had loved, till he dropped in his tracks. He wrote to Archie, himself now ill in hospital: 'I have been reading every damned book in the house. Like a pile-driver, I've gone through the lot. And do you know what they were all trying to say? The Brontës, Casanova, the Trobriand Islanders, the poets, the new stuff alike? They were all trying to say the same thing – how I loved her!'

For weeks the exercise seemed to satisfy him. May fetched the books, first from the shelves in the house, then from the libraries, till one morning his bedroom was found in disorder, the bedside cupboard lying on its side, books and bottles thrown off the chest and strewn across the room. His face was bruised, the eyes bloodshot. He didn't know anything about it, so he said.

The doctor, puzzled at why he should have gone berserk, got him admitted to the London Clinic. There, after a check-over, Tottie bestirred himself to wind up his affairs and sign a Power of Attorney. But he was impatient of any specialist treatment, and remained bursting with violent irascibility, till he was discharged from the Clinic to the familiar John's and Lizzie's a few yards from home, still looking shot to pieces.

Even there everything irritated him, especially the good Sisters and, as May had been prescribed rest, I spent the days with him. On Good Friday he had had a peaceful morning, his body lying unnaturally small; but after a silence in which the cool afternoon had been held as if spellbound, the shaggy head poked straight up, grey-faced; the frame heaved and regained its usual bulk: 'Why do I dream like this about money?' he protested. 'You wouldn't credit the things that passed through my head while I was mad, compounded of evil mixed up with dreadful pain! Evil in money matters, funnily enough, yet I've never done an evil thing in that line. I never cared about money really, nor did Fryn. We didn't bother with it, either of us, though we spent it of course if occasion arose.

'And why do people gather behind me and cause me this agonizing pain that is somehow evil? And these myriads of nurses, surrounding me and fiddling about with my person? I know they are not real, only a product of my dream, but there they are: like a frieze, a chorus for some grotesque play that Fryn might have put on. She could have done something of the sort most beautifully you know, making them prance, making them chant: "The patient is quite comfortable! The patient has no pain!" It would be just the thing for her to stage.' He paused, shaking his head; then started up again: 'But nobody believes I have any pain. Nobody does a thing for it. Even you don't mind my pain. If you did you'd stick a knife in my heart. If I had a knife in my hands, I'd stick it in my heart now. I'd stick a rake in my bowels if I had a rake.' He was bellowing.

'Don't, Tottie. Blow off steam if you like, but don't hate yourself like this,' I pleaded.

'Hate myself? I don't hate myself,' he sounded amazed. 'I just want an overdose. Tell me who has a better right? Why won't they kill me? I want to die! Oh well . . . I suppose I must just leave you to do the best you can for me about an overdose. It's these dreadful nurses – the doe-eyed virgins! They won't help me, yet they never leave me alone.' Mischief lighted up his face. Then, very graciously, the jaw retired until it was no more aggressive than any bulldog, he confided: 'Now, I am going to ask you if you will light me a cigarette? . . . Mmm, this is nice. I haven't had one for a long time, I wonder why. There, keep the rest of this for me, eh? I'm going to have a sleep.' He snuggled down, but at once the eyes shot open while he said threateningly: 'Don't go away, whatever you do.'

Quite soon, he started up with a 'Hey! Oh, there you are. I've been dreaming a strange and rather horrible story; the sort of story that Fryn could produce from her brain. Fryn had a capacity for vindictive enmity, do you know that? She could be inimical to a rare degree. She was capable too of malicious hatred, and she maliciously hated an illegitimate son of mine. There was nothing to be done about it. Nothing made any difference. She couldn't accept that I'd had a child by another woman and not by her. She never forgot it all her life, and sometimes the pain of it drove her mad. Mmm, it's odd that this story of mine should draw you within itself at this late hour. And there's poor little May, right outside it from the beginning, though she was always there.'

Through the window, a squall hit the tall chestnut tree standing in the hospital garden, and its pink glazed buds swung down and away and soared up again. A nun, black-gowned, appeared on the path below and was wafted smoothly off between the bare rose-bushes. 'Shall I wake up tonight in the middle of this evil dream again? Or am I in fact dead? It can't be too soon for me. God damn my body! Do you know that when I walked out of Fryn's room on the morning she died, when she slid down out of my arms and I had to walk away from her alone, I realized that something had broken. I don't know what it was, but it was broken.'

'It can't be very long to wait now, Tottie. You're eighty-five on Sunday, remember?'

For a time he brooded, then: 'Yes. I think I do feel blessedly nearer to my end.' He chuckled softly. 'You know, part of my dream was that when they examined me in the Clinic they found I was hollow; no heart, no bowel left, nothing in there at all! Perhaps I am mad? And I thought it was the doctor who was mad!' He slid his fingers under the pillow and couched his cheek voluptuously, as Fryn always did. He must have realized it, for he said: 'Fryn and I were really very alike. Alike about illness too, I mean. Tell me now, if you had to describe your association with an aged, aged man, how would you set about it? And will you remember all I've been telling you?'

He had come home for Easter, sooner than expected. There was nothing more they could do for him, they said. But he no longer shared in the life of the house, and May wrote to Peter: 'I am lonely and frightened when I think of having to start a new life of my own.' Given over to doctor's visits, to a male nurse by night and Minnehaha by day, the house had just waited for the hairs of Tottie's head to be numbered. He had grown too indolent to evacuate his own bowels, but even his wash-out lady found him charming. He had turned his face to the wall, on which one chubby fist drummed a slow beat, a beat like a signal. Gradually his breathing had taken on the same broken rhythm, and on 19 April 1959 it ceased.

When Fryn died, nothing had changed. A human cornucopia, she had scattered largesse as she breathed, and through her Tottie had been able to do the same. When Tottie died, everything had to change, everyone dispersed. Pear Tree Cottage passed into the hands of Yolande Donlan and her film director husband Val Guest. But May had continued living in it long enough to discover, in Marjorie's comforting presence, that her life had been rich in experience and she wasn't in the least adrift. For the twenty years by which she survived her protectors, a stone's throw from their cul-de-sac, she was to keep the pick of their friends and furniture, her gallows humour, and a priceless collection of prejudices such as they could never have harboured between them.

Neither she nor anybody else had mourned that Tottie should follow his heart. During his last conscious hours, he had smiled a lot of the time. And in the small drawer of his bedside cupboard was found a sheet of Fryn's scribble-paper, tightly folded:

LOVER'S WISH

I would be bread
That you of me might eat;
I would be wine
That I could slake your drouth;
I would be air
To blow as softly sweet
As kisses on your mouth.

Would I were earth
To bear your body up;
Would I were sun
To warm you as you lay,
Or water, I,
To hold you like a cup,
Lapping you every way.

Would I could lie
Close, close within your flesh,
Beat in your pulse,
Brim to your eager eyes,
Burn in your blood —
So, woven in one mesh,
Your breath would be my sighs.

Body and Soul
I would be part of you,
No more myself
But you, the heart of you.

Books by F. Tennyson Jesse

NOVELS: *The Milky Way*, 1913; *Secret Bread*, 1917; *Tom Fool*, 1926; *Moonraker*, 1927; *The Lacquer Lady*, 1929; *A Pin to See the Peepshow*, 1934; *Act of God*, 1937; *The Alabaster Cup*, 1950; *The Dragon in the Heart*, 1956.

SHORT STORIES: *Beggars on Horseback*, 1915; *Many Latitudes*, 1928; *The Solange Stories*, 1931.

POEMS: *The Happy Bride*, 1920; *The Compass*, 1951.

PLAYS: *Quarantine*, 1922; *Anyhouse*, 1925; *Birdcage*, 1949. WITH H.M. HARWOOD: *The Mask*, 1912; *Billeted*, 1917; *The Hotel Mouse* (adapted from the French), 1921; *The Pelican*, 1924; *How to be Healthy though Married*, 1930; *A Pin to See the Peepshow*, 1948.

CRIMINOLOGY: *Murder and its Motives*, 1924; *Comments on Cain*, 1948. NOTABLE BRITISH TRIALS: *Madeleine Smith*, 1927; *Samuel Herbert Dougal*, 1928; *Sidney Harry Fox*, 1934; *Rattenbury and Stoner*, 1935; *Ley and Smith*, 1947; *Evans and Christie*, 1957.

BELLES LETTRES: *The Sword of Deborah*, 1919; *The White Riband*, 1921; *Sabi Pas*, 1935; *The Saga of San Demetrio*, 1942.

LETTERS TO AMERICA (with H.M. Harwood): *London Front*, 1939; *While London Burns*, 1940.

HISTORY: *The Story of Burma*, 1946.

Plays by H.M. Harwood

Honour Thy Father, 1912; *The Confederates*, 1912; *The Mask* (with FTJ), 1912; *The Supplanters*, 1913; *Please Help Emily*, 1916; *Billeted* (with FTJ), 1917; *The Grain of Mustard Seed*, 1920; *A Social Convenience*, 1921; *The Hotel Mouse* (adapted from the French with FTJ), 1921; *The Pelican* (with FTJ), 1924; *The Transit of Venus*, 1927; *The Golden Calf*, 1927; *Excelsior* (adapted from the French), 1928; *A Girl's Best Friend*, 1929; *How to be Healthy though Married* (with FTJ), 1930; *The Man in Possession*, 1930; *Cynara* (with Robert Gore-Browne), 1930; *King, Queen, Knave* (with Robert Gore-

Browne), 1932; *So Far and No Father*, 1932; *The Old Folks at Home*, 1933; *La Foire aux Vices*, 1935; *Married Life Behind the Scenes* (with Harold Dearden), 1936; *The Innocent Party* (with Laurence Kirk), 1936; *These Mortals*, 1935; *A Pin to See the Peepshow* (with FTJ) 1948; *The Thin Line* (with FTJ and Edward Atiyah), 1953.

A Selection of Books Consulted

Eustace Tennyson D'Eyncourt Jesse: *Sonnets*; written from 1880–1922

The Rev Charles Tennyson Turner: *A Hundred Sonnets*; Introduction by Sir Charles Tennyson and Sir John Betjeman. Rupert Hart-Davis, 1960

Mrs Lionel Birch: *Stanhope A. Forbes, ARA and Elizabeth Stanhope Forbes, ARWS*. Cassell and Company Limited, 1906

Crosbie Garstin (later 'Patlander' of the Mudlarks series in Punch): *I.M. The Myrtage*. 1910

Alfred Lord Tennyson: *Poems by Tennyson* 1830–1868; Introduction by T. Herbert Warren, MA Hon DCL, President Magdalen College, Oxford 1910. Oxford University Press, 1918

Jean de Bosschere: *The City Curious*; illustrated by the author and retold in English by F. Tennyson Jesse. Heinemann, and Dodd Mead N.Y. 1920

Jane Starr (Stella Jesse): *Eve in Egypt*; Geoffrey Bles, 1929.

Anthology: *The Post Victorians*, including Joseph Conrad; Ivor Nicolson & Watson, 1933

Alexander Woollcott: *While Rome Burns*; Penguin, 1934. *His Life and Times; the Story of an American Phenomenon*; Hamish Hamilton, 1946

H.M. Harwood: Introduction to *These Mortals*, Heinemann, 1937

Laurence Kirk (Eric Simson); *Rings on her Fingers*; *Treasure on Earth*; Heinemann, 1937. *Halfway to Paradise*; 1951.

Dr Harold Dearden: *The Wind of Circumstance*; Heinemann, 1938

E. Phillips Oppenheim: *The Pool of Memory*; Hodder & Stoughton, 1941

Georgina Battiscombe: *Charlotte M. Yonge*, 1943; *Queen Alexandra*, 1969; *Shaftesbury*, 1974

I.M. C.S. Evans, 1883–1944; Heinemann, 1945

Edward Atiyah: *An Arab Tells His Story*; John Murray, 1946. *The Thin Line*; Peter Davies, 1951.

Josephine Blumenfeld: *Heat of the Sun*: Heinemann, 1948. *Step this Way*; Heinemann, 1951. *Pin a Rose on Me*; Heinemann, 1958

Peter Cotes: *No Star Nonsense*; The Theatre Book Club, 1949

Nikolaus Pevsner: *The Buildings of England (London)*; Penguin Books, 1952

Sir Charles Tennyson: *Life's all a Fragment* (with portraits of Penrose and Julian Tennyson); Cassell, 1953

Basil Dean: *The Theatre at War*; George G. Harrap, 1956

Ludovic Kennedy: *Ten Rillington Place*; Victor Gollancz, 1961

Sir Charles Tennyson and Hope Dyson: *The Tennysons, Background to Genius*; Macmillan, 1974

Madeleine Masson: *I Never Kissed Paris Goodbye*; Hamish Hamilton, 1978

Jocelyn Baines: *Joseph Conrad*; Weidenfeld and Nicolson, 1960; Pelican Books, 1971

Flora Thompson: *Lark Rise to Candleford*; Penguin, 1973

Ardyth Kennelly: *The Peaceable Kingdom*; Penguin, 1973

Hotel Mouse, with FTJ, his marriage to Fryn made public, 118; first crisis over his past, 119–120; Portofino honeymoon, 120–124; life at Cut Mill, 127–131; invited to India by the Viceroy, 131–133; and to Burma by the Governor, 133–134; sold his 11-ton yacht *'Gudgeon'* and bought the 80-ton *'Moby Dick'*, 134–138; *The Pelican*, with FTJ, 139–140, 141; sold *'Moby Dick'* and bought a second house, Sabi Pas, on the Côte des Maures, 144; up the Nile with Fryn, Stella and Somers, 147; *The Transit of Venus*, 149–150; Sabi Pas their winter quarters from 1927–1932, 152–154, 157, 159–160; *Excelsior*, 160; *A Girl's Best Friend*, 163; *The Man in Possession*, 164–165; *Cynara*, 165; Fryn's depression and drug overdose, 168–169; decision to jettison Sabi Pas and the Ambassadors Theatre and go to Hollywood, 170; *So Far and no Father*, and *King, Queen, Knave*, 170; sale of Sabi Pas, 171–172; to Hollywood, followed by Fryn and Tiger, 172–175, 177; resigned MGM contract, 178–179; left Fryn, 180–181; *The Old Folks at Home*, 181–182; harmony restored, 185–187; his method of writing; *La Foire aux Vices* and *These Mortals*, 195–196; *The Innocent Party*, with Laurence Kirk, and *Married Life Behind the Scenes*, with Harold Dearden, 197; bought Pear Tree Cottage, in north-west London, 198; sold Cut Mill, 199; his beliefs, 200; life at Pear Tree Cottage, 200–204; his letters to America, with FTJ: *London Front*, 209–212; *While London Burns*, 213–218; wartime cotton-spinner, 219–220; death of Stella, 221–222; Fryn's hysterectomy, 226; her antagonism and suicide attempt, 230–236; her revival, 237–239; to Mississippi, 244–247; to Rio de Janeiro, 251–254; *A Pin to see the Peepshow*, with FTJ, 241–242, 256, 269; a joint literary Company, 258; to Paris and Biarritz,

259–260; laying Fryn's ghost by letter, 261–264; *The Thin Line*, with FTJ, 268–269; her cataracts and his haemorrhage, 272–274, 275–278; awareness of Fryn's spiritual birth, 277–280; her death, 280–283, his death wish, 284–288

Harwood, Margaret (Maggie), younger sister of H.M. Harwood, 66, 71–72, 107–108, 120, 203, 261, 263

Harwood-Murray, Ellen, (Nellie), née Ellen Hopkinson, H.M. Harwood's step-mother, married George Harwood 1904, three children; Georgina, George and Ruth, 109–111

Hawtrey, Charles, actor, producer, 102

Headfort, Rose, Marchioness of, 201, 237, 254

Hearst Corporation, The, paperback publishers, 191

Heath, A.M. (Audrey), literary agent, 229, 239, 257–258, 271

Heinemann, William, publishers, 70, 85, 90, 94–95, 100, 104–105, 115, 117, 138, 140, 144, 148, 156, 160, 163, 167, 191, 196, 199, 228–229, 243

Herlie, Eileen, actress, 241

Hitchcock, Alfred, film director, 222

Hobbs, Carleton, actor, 140

Hodge, Harry, general editor of the Notable British Trials series published by William Hodge and Company, 138; succeeded by his son James 1927, 147–148, 155, 191, 267

Hodge, James (Jim), publisher of the Notable British Trials series, 147–148, 149, 155, 188, 190, 193, 225, 240–241, 270–271, 274–275, 276

Hoey, Iris, actress, 101

Holland-Martin, Robert, banker, 95

Hovey, Carl, editor of the *Metropolitan Magazine*, New York, married to Sonya Levien, its sub-editor, 79, 81, 179, 209–217, 280

Hubble, Professor Edwin, the Mount Wilson astronomer, and his wife Grace, 180, 200, 209–217, 265, 270, 277, 280

Hudd, Walter, actor, producer, 140

Isaacs, Gerald, *see* Reading, Gerald